*The Heroic Idiom
of Shakespearean Tragedy*

The Heroic Idiom
of Shakespearean Tragedy

James C. Bulman

Newark: University of Delaware Press
London and Toronto: Associated University Presses

© 1985 by Associated University Presses, Inc.

Associated University Presses
440 Forsgate Drive
Cranbury, NJ 08512

Associated University Presses
25 Sicilian Avenue
London WC1A 2QH, England

Associated University Presses
2133 Royal Windsor Drive
Unit 1
Mississauga, Ontario
Canada L5J 1K5

The paper used in this publication meets the minimum requirements of the
American National Standard for Permanence of Paper for
Printed Library Materials Z39.48-1984.

Library of Congress Cataloging Publication Data

Bulman, James C., 1947–
    The heroic idiom of Shakespearean tragedy.

    Bibliography: p.
    Includes index.
    1. Shakespeare, William, 1564–1616—Tragedies.
2. Shakespeare, William, 1564–1616—Characters—Heroes.
3. Heroes in literature.   I. Title.
PR2983.B84   1985   822.3'3   84-40061
ISBN 0-87413-271-1 (alk. paper)

Printed in the United States of America

For Nel

Contents

Acknowledgments

When a book takes as long to write as this one did, the writer runs the risk of forgetting some of the ways, both big and small, in which friends over the years have helped him to make it better. I hope I have forgotten few. My gratitude to my two mentors, the only begetters of the book, is boundless. The late J. M. Nosworthy inspired my love of Shakespeare by both kindness and example. Furthermore, he urged me at every opportunity to take my old Morris over the Welsh hills to visit Stratford-upon-Avon and the Royal Shakespeare Company: he must have known that where Shakespeare is concerned, there is no teacher like the theater. Later, Eugene M. Waith—himself the Hercules of humanist scholarship—spent countless hours nurturing that love. With characteristic generosity and precision, he guided me through the study in which ideas for the book first took shape. Gerry Richman proofread that early draft with an alacrity and good humor born of true friendship.

I am grateful to Nicholas Brooke, Maynard Mack, and Marvin Rosenberg, all of whom shared their wisdom with me by reading embryonic chapters and suggesting ways in which I could develop them. I am grateful, too, to Ruby Cohn, who, one glorious summer at the National Theatre in London, cast more pearls before me than I can remember. The last chapters bear the marks of her incisive criticism. My colleagues likewise have proved unfailingly obstinate in their refusal to understand what was not clear: Fred Frank and Dick Madtes in particular, playing the Palmer to my wavering Guyon, helped me find my way through many thorny passages without bloodshed. More recently, Al Braunmuller and Barbara Mowat read the entire manuscript with a care one expects only of saints and thus saved me from making egregious errors of style and judgment. The book is immeasurably better for their insights. And throughout the process of publication, Jay Halio's advice and encouragement have been more rewarding than he knows.

Portions of chapter 6 first appeared as "Shakespeare's Use of the 'Timon' Comedy," in *Shakespeare Survey* 29 (1976), and portions of chapters 1 and 5 as "Coriolanus and the Matter of Troy," in *Mirror up to Shakespeare,* edited by

9

J. C. Gray (Toronto: University of Toronto Press, 1984). I am indebted to the editor of the *Shakespeare Survey* and to the University of Toronto Press for allowing me to reproduce that material here. I am equally indebted to the Faculty Development Committee of Allegheny College for their assistance in financing my research trips to the Folger Shakespeare Library, the British Library, and the Senate House Library at the University of London.

My greatest debt, however, is recorded in the dedication. I owe it to my wife, who, for the sake of this book, has borne, and borne, and borne, and been fubb'd off, and fubb'd off, and fubb'd off, from this day to that day, that it is a shame to be thought on. I am an infinitive thing upon her score.

James C. Bulman
Allegheny College

Shakespeare quotations throughout are from *The Complete Works of Shakespeare,* ed. David Bevington, 3d ed. (Glenview, Ill.: Scott, Foresman & Co., 1980).

*The Heroic Idiom
of Shakespearean Tragedy*

1

Heroic Mimesis: The Poor Itch of Your Opinion

*O*urs is not a heroic age. Nurtured on skepticism, caught up in questions of unconscious motivation, and rent by moral uncertainty, we are reluctant to take greatness at face value. We rationalize exceptional achievement, explain it as the logical consequence of certain preconditions. Heroism, we suspect, is a figment of the imagination, born of our collective will to idealize manly behavior and propagated in myth and legend, not in life. Even those historical personages we usually regard as heroic—an Alexander, a Julius Caesar, a George Washington—have been so filtered through our myth-making faculties that the hyperbolic deeds for which they are celebrated may, as revisionist historians are quick to tell us, bear little resemblance to their actual performance. Our will to believe in heroes—to make of John Kennedy an Arthur in his Camelot, or of Charles de Gaulle another Charlemagne—is countered by an equally strong will to reduce great men to human proportions. Shakespeare understood the tension between these impulses well. He allows us to share Cleopatra's wish for a superhuman Antony—"Think you there was, or might be, such a man / As this I dreamt of?"—but to answer in Dolabella's voice, "Gentle madam, no."

Shakespeare lived in an age that, unlike ours, still had access to heroic traditions. The codes of chivalry were not long dead—still lived, if anachronistically, in men such as Philip Sidney and Walter Raleigh; and every good schoolboy was versed in Homer, Virgil, and Ovid. Small wonder, then, that heroic poetry came to be regarded in England, as it had been in Italy, as the highest form of art: an imitation of brave and noble deeds capable of moving the reader to admiration and spurring him on to his own acts of valor, justice, magnanimity. The didactic aims of "the *Heroicall*" are succinctly expressed by Sidney in his *Defence of Poesie:*[1]

> For by what conceit can a tongue bee directed to speake evil of that which draweth with him no lesse champions then *Achilles, Cirus, Aeneas, Turnus, Tideus, Rinaldo,* who doeth not onely teache and moove to a truth, but

teacheth and mooveth to the most high and excellent truth: . . . For as the
Image of each Action stirreth and instructeth the minde, so the loftie
Image of such woorthies, most enflameth the minde with desire to bee
woorthie: and enformes with counsaile how to bee woorthie.

Thomas Heywood, some thirty years later, applied this theory of poetry
to the more lively images of drama. In *An Apology for Actors,* he invented an
account of the genesis and transmission of heroism. The process, he suggests, involves emulation. From the time Hercules' tutor inspired him with
a show to emulate "the worthy and memorable acts of his father *Iupiter,*" the
heroes of every generation have learned to pattern their behavior on the
admirable performances of heroes past.[2] The "bold English man" of "our
domesticke hystories" patterned his great deeds on those of ancient heroes
such as Alexander, just as Alexander was inspired by even more ancient
models: "had *Achilles* never lived, *Alexander* had never conquered the whole
world." Elizabethans, thus conditioned to think that history existed on a
continuum with the matter of heroic poetry, could draw ready correspondence between factual accounts and myth. Holinshed could characterize
figures of the recent past as epic conquerors; Daniel could write of English
Palladins out of whose deeds "new immortal *Iliads* might proceed";[3] and
North could employ a distinctly Homeric idiom to assess the human frailties of Plutarch's noble Greeks and Romans. By honoring the patterns of
epic poetry in their histories, chroniclers created a heroic reality firmly
predicated upon fiction. Myth and history merged to make legend, and
great men acquired the patina of their bronze-age prototypes. In the
Elizabethan imagination, Henry V *was* an Alexander; Talbot *was* a Hector;
Essex, at least for Chapman, *was* an Achilles.

The dramatist's problem of how to depict a hero is different from the
chronicler's or even the epic poet's, however. His art is more mimetic than
narrative; and if he attempts to draw a hero of real flesh and blood—a
credible human being whose greatness emerges from the complexities of
historical situation—some of the mythic patina is bound to be dulled. How,
then, is he to present heroism on the stage? If he resorts to simple patterns
to define the hero, as many of Shakespeare's predecessors did, he risks
caricature and destroys mimetic credibility. The patterns Heywood describes had, after all, long been hardening into conventions: what once had
made a deed heroic and its doer exceptional had become, through repetition, the rule. The "lively and well-spirited action" Heywood admired—"to
see a souldier shap'd like a souldier, walke, speake, act like a souldier"—
had, as this passage suggests, devolved into typical behavior. Certain ways
of speaking and acting had become so ingrained in heroic drama that they
were part and parcel of the myth, no longer capable of dramatizing authentic greatness within an historical context, no longer capable of distin-
guishing the individual from the species. Yet to cast off the conventional

patterns would be as risky for the dramatist as to become their slave. Without them, he would have to find new criteria unrelated to stage tradition by which an audience could appraise heroism. The hero would virtually have to create himself; and in two hours' traffic, that feat is well-nigh impossible—even for a Hercules.

Adherence to stage conventions and imitation of reality need not, however, be mutually exclusive. Although conventions may codify reality, they do not preclude it. In fact, reference to heroes past and imitation of their deeds and language provide a convenient dramatic shorthand. A particular behavior or style of speech—some act of note; a little scene to monarchize or kill with looks—when repeated over and over again through time begins to acquire a significance beyond its immediate context: all past uses endow it with a world of accumulated meaning. Conventions, then, are not at odds with reality, but are agreements about how to perceive reality. For an audience, they have the power to suggest ideas and establish values in an easily comprehensible manner. Too slavish an adherence to them will, of course, make it impossible for the hero to achieve that strongly individual identity he requires in order to appear real; but without them, it would be difficult to find enough traditional points of reference—to get enough dramatic bearings—to establish a convincing heroic mimesis. The need simultaneously to embrace and reject heroic conventions is a paradox that Shakespeare wrestled with throughout his career, but never with more dexterity than in *Troilus and Cressida* or more muscle than in *Coriolanus*.

Ulysses, in his famous scene with Achilles, meditates on the power of conventions to create value in the viewer's eye—in Heywood's terms, to move the audience to admiration. At stake is Achilles' worth as a warrior. By pouting in his tent, he has brought the war to a standstill. Ajax, his envious rival, asks the crucial question, "What is he more than another?" (2.3.141); and Ulysses weighs it carefully. On the one hand, he affirms that Achilles is heroic by nature, apt to determine his own value without having to rely on the conventional bases of judgment insisted on in the public forum:

> He doth rely on none,
> But carries on the stream of his dispose
> Without observance or respect of any,
> In will particular and in self-admission.

> (2.3.162–65)

But determined to get Achilles back to battle, Ulysses plots to make him sensible that his is only an "imagin'd worth" (l. 171). At Ulysses' behest, the generals pass by Achilles' tent without their accustomed deference, like an audience unable to recognize the hero because he no longer fits the traditional pattern of brave deeds. Achilles observes the change and, in a moment of doubt, considers what it may mean:

'Tis certain, greatness, once fall'n out with fortune,
Must fall out with men too. What the declin'd is
He shall as soon read in the eyes of others
As feel in his own fall.

(3.3.75–78)

He acknowledges the role public opinion plays in making him what he is—a remarkable concession for one who believes in the absoluteness of his own greatness and who will keep insisting, in the face of all evidence, that it is unassailable. Ulysses is quick to interpret the evidence for him:

no man is the lord of anything,
Though in and of him there be much consisting,
Till he communicate his parts to others;
Nor doth he of himself know them for aught
Till he behold them formed in the applause
Where th' are extended.

(3.3.115–20)

The vocabulary in these lines hints at Shakespeare's darker purpose: to probe an actor's relationship with his audience in creating dramatic identity and to assess the efficacy of stage conventions in persuading an audience that it is watching an authentic representation of heroism. Ulysses argues that identity can be determined only by the collective will: without that will, no man can claim rightly to be great. Analogously, without winning an audience's approbation by communicating "his parts," no character can achieve mimetic credibility. The trouble is, public opinion is fickle; it doles out applause arbitrarily: "The present eye praises the present object" (l. 180).

The point made, Ulysses presses home. Achilles must honor custom, and keep honoring it, if he wishes to be a hero at all. "Time hath, my lord, a wallet at his back, / Wherein he puts alms for oblivion" (ll. 145–46): brave deeds, once forgotten, cannot maintain a hero in the public eye:

Perseverance, dear my lord,
Keeps honor bright; to have done is to hang
Quite out of fashion, like a rusty mail
In monumental mock'ry. Take the instant way . . . .

(3.3.150–53)

The devastating image of armor no longer in use clarifies what Achilles must do if he is to preserve his value: fight, and fight valiantly. The public expects a hero to do it, custom requires it, and custom has validity only so long as the public subscribes to it.

Herein resides the paradox of the scene. Ulysses espouses a theory that heroic value is at the mercy of an inconstant public will, but that theory contravenes his apparent belief in Achilles' intrinsic value as a warrior.

Ulysses, after all, stages the scene as a ruse to make Achilles *think* that he has lost his reputation, whereas in fact the Greeks prize Achilles as highly as he prizes himself. What motivates them to go to such lengths to get him back on the field is an unspoken faith in his absolute worth. One can detect this paradox even in Ulysses' assertion that all value is relative: "no man is the lord of anything, / Though in and of him there be much consisting." The subjunctive clause affirms an intrinsic merit that the main premise denies. Shakespeare further complicates the problem by showing Achilles, in the deeds he does once he leaves his tent, to be hardly worthy of the faith the generals have in him. The paradox thus remains vital in the theater: Ulysses' ostensible belief in Achilles' absolute worth is at odds with his conviction that only adherence to custom can maintain that worth in the public eye. And as we the public watch, Achilles' brutal disregard for everything traditionally valued as heroic persuades us that he is unworthy; yet Achilles is Achilles still.

Ulysses' counterpart in *Coriolanus* is Volumnia, who, in describing how she educated her son in the ways of heroism, echoes Ulysses' image of rusty mail as a heroic mockery:

> I, considering how honor would become such a person, that it was no better than picture-like to hang by th' wall, if renown made it not stir, was pleas'd to let him seek danger where he was like to find fame. (1.3.9–13)

Only in public acclaim, she implies—in the fame and renown attendant upon brave deeds—can he find honor. As a dramatic analogue to the playwright himself, Volumnia seems to defend the legitimacy of convention to define her son's heroic identity. She gloats that the wounds he has sustained in battle will provide the evidence necessary to persuade the Roman citizens to elect him consul. "O, he is wounded, I thank the gods for 't," she exults bloody-mindedly; "He receiv'd in the repulse of Tarquin seven hurts i' th' body"—hurts that Menenius, in best Falstavian fashion, delights to increase for the wonder of it: "One i' th' neck, and two i' th' thigh—there's nine that I know." And to these he now adds two more, "I' th' shoulder and i' th' left arm," according to Volumnia's anatomical record: *"There will be large cicatrices to show the people, when he shall stand for his place"* (2.1.120–51, passim, my italics). At issue is the time-honored assumption, shared by Romans and Elizabethans alike, that the bearer of wounds is worthy of reward: outward shows of honor always signify intrinsic merit. Rome had codified this assumption in a ceremonial peep-show in which the hero, according to tradition, donned a gown of humility, showed his wounds to the citizens, and thereby won their voices. Custom, in a sense, validated noble deeds and assured the hero of who he was.

When Volumnia later bids Coriolanus to bow to the people, or, to borrow Ulysses' phrase, to "communicate his parts to others," she indicates that customs such as these have more than a little theatrical deception in them:

"for in such business / Action is eloquence, and the eyes of th' ignorant / More learned than the ears" (3.2.77–79)—an astute apologist for drama, she, who might agree with Heywood when he says, "so bewitching a thing is lively and well spirited action, that it hath power to new mold the harts of the spectators." Although she finds it distasteful that the mob should be in a position to pass judgment on a heroic merit far beyond their powers to comprehend, she nevertheless, like Ulysses, has a practical grasp of the political situation and is not above urging Coriolanus to "dissemble with [his] nature" (1. 64) if it will win him the reward she thinks is his by right. Volumnia advises him, as Ulysses had Achilles, to act according to custom and bring to popular attention conventional "proofs" to aver a heroism that she believes is intrinsic. Thus, like Ulysses, she obfuscates the psychological and the social determinants of heroic character. She assumes that a hero may exist apart from the conventions by which the public seeks to know him, yet she also counts on those conventions to play an integral part in mediating the hero's reality.

The problem is that such a mediation traps the citizens into making a judgment that, in this case, they would rather not make: that Coriolanus is fit to be consul. Custom binds them to it. They must be a loyal audience to the heroic interlude: "for if he show us his wounds and tell us his deeds, we are to put our tongues into those wounds and speak for them." The long-standing tradition of show-and-tell has all the power on its side. As for their power to deny it, "it is a power that we have no power to do" (2.3.5–8, passim).

More ominously, custom traps Coriolanus in the unsavory position of knowing his heroic worth only by seeking it in the estimation of an incon-stant mob. For one who believes, like Achilles, that the individual will is sacrosanct and that a man is "author of himself" (5.3.36), who recognizes the power of deeds to speak for themselves and loathes to hear his "noth-ings monster'd" (2.2.77), such submission to the popular will is heresy.

When Menenius admonishes him to "go fit you to the custom and / Take to you, as your predecessors have, / Your honor with your form" (11.142–44), he insists on the pattern of emulation so central to the Renaissance aesthetic. But Coriolanus detects a contradiction in it: honor, or the mainte-nance of his heroic integrity, is antithetical to the form that Menenius urges on him. He is averse to bragging to the citizens, showing them

> th' unaching scars which I should hide,
> As if I had receiv'd them for the hire
> Of their breath only!
>
> (2.2.148–50)

His vocabulary of commodity indicates the demeaning results such behav-ior would have: all value would be relative, and the hero, once having relinguished his fixed worth to the popular will, would be no better than a pawn in the marketplace. When he finally submits to the custom, there-fore—dons the gown and stands before the citizens, as he had vowed never to do, begging—he dramatizes the paradox of heroic mimesis more elo-quently than any previous Shakespearean hero, and most appropriately, because he comes last:

> Why in this woolvish toge should I stand here,
> To beg of Hob and Dick, that does appear,
> Their needless vouches? Custom calls me to 't.
> What custom wills, in all things should we do 't,
> The dust on antique time would lie unswept,
> And mountainous error be too highly heap'd
> For truth to o'erpeer. Rather than fool it so,
> Let the high office and the honor go
> To one that would do thus.
>
> (2.3.115–23)

His sarcastic references to truth and honor point up the patent absurdity of his situation. He confesses to perpetuating error by honoring custom; but in doing so, he lends to custom a certain legitimacy and tacitly acknowl-edges that popular opinion counts.[4]

Coriolanus's question recapitulates the question Shakespeare had been asking and boldly answering throughout his career: To adhere to conven-tions or to flout them? On the one hand, conventions draw so explicitly from the stock-in-trade of stage tradition that when we spot them we, like good Roman citizens, immediately recognize their significance as long-standing agreements about how to perceive reality. To discredit them, as Coriolanus wishes to do, would be to deny a potent source of theatrical definition. On the other hand, the danger Coriolanus spies in them is real: they depersonalize the hero by forcing him to conform to established pat-terns of behavior whose very sameness calls attention to itself as typical, even artificial. Such patterns may provide an adequate mimetic idiom for the exploits of soldiers in early chronicle plays, the grand ambitions of epic conquerors, or the rant of Senecan revengers, but they hardly serve to convey the individual greatness of Shakespeare's tragic heroes.

Coriolanus argues, like Plato, that outward shows often lie. The wound he shows to please the public eye today may signify no more than the wound Falstaff is pleased to show tomorrow. He is suspicious of theatrical effects and abjures the actor's profession: to turn his throat of war into a supplicant's voice, to speak with a beggar's tongue, to force his armed knees, who bowed but in his stirrup, to bow to the mob—

> I will not do 't,
> Lest I surcease to honor mine own truth
> And by my body's action teach my mind
> A most inherent baseness.
>
> (3.2.122–25)

He believes that the truth of heroic character is something more profound than conventions have the power to signify or the public to comprehend. But the theater is, after all, a public forum; and when Coriolanus rejects conventions, he in a sense is dismissing a heritage on which the audience has come to depend as a means for evaluating character.

No one understood this better than Shakespeare. Had he not employed heroic conventions, we would not have *Coriolanus*. Coriolanus's battles are the more credible for invoking the alarums and excursions of early chronicle plays; his exhortations to his men the more stirring for echoing the rhetoric of Tamburlaine and his progeny; his one-on-one fight with Aufidius the more epic for recalling Hector's encounter with Achilles; his hyperbolic assertion of constancy as the citizens clamor for his death—

> Let them pull all about mine ears, present me
> Death on the wheel or at wild horses' heels,
> Or pile ten hills on the Tarpeian rock,
> That the precipitation might down stretch
> Below the beam of sight, yet will I still
> Be thus to them.
>
> (3.2.1–6)

—the more suggestive if one remembers that the modes of death he mentions are those of epic mythology, that the piling of hill on hill harks back to Homer, to Virgil, to Ovid's assertion that the giant race piled Pelion upon Olympus, and that Hamlet and Laertes echoed Ovid's lines in their vaunting declarations of heroic purpose at Ophelia's grave. And when Cominius awards Coriolanus a Homeric pedigree in his long encomium beginning, "The deeds of Coriolanus / Should not be utter'd feebly" (2.2.82–83), he may be indulging in another convention Coriolanus thinks he can do without;[5] but it serves both to define the Graeco-Roman idiom in which Coriolanus is conceived and to set a rhetorical standard against whose use he can rebel in order to achieve a more authentic voice of his own.

The verisimilitude of Shakespeare's heroes, then, depends on their relationship to heroic tradition. Shakespeare could not, like Swift's spider, spin new forms of heroism out of the web of his imagination without recourse to the ancient matter that had shaped his audience's expectations. On the contrary, he relied heavily on those expectations: in each of his heroic plays he incorporated allusions to and conventions from his literary and dramatic heritage to serve as models from which to evolve a more authentic representation of heroism. From the play's formal relationship to tradition emerges its reality; in the hero's personal response to it resides his.

The representational power of any work of art springs not so much from its truth to life—evasive phrase—as from its struggle to embrace and at the same time transcend its literary model. As Howard Felperin provocatively argues, "the notion that poetry imitates 'life' leads nowhere, in so far as we have no way of conceiving of, much less comprehending, life except through the mediation of sign-systems . . . that is to say, through the necessary aid of art."[6] Each new work must incorporate models that provide "mimetic points of reference" (39); by discarding them, it may achieve a greater illusion of reality. A credible representation of heroism, therefore, would involve a "restless dialectic between convention and the repudiation of convention" (10) and expose as inadequate, however necessary, "the established and stable forms of prior art and the life they can but stiffly gesture toward" (9). Shakespeare finds a dramatic analogue for the way in which the audience perceives a work of art in the "restless dialectic" with which the characters in *Coriolanus* respond to the conventions of heroism, and in particular to Coriolanus's donning the gown of humility to show his wounds. The citizens require the mediation of such "established and stable forms" to affirm the reality of the hero, whereas he, who declares that such forms have become ossified and thus meaningless, repudiates them in order simply to play "the man I am" (3.2.16), as if the reality of his manhood were theatrically unprecedented. The patricians, accepting these forms both as artificial expedients and as adequate and necessary signs of an intrinsic merit, reward them with a leap of faith: Coriolanus is their god. The tribunes, however, regard the forms as shams, glorified by the patricians (and there is justice in their accusation) to keep the citizens in awe, but inadequate to represent a man's true nature—especially when that man is Coriolanus. The audience may choose to respond to the heroic conventions with simple assent, like the citizens, or simple dissent, like Coriolanus; or it may choose, like the patricians and the tribunes, to respond in a more complex fashion. The fact that the play dramatizes all these options seems to suggest that the most fitting response would embrace and transcend them all: in other words, it would involve an ongoing "restless dialectic" within us between assent and dissent, faith and skepticism. The choice—and ultimately one's attitude toward the hero and the play that contains him—depends on the ability to pick up the dramatic cues that Shakespeare offers; and that ability presupposes some familiarity with heroic traditions.

Much of the misunderstanding of Shakespeare's representation of heroism is caused by his reliance on these traditions. He uses an idiom that we view through a glass darkly—an aggregate of archaic modes of speech and codes of conduct, gleaned from a multitude of heroic sources, that assumes in the audience a shared response, but in fact is now lost to us and difficult to recapture. I do not mean to discount the value of contemporary response to the heroism in Shakespeare's plays: they would lose their vitality if each age could not reinterpret them in light of its own biases. Nevertheless, a familiarity with heroic traditions may allow us to regard certain plays, certain scenes, certain characters, with more tolerance than such biases do. Because the heroic idiom of the plays appears remote and perhaps inaccessible, it sometimes seems ludicrous. We project our prejudice onto Shakespeare, call him Shakespeare our contemporary, and assume that he could not be using the idiom seriously as a means to dramatize heroism, that he must intend it to serve as a disguise for qualities more compatible with the unheroic or antiheroic ethos of modern drama. Like tribunes skeptical of all shows of greatness, we are inclined to disavow any consonance between tenor and vehicle: a heroic idiom must, we argue, be meant to obscure rather than reveal a character's inner being. For this reason, reductive interpretations of Shakespeare's heroes abound. Henry V indulges in public displays of chivalry only to advance his Machiavellian ambitions. Othello? Not a noble Moor at all: just a gull, a dolt, ignorant as dirt, whose assured and rotund Virgilian language hides the ignoble fears and base jealousies that lurk within the gates of his unconscious. Macbeth's resonant epic diction likewise ill conceals the fact that he is but a dwarfish thief in borrowed robes; and Coriolanus's tenacious clinging to heroic principle betrays him at last as a boy of tears—nothing more. The arguments are familiar. Many of them are compelling. But on the whole, they tend to be lopsidedly skeptical. They reflect too consistently, almost predictably, an antiheroic bias, as if Shakespeare incorporated heroic traditions *only* to repudiate them. But the heroic idiom that Shakespeare inherited had richly served the Elizabethan theatre as a rhetorical basis of characterization. A rhetorical conception of reality may, of course, affront our acquired taste for the Beckett nonsequitur, the Albee subtext, and the Pinter pause that are the current measures of theatrical representation; but one must be careful not to let those measures call "bastard" an idiom that functioned perfectly legitimately four hundred years ago. If the heroic idiom ever grew to be something more than merely a conventional means of characterization, it did so in the shaping hands of Shakespeare, who found it a random collection of untuned strings and left it a lyre, who fashioned it as an instrument mutable and varied, explored its resonances, and played it with increasing sophistication during the course of his career. We owe it to him to study the idiom more carefully in the context of each individual play before determining that his heroes, and his heroic plays, do not really mean what they say.

I intend this study as a modest supplement to those indispensable works that have already illuminated the heroic background of Shakespeare's plays: his reading of Homer and Virgil, Ovid and Plutarch; his knowledge of Senecan drama and philosophy, both in the original and in Elizabethan imitations; his immersion in moral historians whose heroes unfailingly illustrated some sententious point; his appreciation of how classical heroes and antique legends were adapted, embellished, and transformed by writers of medieval romance; his more immediate reliance on contemporary dramatists—Kyd, Peele, Greene, Marlowe—to furnish him with prefabricated forms of stage heroism.[7] I depart from those works to examine the ways in which Shakespeare's use of the heroic idiom changed and

developed through his career—how in the early plays he drew on traditional narrative and dramatic sources to create the illusion of heroic reality;
how in the later plays he borrowed increasingly from his own earlier work,
the reference to which, whether conscious or unconscious, complicates any
appreciation of the heroic in them. It may be instructive to study how
Shakespeare in time became his own best resource for establishing more
authentic representations of heroism; but to do that, we first must look at
how, in the early plays, he ransacked the material at hand, borrowed from
other writers, and tested the established modes of heroic mimesis. To his
apprenticeship, then, I now turn.

2

Emulation Hath a Thousand Sons: Heroism in the Early Plays

To open what may have been his first play, Shakespeare chose to dramatize the funeral of Henry V, a patriot king whom chroniclers had already made legendary and who had recently trod the boards in *The Famous Victories of Henry V.*[1] Shakespeare's problem was to translate that funeral into the heroic terms his audience would expect. Into the mouths of the mourners who attend Henry's coffin, therefore, he put conventional panegyric. Cosmic imagery that attends the fall of a great man—injunctions to comets to "brandish your crystal tresses in the sky / And with them scourge the bad revolting stars" (*1 Henry VI*, 1.1.3–4)—functions here as it will in later plays such as *Julius Caesar* to elevate a human death into something of mythic proportions. Words such as "brandish" and "scourge," though applied here to comets, nevertheless call to mind the heroic deeds done by Henry and are applied specifically to him by the second mourner:

> His brandish'd sword did blind men with his beams;
> His arms spread wider than a dragon's wings;
> His sparkling eyes, replete with wrathful fire,
> More dazzled and drove back his enemies
> Than midday sun fierce bent against their faces.
> What should I say? His deeds exceed all speech.
>
> (1.1.10–15)

Such a *laudatio* is recognizably in the epic vein, the sort of verse that Surrey, inspired by unrhymed Italian versions of the *Aeneid,* had developed in his translation of Virgil, that Sackville had made more striking by allying it with lurid images of blood in the *Complaint of Buckingham* and *Gorboduc,* and that had been made more dramatically sensational by Kyd and Marlowe.[2] It transforms the passage from Hall on which it was based:

26

What should I say, he was the blasying comete and apparant lanterne in his daies, he was the myrror of Christendome & the glory of his countrey, he was the floure of kynges passed, and a glasse to them that should succede.[3]

Hall conveys Henry's greatness in terms befitting a Christian prince and suitably casts his life in the Mirror tradition. Shakespeare's embellishment makes Henry more pagan, more Homeric, of an awful, almost Achillean nature—arms like dragon's wings, eyes sparkling with wrathful fire; the description is like that of a Spenserian basilisk—and his emphasis is not on praise for a Christian prince, but on admiration for an epic warrior. The language is not, like Hall's, courtly: in its gaudy allusions it must have sounded to an Elizabethan audience very much like Marlowe.

The most immediate and influential model for such a portrait would have been Tamburlaine, whose high astounding terms Edward Alleyn had brought to life in the year or two before *1 Henry VI* and who continued to hold the stage. A conqueror of no Christian sensibility, Tamburlaine was a scourge of Asia about whom it could be said, as Gloucester says of Henry, "He ne'er lift up his hand but conquered" (l. 16). The staging of Henry's funeral may in fact allude to the spectacular scene of mourning for Zenocrate in *Tamburlaine: Part Two,* for which the stage was draped in black, and during which Tamburlaine vented his spleen against the town where she died in language—"fiery meteors" that "presage / Death," "a blazing star / That may endure till heaven be dissolved," "Flying dragons, lightning," and "fearful thunder-claps" (3.2.1–14)[4]—that anticipates the language of Henry's panegyrics. In the first line of *Henry,* Bedford recalls Marlowe: "Hung be the heavens with black, yield day to night!"; and the recollection is even stronger when Exeter intones,

> And death's dishonorable victory
> We with our stately presence glorify,
> Like captives bound to a triumphant car.
>
> (1.1.20–22)

—lines that would have conjured up for the audience the memorable image of Tamburlaine being drawn across the stage in his chariot by captive kings.

This epic diction yields to something more biblical as Winchester portrays Henry as "a king bless'd of the King of kings" who fought "the battles of the Lord of hosts" and brought "unto the French the dreadful Judgment Day," but whose death may cause England to endure, in civil broils, another Flood: "Our isle be made a nourish of salt tears" (ll. 28–32, passim; l. 50). The mourners' final consolation, however, is not scriptural, but Ovidian. Henry is to undergo a classical metamorphosis: "A far more glorious star thy soul will make / Than Julius Caesar or bright—" (ll. 55–56). Just as Ovid had apotheosized Caesar in a triumph over death, so Henry here is not only deified as a conqueror—another Caesar—but even outdoes him: "*more glorious.*" The historical association of Rome and England had become legend.

In Henry's funeral, Shakespeare creates a dramatic correlative for the chronicle's narration: he translates Hall into heroic drama by using language he had inherited from epic tradition and from conqueror plays. This language, in its conventional appeal to one's instinct for admiration, re-creates the picture of a golden age of English heroism against which the mourners themselves jar and wrangle, striving to take charge of a now-headless realm. But the language is still essentially undramatic: formal encomium that defines heroism but is not yet allied to stage action and is spoken by as yet unidentified dramatis personae. Only in scenes with Talbot does it operate in conjunction with heroic performance.

Talbot, the play's English champion, embodies the qualities that the mourners had valued in Henry V and so becomes the dramatic surrogate for England's god of the golden age. Less well known than Henry, Talbot had nevertheless been immortalized by chroniclers as the "English Hector."[5] Shakespeare was thus free to take command of his dramatic resources to fashion forth a man of heroic greatness, not just in elegiac recollection, but in fully fleshed stage representation.

Shakespeare introduces Talbot significantly in the same scene in which Henry is eulogized, and by the Senecan convention of a Nuntius who delivers a long narrative account of his victories in battle. Shakespeare resorted to this convention throughout his career to insure admiration of heroes, perhaps most notably in the Bleeding Captain's account of Macbeth's deeds and Cominius's account of Coriolanus's. For Talbot, he drew his material from the Chronicles but, as in Henry's panegyric, transformed it with epic diction:

> More than three hours the fight continued,
> Where valiant Talbot above human thought
> Enacted wonders with his sword and lance.
> Hundreds he sent to hell, and none durst stand him;
> Here, there, and every where, enrag'd he slew.
> The French exclaim'd the devil was in arms;
> All the whole army stood agaz'd on him.
>
> (1.1.120–26)

Sidney would approve: the passage begs for admiration. The army stood "agaz'd" at this Herculean war machine; and so, the language suggests, should we, in our imaginations. The style owes a good deal to the "epic stateliness combined with the turgid sensationalism" that had become characteristic of Nuntii and had been employed to dramatic effect in the reports of battle in Kyd's *The Spanish Tragedie.*[6] Hamlet's attempt to reconstruct the speech of Pyrrhus's slaughter of Priam marks Shakespeare's extreme descent into the style. But the representation of Talbot as hero, as scourge of France, owes more to *Tamburlaine* and its progeny— plays such as Greene's *Alphonsus, King of Aragon* and Peele's *The Battle of Alcazar*—than to epic narration.[7] These plays dramatize aspiring heroes so near to Homer's Achilles in spirit that they pay allegiance to no higher law than self-will. Talbot's assertive rhetorical style distinctly echoes that of Tamburlaine: he vaunts, he dares, he vows to outdo. Against the French he hurls abuse with all the fervor of a Tamburlaine raging against the world's tyrants:

> Your hearts I'll stamp out with my horse's heels,
> And make a quagmire of your mingled brains.
>
> (1.4.108–9)

Heroic hyperbole frequently has such grotesque overtones. They form a part of the threat, the claim of superhuman scourging power, that Tamburlaine uses against all his enemies, but never so confidently as against the Turkish kings:

> I will, with engines never exercised,
> Conquer, sack, and utterly consume
> Your cities and your golden palaces,
> And with the flames that beat against the clouds,
> Incense the heavens and make the stars to melt,
> As if they were the tears of Mohamet,
> For hot consumption of his country's pride.
>
> (*Part Two:* 4.2.117–23)

The sublime egotism of Tamburlaine's vaunt—his ornately Ovidian hyperbole, his recurrent claim that he is another Mars—gives him a dramatic definition akin to that of mythic figures, untamed by the social contexts in which one must judge the actions of lesser men.[8] Much of Talbot's verse bears this stamp. Before the walls of Bordeaux he vaunts as brazenly as Tamburlaine before the walls of Babylon. His three personified attendants—famine, steel, and fire—indicate that he, too, is a god of war; and his reference to "air-braving towers" clearly invokes the topless towers of Ilium:

> if you frown upon this proffer'd peace,
> You tempt the fury of my three attendants,
> Lean famine, quartering steel, and climbing fire,
> Who in a moment even with the earth
> Shall lay your stately and air-braving towers . . . .
>
> (4.2.9–13)

It is a type of verse to which Henry V will have recourse, though with a greater sense of role-playing, before the walls of Harfleur. Here, there is no evidence that Talbot is role-playing, self-consciously adopting a particular style to achieve his ends. Instead, the verse defines him; the only selfhood he has, as a dramatic character, comes from it; and the General at Bordeaux responds to it in kind by addressing him as a Tamburlaine: "Thou ominous and fearful owl of death, / Our nation's terror and their bloody scourge" (ll. 15–16). The heroic "reality" of the scene thus depends on our recognition of a familiar style of rhetorical self-assertion. That style encourages us to regard Talbot with wonder and awe, not with the moral censure that might otherwise frown upon his deeds; for as Eugene Waith observes of other Herculean heroes, the verse filters historical figures through myth so hyperbolically that their deeds can no longer be measured by the rod of conventional morality.

Epic narration and conqueror drama were not the only sources for heroic patterns in *Henry VI*, however. The expectations raised in an audience by reference to Tamburlaine were crossed by reference to other heroic traditions that made the play's mimesis far more complex: chief among them, the nationalism sprung of English chivalry. As if to provide a genealogy for the tradition, Shakespeare traces his English conqueror back to forebears in Froissart's fourteenth-century *Chroniques*—works that canonized courtly traditions for the court of Edward III—and, behind them, to epic figures in *chanson de geste:* "Froissart, a countryman of ours, records / England all Olivers and Rowlands bred / During the time Edward the Third did reign" (1.2.29–31); and the tradition of chivalry lives even more nobly, Shakespeare suggests, in Talbot: "More truly now may this be verified" (l. 32). But mention of the English king tempers the spirit of independent achievement associated with knightly quests. A soldier fights not for himself, but for his country: he is foremost a patriot, and his *res gestae* cannot be divorced from the welfare of the king whom he serves.

According to chivalric tradition, honor is directed both inward, to a preservation of one's own heroic constancy, and outward, to a preservation of the social order: it requires both a private and a public commitment.[9] In this dual commitment, Talbot differs from the less chivalrous Tamburlaine. True, both of them believe that a hero must be as good as his word. Honor, as its core, involves a consonance of word and deed through which a hero insures his integrity—inseparable, in terms of dramatic representation, from his heroic "reality." Talbot and Tamburlaine could speak in the same voice: "Nor are Apollo's oracles more true / Than thou shalt find my vaunts substantial" (*Part One:* 1.2.211–12), and their actions would bear them out. The oaths, vows, and pledges of faith that riddle such conquerors' speech are a conventional means by which they express their honor and, along with it, manifest their epic selfhood. But Talbot's conception of honor also bows to the more public requirements of state. He does not, like Tamburlaine, exist in a moral and political vacuum; rather than play God and King, he serves God and king. His private honor is subservient to the honor owed to a higher order and, as such, is in accord with the Tudor historians' modification of the chivalric ethos.[10] The social and political context they provide for Talbot makes his ethos more complex than that of conquerors who, conceived in the isolated circumstances that remove legend from history, are free to act on their individual wills unbounded. Even when Talbot seems bent on a most private course of honor to avenge the death of his friend Salisbury, using the images of grotesque bravado to which I have already referred (stamping out hearts with horses' heels, making a quagmire of mingled brains) to assert his purpose, he nevertheless conceives of it as consistent with his patriotic duty: "Now, Salisbury, for thee, and for the right / Of English Henry, shall this night appear / How much in duty I am bound to both" (2.1.35–37).

In an emblematic scene that could have no place in the conqueror drama of Marlowe's ilk, Shakespeare further adjusts our perspective on the public orientation of Talbot's heroism. Accompanied by his soldiers, Talbot marches onstage with great pomp to lay down his sword and to kneel before his king: a ceremonial affirmation of the order of state, and the individual's submission to it, that Shakespeare would use again in *Titus Andronicus* and much later, with tragic irony, in *Macbeth:*

> this arm, that hath reclaim'd
> To your obedience fifty fortresses,
> Twelve cities, and seven walled towns of strength,
> Beside five hundred prisoners of esteem,
> Lets fall his sword before your Highness' feet,
> And with submissive loyalty of heart
> Ascribes the glory of his conquest got
> First to my God and next unto your Grace.
>
> (3.4.5–12)

The king's rewarding Talbot with the title Earl of Shrewsbury also fulfills convention by matching a hero's dedication with his country's appreciation in a satisfying mutuality.

Such heroic dedication to a patriotic order gives rise to righteous indignation against those who fail so to dedicate themselves. With a fervor that anticipates that of Henry V Talbot rallies his soldiers against the French at Orleans: "Hark, countrymen! Either renew the fight, / Or tear the lions out of England's coat" (1.5.27–28); but when they fail him, he chastises them in a manner that Coriolanus will outdo when he rails against his troops for dishonoring mother Rome by their cowardice:

> Renounce your soil, give sheep in lions' stead.
> Sheep run not half so treacherous from the wolf,
> Or horse or oxen from the leopard,
> As you fly from your oft-subdued slaves.
> ·
> You all consented unto Salisbury's death,

>   For none would strike a stroke in his revenge.
>   . . . .
>   The shame hereof will make me hide my head.
>
> (1.5.29–39, passim)

The ethos of chivalry is dramatized even more explicitly in a scene between Talbot and his son. The family has courtesy in the blood: father and
son are as constant to one another as each is to the state. In their scene
together, the community of values that defines their chivalric heroism is at
stake. Constancy to those values requires that Talbot fight to the death;
policy dictates that he fly. He urges his son to fly in order to avenge his
certain death; his son urges him to fly in order to return with reinforce-
ments.

JOHN:	Is my name Talbot? And am I your son?
	And shall I fly? O, if you love my mother,
	Dishonor not her honorable name
	To make a bastard and a slave of me!
	The world will say he is not Talbot's blood,
	That basely fled when noble Talbot stood.
TALBOT:	Fly, to revenge my death, if I be slain.
JOHN:	He that flies so will ne'er return again.
TALBOT:	If we both stay, we both are sure to die.
JOHN:	Then let me stay, and, father, do you fly.
	. . . .
TALBOT:	Shall all thy mother's hopes lie in one tomb?
JOHN:	Ay, rather than I'll shame my mother's womb.
TALBOT:	Upon my blessing, I command thee go.
JOHN:	To fight I will, but not to fly the foe.
TALBOT:	Part of thy father may be sav'd in thee.
JOHN:	No part of him but will be shame in me.

>   (4.5.12–39, passim)

As they vie to outdo one another in a courtesy that defies all reason, the
Talbots strain rhetorical formulae. Rhetoric, in fact, defines their very being: once each stakes his character on a simple line of argument, Shakespeare uses amplification to sustain it. There is no change, suppleness, or
flexibility to hint that there might be two minds at work behind the
rhetoric. The rhyming couplets and the stichomythia, furthermore, embody in their artificiality the formal antiquity of the Talbots' call to honor.
As both magnanimously choose not to forswear the chivalry that sustains
their heroic being, both die. Die, indeed, like hungry lions doing "rough
deeds of rage and stern impatience" (4.7.8), the echo of alliterative verse
reinforcing an epic resolve; but die, nevertheless. Shakespeare implies that
the rhetorical nature of such heroism itself may, by its very inflexibility,
cause the hero's fall: a hero limited to one idiom is doomed by his inability

to adapt to dramatic circumstances. Within a chronicle frame, then, Shake-speare uses conventions drawn from a variety of heroic sources to define Talbot's tragedy; but through them, he does not succeed in portraying any inner life for Talbot.

Talbot's death takes the form of traditional *de casibus* tragedy wherein a great man falls from a high place, is brought low by fortune. Willard Farnham has traced the tradition from its source, Boccaccio's *De Casibus Virorum Illustrium,* through Lydgate's moralistic redaction of it called *The Fall of Princes,* up to *The Mirror for Magistrates,* which reads like a veritable Madame Tussaud's of War-of-the-Roses' notables, each one exemplifying either virtue victimized by vice, or vice that falls by its own undoing.[11] The *de casibus* tradition underlies most English tragedy before Shakespeare, and Talbot certainly falls as a representative of chivalric virtue victimized by vicious historical necessity. But there is more to it. Marlowe had defied the tradition by dramatizing Tamburlaine's death as a heroic transcendence, his body no longer "of force enough / To hold the fiery spirit it contains" (*Part Two:* 5.3.168–69); and Talbot, too, insists on regarding his own death in this fashion:

> Thou antic Death, which laugh'st us here to scorn,
> Anon, from thy insulting tyranny,
> Coupled in bonds of perpetuity,
> Two Talbots, winged through the lither sky,
> In thy despite shall scape mortality.
>
> (4.7.18–22)

Although the sentiments begin conventionally enough, with a glance at medieval depictions of death as a foul player, they move inexorably into the language of heroic metamorphosis (Ovid's voice always whispers in the early work of Shakespeare) that recalls the play's opening apotheosis of Henry V as a "glorious star," but here functions more dramatically to counterpoint the most mortal scene enacted onstage.

I do not mean to suggest that Shakespeare here is casting an ironic eye on the heroic traditions by which we come to know Talbot. If too absolute a faith in chivalric codes does him in, it does not necessarily follow that Shakespeare is urging us to withhold our admiration from the codes or our sympathy from him. Indeed, the persistence of Talbot's aspiration encour-ages acceptance of a final emphasis on his heroic potential, not on his human limitation; and contemporary evidence, such as Nashe's account of the play in *Pierce Pennilesse,* indicates that the heroic idiom that defined Talbot did move audiences to admiration:

How would it have joyed brave *Talbot* (the terror of the French) to thinke that after he had lyne two hundred yeares in his Tombe, hee should triumph againe on the Stage, and have his bones newe embalmed with

the teares of ten thousand spectators at least (at severall times), who, in
the Tragedian that represents his person, imagine they behold him fresh
bleeding.[12]

In a scene sometimes criticized as extraneous, Shakespeare in almost
paradigmatic fashion dramatizes how the audience is to be won to belief in
Talbot's heroic reality. Thinking she has Talbot trapped in her house, the
Countess of Auvergne challenges him, in cadences Marlowe applied to
Helen, to prove his heritage:

> Is this the scourge of France?
> Is this the Talbot, so much fear'd abroad
> That with his name the mothers still their babes?
> I see report is fabulous and false.
> I thought I should have seen some Hercules,
> A second Hector, for his grim aspect
> And large proportion of his strong-knit limbs.
>
> (2.3.15–21)

In what Sigurd Burckhardt calls a "ceremony of insult,"[13] the Countess
violates every standard of hospitality that chivalry would have her uphold.
But Talbot, with all the self-assurance and *gentilesse* for which Hector was
famous in medieval accounts of Troy, redeems chivalry by showing her that
he is indeed made of that epic mettle. The "silly dwarf" (l. 22) she sees
before her is, he confesses, but the shadow of himself.

> I tell you, madam, were the whole frame here,
> It is of such a spacious lofty pitch
> Your roof were not sufficient to contain 't.
>
> (2.3.54–56)

Stage directions reveal the dramatic process by which he transforms a
seemingly metaphoric boast into "reality" and convinces her of his true
stature: *"Winds his horn. Drums strike up. A peal of ordnance. Enter Soldiers."*
The frame by which he defines his heroic being is, he demonstrates, his
army:

> These are his substance, sinews, arms, and strength,
> With which he yoketh your rebellious necks,
> Razeth your cities, and subverts your towns,
> And in a moment makes them desolate.
>
> (2.3.63–66)

Courtesy gives way to bravado; Hector, to Tamburlaine. Despite Talbot's
physical limitations, the scene, both in language and in action, bids us to
believe in his greatness. The convention of a hero's defining himself by
external measures, such as his army, here raises no question of mutability as
it will later for a Richard II, who calls in vain upon an army of angels to

support his claim to a usurped throne, or a King Lear, who discovers with horror that his daughters can bargain away the hundred knights in whom he vests his royal identity. In this early play, Shakespeare uses the convention without irony: it demonstrates a firm union of sign and significance. Talbot is the sum of his parts. Conventional means of characterization—his modes of speech, his deeds—make the man, and one need look no deeper than they permit.[14] Talbot's display evokes an admiring response from the Countess:

> Victorious Talbot, pardon my abuse.
> I find thou art no less than fame hath bruited
> And more than may be gathered by thy shape.
>
> (2.3.67–69)

Her response provides a model for what the audience's response is to be and, to judge by contemporary accounts, was: a conviction that traditional idioms are equal to the task of depicting authentic heroism onstage.

There are passages, even in this early play, in which Shakespeare allows one to question the legitimacy of heroic conventions to define character; but they are more satirical, their parody of old plays more extreme, than anything he uses in scenes characterizing Talbot. Joan Pucelle in particular reduces the Tamburlainian pattern to its lowest comic denominator. A woman in man's attire who claims to be a virgin but is in fact a slut, she, like Tamburlaine, is "by birth a shepherd's" child (1.2.72); but with divine intervention, or so she says, she metamorphoses into a conquering hero. David Riggs has shown how her first scene in the French camp parodies the recognition scenes in *Tamburlaine: Part One*. Joan declares her heroic worth "through Marlowe's familiar gestures of challenge and vaunt":[15]

> My courage try by combat, if thou dar'st,
> And thou shalt find that I exceed my sex.
> Resolve on this: thou shalt be fortunate
> If thou receive me for thy warlike mate.
>
> (1.2.89–92)

Charles's response is, true to form, admiring: "Thou hast astonish'd me with thy high terms" (l. 93), but the one-on-one combat in which they engage is, like Joan's challenge, laden with sexual overtones; and when Joan overcomes him, the onlookers provide a chorus of bawdy innuendo that cheapens the Marlovian cadences of Charles's infatuated praise— "Doubtless he shrives this woman to her smock; / Else ne'er could he so long protract his speech" (ll. 119–20)—and renders a bit ludicrous Joan's claim to be the French Tamburlaine in a long speech of epic simile beginning, "Assign'd am I to be the English scourge" (l. 129). She is a distorted shadow of Tamburlaine, an impostor basely born whose high astounding terms disguise (in vain) her sexual witchcraft, whose quest for personal glory illuminates the unselfish nationalism of her English rival, and whose ignoble attempt to avoid death in the fire by crying to her incredulous captors, "I am with child, ye bloody homicides!" (5.4.62), underscores the nobility of Talbot's death. This exaggeration of heroics in one "possessed," while it makes fun of conventions, nevertheless sets off their more serious and credible use in representing the heroism of figures such as Talbot.

But Joan is not merely a parody in and of herself; she is the cause of our seeing parody in others. In the scene following Talbot's death, she devalues the traditional forms of encomium that were intoned so convincingly for Henry V by calling attention to their hollowness. In a Homeric catalogue of English pedigree, Lucy identifies Talbot by all his titles, and then some:

> But where's the great Alcides of the field,
> Valiant Lord Talbot, Earl of Shrewsbury,
> Created, for his rare success in arms,
> Great Earl of Washford, Waterford, and Valence,
> Lord Talbot of Goodrig and Urchinfield,
> Lord Strange of Blackmere, Lord Verdun of Alton,
> Lord Cromwell of Wingfield, Lord Furnival of Sheffield . . .
> (4.7.60–66)

And the list goes on. In a confrontation daring for its implicit comedy in a scene of heroic death, Joan ridicules Lucy for his "silly stately style": "The Turk, that two and fifty kingdoms hath, / Writes not so tedious a style as this" (ll. 72–74); and she satirically undercuts hyperbole with reality:

> Him that thou magnifi'st with all these titles
> Stinking and fly-blown lies here at our feet.
> (4.7.75–76)

But Joan's is not the last word. Lucy threatens to revenge Talbot's death by shifting to an equally hyperbolic idiom, that of Kyd and Peele. For the sake of him that was France's "terror and black Nemesis" (l. 78), Lucy rails, "O, were mine eyeballs into bullets turn'd, / That I in rage might shoot them at your faces!" (ll. 79–80). Joan again deflates the hyperbole by sneering, "I think this upstart is old Talbot's ghost" (l. 87), encouraging the audience to hear in him the outmoded diction of Andrea's Ghost trying to awake Revenge, perhaps the ghost of the Ur-Hamlet, certainly the mad Hieronimo's cry for vengeance and the *Vindicta* of *Alcazar*. Joan's confrontation with Lucy ends in a stand-off, he vowing that from Talbot's ashes will rise "a phoenix that shall make all France afeard" (l. 93), she reasserting herself in a "conquering vein" (l. 95). Their scene creates a tension between acceptance of the heroic idiom and criticism of it as overblown and out of date. Shakespeare may have felt both ways about it. But Joan's disparaging voice fails to disqualify the idiom as a legitimate means for dramatizing heroic reality. Through her, instead, Shakespeare only complicates our response to it, so that if we look at it one way, it is fustian; look at it another, it is the real thing.

The Jack Cade scenes in *2 Henry VI* burlesque the traditions of conqueror drama far more prosaically. Cade's parody of Tamburlaine's idiom is so reductive that, as David Riggs observes, it places him squarely in the line of would-be soldiers who comprise the clownish subplots of plays such as *Horestes* and *Locrine*.[16] As in those plays, the Cade subplot mocks but is really too silly to invalidate the serious functioning of heroic traditions in the main plot. Of no noble lineage at all, but claiming to be a Mortimer, Cade would lead an insurrection to put himself on the throne. His goals: to maintain authority by the martial strength required of noble men and, like Tamburlaine, to purge the court of all "false caterpillars" (4.4.37). But his army, "a ragged multitude / Of hinds and peasants" (ll. 32–33), unlike Joan's, poses no threat; and the best of his followers—worthies such as Dick the butcher and Smith the weaver—let the air out of his heroic pretense in their realistic asides. In this vein, the idiom of Cade's death is laughably mock-heroic. "O, I am slain! Famine and no other hath slain me" (4.10.59) he declares, discourteously robbing Alexander Iden of the victory rightly his; and then, in a prose the more absurd because it recalls the heroic transcendence of Talbot, Henry, and Tamburlaine before him, he curses, "Wither, garden, and be henceforth a burying-place to all that do dwell in this house, because the unconquer'd soul of Cade is fled" (ll. 61–64). His bravado yields at last a self-dramatized eulogy that anticipates the heroic farewells of many Shakespearean heroes to come—Hotspur's, Othello's, and Antony's among them; but Cade makes a travesty of the form because his claim is so unfounded: "Tell Kent from me, she hath lost her best man, and exhort all the world to be cowards; for I, that never fear'd any, am vanquish'd by famine, not by valor" (ll. 71–74).

The blatant satire of the traditional conqueror pattern that informs Cade's progress is warranted by the play's rigorous application of that pattern to York, the noble who seduces Cade "to make commotion" (3.1.358) and who thus becomes his companion in anarchy, the man by whose actions one takes the measure of Cade's folly. York's lust for power is not subsumed to the interests of state; therefore Cade's satire of it is less subtle than Joan's satire of Talbot, which depends on contrast to make its point. York's is a self-interested heroism. He indulges a "private grudge" (*1 Henry VI:* 4.1.109) against Somerset that violates the social and political order Talbot has sworn to uphold. Exeter casts York's wrath in indisputably epic terms: "had the passions of thy heart burst out," he tells York, "I fear we should have seen decipher'd there / More rancorous spite, more furious raging broils, / Than yet can be imagin'd or suppos'd" (ll.183–86). York, then, not the French, proves to be Talbot's worst enemy. He is the Achilles who, so wrapped up in his quarrel with Somerset that he fails to come to Talbot's aid, sacrifices this "Second Hector" to a selfish cause.

In the course of *Part Two*, York grows from mere epic hero to aspirant conqueror. He hungers for the sweet fruition of an earthly crown; his brows must deal life and death:

> That gold must round engirt these brows of mine,
> Whose smile and frown, like to Achilles' spear,
> Is able with the change to kill and cure.
>
> (5.1.99–101)

This passage conflates several in which Tamburlaine's regal aspirations and godlike powers are asserted: "To wear a crown enchased with pearl and gold, / Whose virtues carry with it life and death" (*Part One:* 2.5.60–61); "Upon his brows was portrayed ugly death" (3.2.72); "His lofty brows in folds do figure death, / And in their smoothness amity and life" (2.1.21–22).[17] York's is an almost formulaic statement of untrammeled heroic will, and it is anticipated in numerous speeches in the play, such as the long soliloquy in which he takes upon himself a divinity of hell:

> I will stir up in England some black storm
> Shall blow ten thousand souls to heaven or hell;
> And this fell tempest shall not cease to rage
> Until the golden circuit on my head,
> Like to the glorious sun's transparent beams,
> Do calm the fury of this mad-bred flaw.
>
> (3.1.349–54)

Like Talbot, York defines his identity according to the power he wields in his army. But whereas Talbot uses his army to defend England, York uses his obsessively for self-aggrandizement; and the obsession, as he admits, verges on madness: "You put sharp weapons in a madman's hands" (l.347). Such madness finds expression in York's hyperbolic claims of what he *could* do:

> O, I could hew up rocks and fight with flint,
> I am so angry at these abject terms!
> And now, like Ajax Telamonius,
> On sheep or oxen could I spend my fury.
>
> (5.1.24–27)

This is a rhetorical declaration of emotion rather than a dramatic demonstration of it: a language that depersonalizes the speaker by suggesting a *type* of heightened emotion without individualization. The Elizabethans learned it from Seneca. His tragic heroes spoke indulgently and at length *about* passion, but their speeches seldom embodied it: as G. K. Hunter observes, Seneca's plays were not imitations of action, but comments on mental states that would be appropriate to action.[18] His verse, however, was rich in the imagery of implied passion, and a few of Shakespeare's contemporaries, Kyd and Marlowe in particular, molded it into something far more dramatic. At its best, as in Hieronimo's discovery of his son hanging in the garden, it gives voice to an immediately apprehensible, intensely personal *process* of passion: Hieronimo's mad anger seems to emanate from within because his speech treats form dynamically—fluctuates, alters course in midthought, responds to new stimuli as if spontaneously. Shakespeare, however, still found the more static set-speech convenient, on occasion, to register a frozen *type* of heroic passion or pose; and he continued to use the rhetoric of generalization even in his mature plays, as when Hamlet, plucking up his courage to play heroic revenger, uncharacteristically asserts, "Now could I drink hot blood, / And do such bitter business as the day / Would quake to look on" (3.2.389–91). Shakespeare may use the form with greater irony and sophistication when Hamlet speaks, but the form is nonetheless the same as that by which York expresses his fury.

Seneca influences the blood revenges of Clifford and Margaret even more pervasively. Spotting his father lying dead on the field, killed by York's hand, Clifford pauses for a lament that draws on a rich tradition:

> O, let the vile world end,
> And the premised flames of the last day
> Knit earth and heaven together!
> Now let the general trumpet blow his blast,
> Particularities and petty sounds
> To cease!
>
> (5.2.40–45)

Shakespeare would revert to the language of apocalypse to assist the expression of grief throughout his career, not least in Lear's recoiling from filial ingratitude, in Macduff's horror at the murder of Duncan, or in Cleopatra's lament over the dying Antony. But as Clifford speaks, the style of his language undergoes a metamorphosis—

> Even at this sight
> My heart is turn'd to stone; and while 'tis mine,
> It shall be stony.
>
> (5.2.49–51)

—and so closely allied are idiom and characterization in these early plays that when Clifford's style of speech changes, so does his character. He degenerates from a chivalric warrior to a Senecan revenger:

> Henceforth I will not have to do with pity.
> Meet I an infant of the house of York,

> Into as many gobbets will I cut it
> As wild Medea young Absyrtus did.
> In cruelty will I seek out my fame.
>
> (5.2.56–60)

In this rhetorical declaration Clifford aligns himself with a string of Senecan heroes and heroines—Hercules, Medea, Thyestes, and Clytemnestra among them—who perverted their heroism into obsessive forms of cruelty. The sensational details of their revenges, the hacking and hewing, poisoning and seasoning, held great allure for bloody-minded Elizabethans; and in fact, as Inga-Stina Ewbank demonstrates, Clifford's declaration borrows directly from Medea's account of how she slew her brother, "whose shreaded and dismembred corps, with sword [I] in gobbets hewd," according to John Studley's translation of 1581.[19] Clifford thus seals his vow of revenge with an explicit Senecan allusion.

Clifford's desire to win fame in cruelty perverts the Homeric hero's lust for fame in arms, for public recognition of what he is, and that desire is consonant with the diction he uses. His diction defines the character of a revenger, and his audience consents to recognize him as such. The Senecan excess of his self-definition becomes readily apparent on his first appearance in *Part Three,* where he makes good the threat with which he ended *Part Two.* "Had I thy brethren here," he gloats to York's young son Rutland, "their lives and thine / Were not revenge sufficient for me";

> No, if I digg'd up thy forefathers' graves
> And hung their rotten coffins up in chains,
> It could not slake mine ire, nor ease my heart.
> The sight of any of the house of York
> Is as a fury to torment my soul;
> And till I root out their accursed line
> And leave not one alive, I live in hell.
>
> (1.3.25–33)

His morbid allusions to graves and coffins, to the personified fury who torments his soul, are all part and parcel of the diction of those Senecan heroes whose lives were nothing but living hells. Seneca provides a model, too, for Clifford's accomplice in crime, Queen Margaret, that "tiger's heart wrapt in a woman's hide" (1.4.137), whose baiting of York was perhaps inspired by the scene in which Medea confronts Jason with his dead sons.[20]

But if Seneca offered a source for Margaret's outraged bloodlust, Thomas Kyd offered more direct inspiration in his popular adaptation of Senecan images to the actual imitation of those horrors on the stage. Margaret's taunting of York with the blood-stained napkin of Rutland makes bold reference to the handkerchief stained with Horatio's blood that appeared at the most crucial moments of Hieronimo's revenge and had undoubtedly become for contemporary audiences one of the most poignant props in all drama. Leaning down to kiss the corpse of his son shortly after discovering him hanging from the tree, Hieronimo makes the discovery: "Seest thou this handkercher besmerd with blood? / It shall not from me, till I haue reueng'd" (2.6.52–53).[21] He offers the *"bloudie Napkin"* (3.13) to old Bazulto, who also grieves for a dead son: "Here, take my handkercher, and wipe thine eies . . . *Horatio,* this was thine . . . I dyde it in thy deerest blood" (ll.83,86,87). And at the climax, he flaunts it shamelessly as the token of a successful revenge in the faces of other grieving fathers:

> And heere beholde this bloudie hand-kercher,
> Which at *Horatios* death I weeping dipt
> Within the riuer of his bleeding wounds:
> It is propitious, see, I haue reserued,
> And neuer hath it left my bloody hart,
> Soliciting remembrance of my vow
> With these, O, these accursed murderers:
> Which now perform'd, my hart is satisfied.
>
> (4.4.122–29)

Margaret, when she offers *"the bloodstained cloth"* to York, solicits *our* remembrance of *The Spanish Tragedie.* If the napkin she gloats over is tainted with the blood of a revenge crueler and less just than Hieronimo's, that makes our recollection of *The Spanish Tragedie* the more painful and consequently makes Margaret's actions seem the more vicious. Like Hieronimo, she emphasizes how the napkin was dipped in the boy's blood; she gives it to York so that he may wipe his eyes; but above all, she exults in it as an instrument of torment, symbol of an achieved revenge that she flaunts more shamelessly than Hieronimo:

> Look, York! I stain'd this napkin with the blood
> That valiant Clifford, with his rapier's point,
> Made issue from the bosom of the boy;
> And if thine eyes can water for his death,
> I give thee this to dry thy cheeks withal.
>
> (*3 Henry VI*:1.4.79–83)

If her very next line, "Alas, poor York, but that I hate thee deadly," echoes the line Perseda speaks to Soliman as she is about to award him the poisoned kiss of revenge,[22] it only reinforces the extent to which Shakespeare's mind was suffused with Kyd during the writing of this scene and indicates how his art gains power through a creative tension with older plays and the formulas he derived from them.

Against the devolution of epic heroism into obsessive cruelty, Shakespeare in *Part Three,* in a masterful sleight of hand, recreates York in the image of Talbot. No longer the vaunting Marlovian whose heroism is as egotistical (if not so excessive) as Clifford's, York here is positively chivalric.

When he praises his sons' daring in the battle against Margaret, he resembles no one more than old Talbot delivering his final eulogy over young Talbot's passage to heroic manhood:

> My sons—God knows what hath bechanced them;
> But this I know, they have demean'd themselves
> Like men born to renown by life or death.
> Three times did Richard make a lane to me,
> And thrice cried "Courage, father, fight it out!"
> And full as oft came Edward to my side
> With purple falchion, painted to the hilt
> In blood of those that had encount'red him.
> And when the hardiest warriors did retire,
> Richard cried, "Charge, and give no foot of ground!"
>
> (1.4.6–15)

York speaks the kind of epic narration that had so distinguished the patriotism of England's defenders in *Part One;* and if he was not one of them in that play, his new style of verse in *Part Three* nevertheless casts him in a new and more sympathetic role of English chevalier sacrificed to the private revenges of a perverse few. A change of idiom accomplishes this remarkable metamorphosis: York's character is purely a function of his diction. When, in the same scene, he is made to suffer the outrage of the bloody napkin and the humiliation of the paper crown, his voice, in contrast to Clifford's and Margaret's, is full of righteous indignation; and when he is finally moved to express grief over Rutland and give in to their ritual gloating, he does so with a rhetoric that challenges their expectations even as it satisfies them:

> Bid'st thou me rage? Why, now thou hast thy wish.
> Wouldst have me weep? Why, now thou hast thy will.
> For raging wind blows up incessant showers,
> And, when the rage allays, the rain begins.
>
> (1.4.143–46)

The self-consciousness with which he conforms to the idiomatic convention of heroic anguish—questioning it, then answering—anticipates Hamlet's employment of the same device with Laertes at Ophelia's grave: "'Swounds, show me what thou't do. / Woo 't weep? Woo 't fight? Woo 't fast? Woo 't tear thyself? . . . I'll do 't. . . . Be buried quick with her, and so will I. . . . Nay, an thou 'lt mouth, / I'll rant as well as thou" (5.1.274–84, passim). The difference lies in the quality of self-awareness. Hamlet's decision to use the idiom is, I feel, his own—one of many voices tried out and cast off, none capable of fully expressing his character; York's decision to use it is, in effect, Shakespeare's. The apparent self-consciousness with which York questions it in no way suggests that there is an autonomous self apart from the idiom that defines him.

In death, York is enshrined in conventional epic hyperbole by a Messenger, a Nuntius of the sort who first introduced Talbot in a report of battle:

> Environed he was with many foes,
> And stood against them, as the hope of Troy
> Against the Greeks that would have ent'red Troy.
> But Hercules himself must yield to odds;
> And many strokes, though with a little axe,
> Hews down and fells the hardest-timber'd oak.
>
> (2.1.50–55)

The references to Hercules and to Hector, "the hope of Troy," hark back to the Countess of Auvergne's comparison of Talbot to the same two mythic figures and argue all the more persuasively for what Shakespeare had in mind: an imaginative metamorphosis of York's character from wrathful Marlovian conqueror, defender of himself alone, to chivalric paragon, courteous defender of the commonweal. When Edward cries, "O Clifford, boist'rous Clifford! Thou has slain / The flow'r of Europe for his chivalry" (ll. 70–71), York's metamorphosis is complete: Achilles has become Hector. The association resonates with the sound of a medieval Troy, once towering in glory, now falling to rubble at the feet of men for whom cunning and brute force are the only reality.

In a recent essay entitled "The Changes of Heroick Song,"[23] Herbert Howarth, an eloquent spokesman for contemporary critical attitudes, argues that self-criticism is implicit in the English heroic, especially as presented in the history plays. Whereas Sidney and Spenser idealize heroism in their epic narratives and, through them, urge men to emulate the heroic patterns of old, be they patterns of military honor or religious knighthood, Marlowe and Shakespeare refuse to idealize. In making the stage a medium for English epic, they choose to present history as crime: they go to chronicles, not legend, to seek truth, and find there not glorious enterprises to inspire emulation, but only the vicious reality of men. Against the evil of self-interest in *Henry VI*, Howarth observes, Shakespeare sets no vision of the good life, no coherent system of values. Faith in the great chain of being that had served poets like Spenser does not serve Shakespeare; and the instructive delight of heroic poetry yields, in the theater, to the intellectual foment of violent realism. Howarth's argument is shrewd; but by embracing a modern bias, he (as I hope should be clear by this point) exaggerates the histories' "realism." Shakespeare does allow certain epic values to stand as ideal, even if not easily emulated: they achieve dramatic vitality in characters such as Talbot and York. And when he wishes to show how such values are overwhelmed by historical reality, he still conveys that reality through the medium of heroic convention. The reality Howarth sees in the plays is, I think, inextricably bound up with the epic models that he claims Shakespeare rejects.

The reality that Shakespeare achieves in his *Henry VI* plays, then, is created by a tension among heroic idioms. He pits the conventions of chivalric heroism against those of conqueror drama, and pits the epic strain of both against the lurid heroics of private revengers to whom the nobility of England in this trilogy finally succumbs. Shakespeare does not distinguish between character and idiom: conventional modes of speech and action are sufficient to define heroic character, and each hero functions more as a representative of a certain *type* of heroism than as a distinguishable tragic personality. By the time Shakespeare wrote these apprentice plays, the English stage had developed a rich variety of heroic dictions and typical, even emblematic, scenes by which an audience could identify heroic character; and Shakespeare was not ready to dismiss this heritage. Not that he stuck rigidly within the boundaries of each idiom: even this early in his career, he displayed a virtuoso's flexibility in mixing idioms or, as in the case of York, applying more than one to a character. But heroic reality was still a function of them. Authenticity and convention were inseparable.

If the reading of history in the three parts of *Henry VI* is determined in part by the heroic conventions Shakespeare found at hand, then *Titus Andonicus* manipulates those conventions more dynamically to represent aspects of and shifts within an individual character.

In the play's ceremonial opening, Titus returns in triumph as a conquering hero, but not in the Marlovian vein. Called "the good Andronicus, / Patron of virtue, Rome's best champion" (1.1.67–68), Titus is a sort of Virgilian Talbot so dedicated to his city that his idiom is akin to that of the chevaliers in the *Henry VI* plays. His notion of honor is public as well as private: he spurns the heroic individualism of a Tamburlaine in order to lay his sword, his conquests, his very self, at the feet of his emperor: "Give me a staff of honor for mine age, / But not a scepter to control the world" (ll. 201–2) he asks in deliberate contrast to the ethos of aspiring conquerors in plays by Marlowe, Peele and Greene:

> to Saturnine,
> King and commander of our commonweal,
> The wide world's emperor, do I consecrate
> My sword, my chariot, and my prisoners,
> Presents well worthy Rome's imperious lord.
> Receive them then, the tribute that I owe,
> Mine honor's ensigns humbled at thy feet.
>
> (1.1.250–56)

The scene emblematically conveys, as did Talbot's kneeling before Henry, the right relationship between a conqueror and his king. Already, Shakespeare is borrowing a scenic form from his own earlier work in order to adjust the perspective on a particular type of heroism; and one's awareness of the borrowing, on hearing the echo, can only clarify and enrich an understanding of that adjustment.

To honor Rome means, for Titus, to honor himself, for he sees in Rome a reflection of himself; and by Rome's constancy he looks to verify his own heroic identity. He is nobly innocent, confident that his faith in Rome will be reciprocated. Thus, in addition to being a Hector on the field, he sees himself as a martial patriarch, a "King Priam" who willingly sacrifices "five and twenty valiant sons" (ll. 82–83) to defend the city that defines him. For this reason, too, when other of his sons undertake to defend Bassianus's claim to Lavinia, the daughter whom Titus has promised to Saturninus, Titus interprets their action as an attack on his own honor: "The dismall'st day is this that e'er I saw, / To be dishonored by my sons in Rome!" (ll. 388–89). He has given his word to the emperor, and the essence of his honor lies in fidelity to his word, as it does for any hero. To be forsworn is to be undone. Rather than risk that, Titus lets a point of honor supersede even a bond of blood: he kills his son Mutius in order to confirm his loyalty to the emperor. Even Talbot does not do so much.

When Saturninus accuses him of mockery and contempt, however, Titus is suddenly threatened with a disintegration of his heroic selfhood. The Rome whose immutable honor he has sworn to defend proves mutable; the world of absolutes begins to tremble beneath his feet; and with Aaron and Tamora impelling Saturninus to take a quick and insidious revenge on the Andronici, Titus, using the image with which the chivalric York has chastised the vengeful Margaret, recoils in horror "that Rome is but a wilderness of tigers" (3.1.54). Aaron and Tamora, in fact, bear a certain resemblance to Clifford and Margaret, sadistically opposing the nobler humanity of Titus as the earlier pair had opposed York. Tamora has the blood of both Medea and Margaret coursing in her veins: it makes her disposition tigerish and her maternity marble-hard. Lavinia addresses Tamora's two sons as "the tiger's young ones": "The milk thou suck'dst from her did turn to marble" (2.3.142, 144). But at other times, Tamora acts more like a lascivious Dido bent on ensnaring her black Aeneas; and it is on him that Shakespeare concentrates his effort to provide a dramatic counterforce to Titus. Aaron is as ambitious as any Tamburlaine. Though not a conqueror of the coventional sort, he still covets an earthly crown and knows the surest way to get it. His first soliloquy is couched almost parodically in high astounding terms; and if the epic simile he uses applies to Tamora's rise to power rather than his own, he nevertheless plans to mount aloft with her, and it is he, not she, who will imitate Tamburlaine's metamorphosis from shepherd to demigod: "Away with slavish weeds and servile thoughts!":

> Now climbeth Tamora Olympus' top,
> Safe out of fortune's shot, and sits aloft,
> Secure of thunder's crack or lightning flash,

Advanc'd above pale envy's threat'ning reach.
As when the golden sun salutes the morn,
And, having gilt the ocean with his beams,
Gallops the zodiac in his glistering coach,
And overlooks the highest-peering hills,
So Tamora.
. . . .

Then, Aaron, arm thy heart, and fit thy thoughts,
To mount aloft with thy imperial mistress,
And mount her pitch, whom thou in triumph long
Hast prisoner held, fett'red in amorous chains
And faster bound to Aaron's charming eyes
Than is Prometheus tied to Caucasus.

(2.1.1–18, passim)

If this vaunt was bred in Marlowe's house, it does not slavishly imitate Tamburlaine's manner. True, the allusions to Olympus and Phoebus bear the stamp of Tamburlaine's myth-making; the thunder and lightning are his; the fett'red prisoner led in triumph, his. But the style fails to maintain his high seriousness. In Aaron, the lofty assertion of a conqueror declines to mere cock-suredness in the bedroom: the bawdy innuendo of "mount her pitch" recalls the asides by which Shakespeare deflated Joan's Marlovian vaunt, except that the deflation now occurs within the vaunt itself. Aaron, unlike Joan and Tamburlaine, has a sense of humor; he relishes lecherous scheming as much as Ithamore does in *The Jew of Malta.* His speech grows more playful as he goes: "To wait, said I? To wanton with this queen . . ." (l. 21). He revels in the thought that he will mate the empress to his own purpose: that purpose, it should be recognized, is not so much revenge—Aaron after all has no grudge, only ambition—as a diabolical delight in villainy. He in fact is much more kin to the Vice of Morality plays or to the Elizabethans' Machiavellian version of the Vice than he is to a revenger; and though he starts life in a Marlovian idiom, he grows up a bastard begotten of many parents. This eclecticism may be regarded as a virtue: it makes him the most compelling and, in a sense, "real" character in the play. But it does not allow him to function with dramatic integrity in Titus's tragedy. Aaron exists on the periphery of the main action; he does a burlesque turn on the heroic theme; but Shakespeare has not yet learned how to yoke his brand of villainy to heroic tragedy.

In disillusion, Titus strives to maintain his heroic identity by taking the ideal of Rome, the constant Rome in which public and private pursuits are one, upon himself. In this defiance of the Roman reality, he anticipates Coriolanus's "I banish you!" The Andronici, Titus chivalrically resolves, will preserve the old Roman integrity to spite the new ethos of private revenge. He instinctively preserves a mythic sense of himself and his mission: he will continue to be a Priam in whom Trojan values flourish. But the role is difficult to play. At the sight of his mutilated Lavinia, he likens the destruction of his family to that of Troy—

What fool hath added water to the sea,
Or brought a faggot to bright-burning Troy?

(3.1.68–69)

—and vows to chop off his own hands, the instruments of all his heroic deeds, in protest, "for they have fought for Rome, and all in vain" (l. 73).

Aaron gives Titus the chance to prove that he is as good as his word when, in a vicious lie, he reports the Emperor's condition: one severed hand sent from the Andronici will ransom Titus's two captive sons. This condition spurs Titus, Marcus, and Lucius once more to chivalric idealism. It gives them a rallying point to restore their heroic faith. As each vies with the other in an almost comic display of magnanimous self-sacrifice, the scene recreates that in which Talbot and his son, each outdoing the other in courtesy, wind up effacing themselves in the name of honor:

MARCUS: My hand shall go.
LUCIUS: By heaven, it shall not go!
TITUS: Sirs, strive no more. Such with'red herbs as these
         Are meet for plucking up, and therefore mine.
LUCIUS: Sweet father, if I shall be thought thy son,
         Let me redeem my brothers both from death.
MARCUS: And, for our father's sake and mother's care,
         Now let me show a brother's love to thee.
TITUS: Agree between you; I will spare my hand.

(3.1.176–83)

In its grotesque subject, with a grinning Aaron looking on, the scene perhaps unintentionally points to a humorous absurdity in such antique heroism. Certainly the context makes the Andronici look even more foolish than the Talbots. Titus sacrifices his hand as a token of abiding allegiance, perhaps sanguine that it may revive in the emperor a reciprocal sense of honor: "Tell him it was a hand that warded him / From thousand dangers" (ll. 194–95). But his hope is vain; his sacrifice, meaningless. Instead of returning with Titus's two sons, Aaron returns with their two heads. Desperately trying to ward off despair, Titus clings to the myth of himself as a Trojan:

Ah, wherefore dost thou urge the name of hands,
To bid Aeneas tell the tale twice o'er
How Troy was burnt and he made miserable?

(3.2.26–28)

But his tone is elegiac, sorrowful for the passing of an age, a belief, an idiom. The lines convey a Virgilian sense of a heroic past akin to the elegies on the passing of England's golden age spoken at the funeral of Henry V. In Titus, the Virgilian strain gives way to the Senecan. He becomes a tower of heroic passion: martial glory yields to lament, and then to cruelty. But the process is organic. The shifts in idiom convey a semblance of psychological development, not, as in the *Henry VI* plays, an interplay of static heroic alternatives.

Titus's lament is typical of the Senecan set-speech, extreme in its description of passion, laden with elemental metaphors:

> If there were reason for these miseries,
> Then into limits could I bind my woes.
> When heaven doth weep, doth not the earth o'erflow?
> If the winds rage, doth not the sea wax mad,
> Threat'ning the welkin with his big-swoll'n face?
> And wilt thou have a reason for this coil?
> I am the sea; hark, how her sighs doth flow!
> She is the weeping welkin, I the earth.
> Then must my sea be moved with her sighs;
> Then must my earth with her continual tears
> Become a deluge, overflow'd and drown'd. . . .

> (3.1.219–29)

The speech, I think, is a deliberate conflation of two famous laments spoken by Hieronimo, whose grief for a child Shakespeare must have likened to Titus's. In one, Hieronimo asks a rhetorical question much like Titus's and embellishes it with similar metaphors for his state of mind:

> Where shall I run to breath abroad my woes,
> My woes, whose weight hath wearied the earth?
> . . . .
> The blustring winds, conspiring with my words,
> At my lament haue moued the leaueles trees,
> Disroabde the medowes of their flowred greene,
> Made mountains marsh with spring tides of my teares, . . .
> (3.7.1–8, passim)

Titus's image of himself as a sea maddened by wind and rain, however, springs more directly from a later lament in which Hieronimo speaks of himself "as a raging Sea" that, "Tost with the winde and tide, ore turnest then / The vpper billowes course of waues to keep, / Whilest lesser waters labour in the deepe" (3.13.102–5). In the same speech, Hieronimo vows to go as far as hell, "knock at the dismall gates of *Plutos* Court" (l. 110), to retrieve the justice that has fled the earth. This might have been the germ for the scene in which Titus, declaring that "Terras Astraea reliquit," vows to plumb the ocean's depth and "pierce the inmost center of the earth" as far as "Pluto's region" to find justice out (4.3.4, 12–13). Certainly Kyd's rhetoric fired Shakespeare's imagination when he was composing a play on the fall of a noble mind to madness.

It is easy to disparage such laments by belaboring their conventional hyperbole, their artificial heightening of sorrow. By modern standards, of course, they are rhetorical *shows* of grief, windy suspiration of forc'd breath. But Hieronimo's were memorable for Elizabethans because they gave a distinctive personal voice to the generalized emotion of their Senecan originals. Linked to stage action, his laments arose out of an immediate dramatic context, responded to objects—a corpse, a bloody napkin, a letter—that assaulted his senses, and thus embodied his *individual* grief. For this reason, Shakespeare turned to them as models. If Titus's lament does not convey his grief with quite the same intensity as Hieronimo's, if his metaphor is pressed to the point of conceit, it nevertheless has more theatrical vitality—responding as it does to the presence of Lavinia kneeling before him, weeping—than the more conventional lament Clifford utters over his father. And one has only to look at the Ovidian excesses of Marcus when he discovers Lavinia ravished (a crimson river of warm blood, or lily hands, now lopped, trembling like aspen leaves on a lute: such images as render passion static, an object of aesthetic contemplation)[24] to realize how far Shakespeare advanced in dramatizing a more *felt* passion in Titus.

This lament marks Titus's descent into madness. But even in madness, his heroic integrity is given new life by his outraged sense of injustice. With the model of Hieronimo before him and, further back, such Senecan worthies as the mad Hercules, Titus withdraws from a dependence on the social order and dedicates himself instead to an insane private revenge. Revenge, too, has its code of ethics, its rules, its heroic ideals. Titus's heroic metamorphosis is thus a matter of degree, not kind. He invokes the honor of an oath as he once had done in the name of Rome, now to ally his family against Rome:

> You heavy people, circle me about,
> That I may turn me to each one of you,
> And swear unto my soul to right your wrongs.
> [*They form a circle about Titus, and he pledges each.*]
> The vow is made.
>
> (3.1.276–79)

Here, too, Shakespeare returns to an emblematic scene he had used before in *3 Henry VI,* when Warwick, Richard, Edward, and Clarence, in a grouping of generations resembling that of the Andronici, all vow in the name of family honor to avenge the death of York:

> Here on my knee I vow to God above
> I'll never pause again, never stand still,
> Till either death hath clos'd these eyes of mine
> Or fortune given me measure of revenge.
>
> (2.3.29–32)

The lines are Warwick's; and but for the presence of God, they could be Titus's. The mutual vows, the pledges, the handshakes, the swearing by sword or on bended knee not to rest till the deed is done—"I shall never come to bliss / Till all these mischiefs be return'd again" is Titus's way of putting it—are a part of the ritual of blood tragedy. Although Shakespeare has managed to create for Titus a heroic voice far more distinct than the voices heard in *Henry VI,* and a stature more humanly comprehensible, nevertheless as Titus falls further into madness, he loses that voice, that stature, and becomes at one with his genre: he quotes Seneca's *Hippolytus* and cries to the gods for justice; he plots, he schemes, he puts on an antic disposition; he kills, he minces, he seasons, he bakes. And with him falls the play. Like others of its genre, it focuses on perverse manifestations of revenge rather than on the psychological development of the revenger. It fails to live up to its early promise.

Even so, by allowing the idioms that had stood in bald opposition to one another in *Henry VI* to evolve *out* of one another in Titus, Shakespeare makes some progress in characterization. The confrontation of values implicit in the various idioms—chivalric, Marlovian, Kydian—as they jockey for priority in Titus's character helps to define his tragedy. Through that confrontation, Shakespeare dramatizes a credible motivation for a man who must go mad in order to preserve his heroic integrity, a motivation denied the more conventional revengers of *3 Henry VI.* And if Shakespeare at last allows *Titus* to deteriorate into a grotesque display of cruelty inspired by *Thyestes* and thus to satisfy, not challenge, crude expectations of the genre, he nevertheless takes a significant step towards working out the shape of a mind beneath the heroic idiom before this happens.[25]

But idiom is still not submerged in the psychology of character. Even Titus's character, the most developed so far, consists largely of rhetorical exercises, conventions juggled with striking effect, but not revolutionary. Shakespeare does not synthesize them with enough mastery in these early plays to arrive at a new, more authentic way of dramatizing heroism. Heroes are heroes because they speak and act like other heroes—like Tamburlaine or Hieronimo, like Hector or Achilles, like Medea or Hercules. Shakespeare manipulates conventions with skill to make heroes within each play rhetorically distinct from one another. But none of them is distinct enough to pass the test for which Shakespeare's later heroes set the mimetic standard: self-consciousness. Their emotions, values and actions are determined by the types of language and scenes Shakespeare chooses from the grab bag of tradition; their deaths conform to the patterns of *de casibus* or revenge tragedy. Their idiom is indivisible from their dramatic being. Their perspective on heroic value or on the nature of heroic identity does not inform their tragedies, as it will inform the tragedies of Shakespeare's later heroes, because they *have* no perspective, no autonomy. *Shakespeare* may, through them, question the morality of a heroic tradition or the legitimacy of a heroic code; *they* do not. Heroic reality has yet to extricate itself from the tyranny of the past.

3

Ironic Heroism: A Repudiation of the Past

The idioms Shakespeare employed to delineate heroism in his early plays were too restrictive to allow him a personal signature. It is not by chance that these plays for years were thought to be the work, or at least to contain the work, of other dramatists: they fully partake of the conventions that were the stock-in-trade of stage heroism. But together they constitute only Shakespeare's apprenticeship to already-established writers. Within a few years, he was forging a mimesis more sophisticated than any that had yet been tried and, as a consequence, was recutting the heroic patterns that only yesterday he had found fashionable enough. His new heroes were characterized by their awareness of conventional expectations, and their tragedies arose from their failure to live up to them—from their inability to wear hand-me-down roles with any comfort or conviction. The authenticity of the plays themselves sprang likewise from their simultaneous employment and repudiation of the conventions that had bodied forth a heroic reality in the "old plays."

The death of Caesar illustrates how Shakespeare had come to use conventions with detachment, even irony. *Julius Caesar* is often labeled a sort of revenge play, harking back to various Senecan plays on the theme of Caesar's hubris and perhaps directly to an academic play called *Caesar's Revenge.*[1] Certainly it has the ethical confrontations and at times the rhetorical style of Senecan offshoots; and the trappings of portentous storms, daggers, ritual murder, and a vengeful ghost cast it in the mold of the more popular *Spanish Tragedie* and *Locrine.* Caesar himself bestrides the stage like a conquering colossus. He has an egotistical self-assurance to rival Tamburlaine's—"for always I am Caesar" (1.2.212)—and an imperious will that bends to no external persuasion—"The cause is in my will. I will not come" (2.2.71). His epic hubris, the insolent pride that dares fate to match him in a test of strength, finds apt expression in the conventional outdoing topos:

51

> Danger knows full well
> That Caesar is more dangerous than he.
> We are two lions litter'd in one day,
> And I the elder and more terrible. . . .

> (2.2.44–47)

And his passionate assertion of heroic selfhood is supremely embodied in the rhetorical set-piece he delivers just prior to his murder. The epic simile, with enough Ovidian fire to make the gods blush, is strongly reminiscent of Tamburlaine:

> I am constant as the northern star,
> Of whose true-fix'd and resting quality
> There is no fellow in the firmament.
> The skies are painted with unnumb'red sparks,
> They are all fire and every one doth shine,
> But there's but one in all doth hold his place.
> So in the world: 'tis furnish'd well with men,
> And men are flesh and blood, and apprehensive;
> Yet in the number I do know but one
> That unassailable holds on his rank,
> Unshak'd of motion. And . . . I am he.

> (3.1.60–70)

With the hyperbole that has characterized all conqueror heroes, Caesar ingenuously identifies in himself an absolute integrity of self and self-image. Like Talbot, he is what he says he is—a godlike hero of mythic proportions. The language defines him as such; and public acclaim, heard offstage each time he refuses the crown, affirms it. But Shakespeare does not let this assertion stand unchallenged. Against that offstage acclaim, he gives us an antiphonal voice *on*stage that relentlessly, right up to the time of the murder, points out Caesar's naked frailties: he is deaf in one ear; he has epilepsy; Cassius once had to save him from drowning. Even his wife Calpurnia qualifies our admiration by gently mocking his vaunt as unwise boasting: "Alas, my lord, / Your wisdom is consum'd in confidence" (2.2.48–49). In the judgment of various Renaissance historians, such hubris provided ample justification for Caesar's murder; and so Brutus characterizes it: "People and senators, be not affrighted. / Fly not; stand still. *Ambition's debt is paid*" (3.1.82–83, my italics).

But much as Brutus would like to conceive of Caesar's death as a moral exemplum, a just retribution in the tradition of the *Fall of Princes,* he cannot: he is too circumspect to believe in the public construction he puts on it. Like a chivalric defender of national honor in the early histories, or even more like Titus who takes great risks to preserve Rome's honor, Brutus would define his role in Caesar's death as that of heroic justicer. He would prefer to regard the murder as consonant with public rather than private honor—

> If it be aught toward the general good,
> Set honor in one eye and death i' th' other,
> And I will look on both indifferently;
>
> (1.2.85–87)

—but he senses more deeply that his role likens him to a revenger who calls wrongs to a private accounting without recourse to law.

Brutus is aware that he has insufficient evidence of those "wrongs" to justify the murder. "To speak truth of Caesar, / I have not known when his affections sway'd / More than his reason" (2.1.19–21). Thus, in order to persuade himself, he must conjecture some future cause and proceed to act on that conjecture as if it were proof:

> And, since the quarrel
> Will bear no color for the thing he is,
> Fashion it thus. . . .
>
> (2.1.28–30)

The vocabulary of his internal debate, "Fashion it thus," reveals in him an active will to dissemble. He will seek no "cavern" to mask the "monstrous visage" of conspiracy, but rather will "hide it in smiles and affability" (ll. 80–82, passim). Beyond the mask of smiles, he advocates a grander imposture that would disguise blood revenge in the cloak of ceremony. "Let's be sacrificers, but not butchers," he urges his fellow conspirators (l. 166):

> And let our hearts, as subtle masters do,
> Stir up their servants to an act of rage,
> And after seem to chide 'em. This shall make
> Our purpose necessary, and not envious;
> Which so appearing to the common eyes,
> We shall be call'd purgers, not murderers.
>
> (2.1.175–80)

Brutus's advice to his coconspirators is remarkably like Volumnia's to Coriolanus: as the public eye alone will determine the legitimacy of your heroic fame, act the part nobly, even if you do not believe in it. The pretense to heroism, reflected in the "seem" and the "so appearing," is ironic because Brutus would include his own among the "common eyes" he is trying to deceive. With a duplicity of which the more conventionally drawn heroes of Shakespeare's earlier plays were incapable, Brutus teaches his fellows to play a role to convince the audience of their integrity, and at the same time he would convince himself that the role is perfectly consistent with his ethical selfhood. He would be as absolute as Caesar in believing himself a hero. The traditional heroic vocabulary he uses conveys that wish: "our hearts," seats of the will, must stir "their servants," the passions, to "an act of rage," an essential component of heroes from Achilles onward. And why? Because murder resulting from a noble wrath will always be condoned as a heroic deed. So strong is Brutus's wish, in fact, that it almost fathers self-delusion.

His wish is undermined by the self-consciousness with which he uses the heroic idiom, however. In his attempt to use the idiom to effect only an *appearance* of heroic purpose, its credibility as a means of representing reality suffers. Brutus tries hard to convince us otherwise. To reinforce the legitimacy of his purpose, he resorts to a form of traditional oath-taking; but he metamorphoses it into a fellowship of honesty, suggesting that the reality of the oath transcends mere words: "What need we any spur but our own cause . . . And what other oath / Than honesty to honesty engag'd . . . ? (ll. 123, 126–27). Shakespeare recalls for us the moment when the Andronici, with no discrepancy between a heroic sign and its significance, took vows against Saturninus, and the even earlier episode when York's family vowed revenge against Clifford. Brutus adopts the ritual—"Give me your hands all over, one by one" (l. 112)—only to try to outdo it in high-minded pretense: "No, not an oath. If not the face of men, / The sufferance of our souls, the time's abuse—" (ll. 114–15). But in declining the oath itself, in reaching instead for something more universal, he fails to engage himself with the form and with the power of its accumulated meaning that generations of heroes had counted on for sustenance. The self-consciousness with which he manipulates the form betrays his detachment from the ethos it signifies.

Brutus's failure to be engaged with the forms he enacts is dramatized even more explicitly in the murder of Caesar. Ritual murder scenes were a popular part of the revenge tradition. Shakespeare had played them to the hilt in his *Henry VI* plays, especially when Edward, Richard, and Clarence one by one stab young Prince Edward before his mother's eyes (*Part Three:* 5.5)[2] and again, even more sensationally, in the Thyestian banquet of blood that concludes the festivities in *Titus Andronicus*. Caesar himself had been ritually murdered in the academic *Caesar's Revenge,* falling to the music of Cassius's couplet, "Stab on, stab on, thus should your Poniards play, / Aloud deepe note upon this trembling Kay" (ll. 1699–1700), and confronted at the last by Brutus's stern rebuke:

> But lives hee still, yet doth the Tyrant breath?
> Chalinging Heavens with his blasphemies,
> . . . .
> I bloody *Caesar, Caesar, Brutus* too,
> Doth geeve thee this, and this to quite *Romes* wrongs.
> (ll. 1723–24, 1729–30)[3]

Shakespeare's Brutus, unlike his earlier counterpart, is not content simply to do the deed out of moral conviction. Rather, he arranges Caesar's murder as a theatrical event. He directs his accomplices to play their parts "as our Roman actors do, / With untir'd spirits and formal constancy"

(2.1.226–27)—an admission that constancy is no more to him than outward form—and bestows legitimacy on the murder by bidding them to bathe their hands in Caesar's blood, besmear their swords, then walk with him to the market-place,

> And, waving our red weapons o'er our heads,
> Let's all cry, "Peace, freedom, and liberty!"
>
> (3.1.109–10)

Through these conventional signs of ritual sacrifice, Brutus hopes to persuade his audience of Romans that Caesar's murder was a heroic act—a purge of tyranny, as in the old play—and that he and his accomplices are liberators, Rome's saviors, not butchers. He and Cassius even speculate that players in "ages hence" will reenact this "lofty scene" to the glory of their memory. "How many times shall Caesar bleed in sport," Brutus ponders (l. 114); and in so pondering, he "places" the event in a theatrical context and attempts to convince us, as well as himself, that outward shows may *create* a substantial reality.

Allusion to the theater was not new to a Shakespearean hero. As far back as *3 Henry VI*, Warwick, in his scene of oath-taking, had asked in agitation,

> Why stand we like soft-hearted women here,
> Wailing our losses, whiles the foe doth rage,
> And look upon, as if the tragedy
> Were play'd in jest by counterfeiting actors?
>
> (2.3.25–28)

Warwick's rejection of jest and counterfeit, however, affirms the reality of himself, his friends, and their cause: they must not act, but *be*, revengers. Brutus's use of theatrical imagery is far more complex. He tries to make acting and being inseparable. He instructs his friends to counterfeit like actors; he embraces the ritual shows by which he will win public approval; he conceives of the murder throughout as a scene played for posterity. Reality, for him, may be no deeper than the stage. But if the audience sees that Brutus can manipulate conventions to give a false appearance of heroism, then one's faith in conventional criteria for judging the reality of heroism on the stage cannot rest secure. The nature of dramatic illusion shifts. We do not trust, as Brutus hopes the Romans will trust, in the absolute correspondence of sign and significance. We may see more heroism in Brutus's struggle to come to terms with the heroic idiom than we see in the idiom itself. His self-consciousness becomes more compelling than his actual deeds. And the tension he feels between aping heroic forms and knowing that those forms are, for him, counterfeit, *makes* him real in a way that no conventionally drawn hero, not even Caesar himself, could ever be.

Shakespeare treats the heroic idiom with more irony in the various voices

Antony adopts following Caesar's death. Most famous of these is the voice of heroic revenger. Left alone, after the conspirators have departed, Antony addresses Caesar's corpse in a lament that harks back to Clifford's lament over the corpse of his father, in which he vows to dry up all tears of pity in a "flaming wrath" and to find solace in cruelty. But Antony's prophecy is more universal:

> A curse shall light upon the limbs of men;
> Domestic fury and fierce civil strife
> Shall cumber all the parts of Italy;
> Blood and destruction shall be so in use
> And dreadful objects so familiar
> That mothers shall but smile when they behold
> Their infants quartered with the hands of war,
> All pity chok'd with custom of fell deeds.
>
> (3.1.263–70)

It stems from a long tradition of curse and threat of the sort that Shakespeare sprinkled liberally through his histories. Tamburlaine had called on it, "threatening a death and famine to this land," at the death of Zenocrate. Talbot had threatened to "conquer, sack, and utterly consume" Bordeaux; and Henry V, to shut up the gates of mercy and mow "like grass" the "fresh-fair virgins" and "flow'ring infants" of Harfleur. Behind these manifestations lie imprecations in earlier English tragedies that invoke both biblical sources, such as this in *Gorboduc:* "But dearth and famine shall possesse the land! / The townes shall be consumed and burnt with fire"; and classical sources, such as this in *Jocasta:* "And angry *Mars* shall ouercome it all / With famine, flame, rape, murther, dole and death."[4] But Antony does not forget the more Senecan elements of revenge tragedy either. The ghost that appeared three times in *Caesar's Revenge,* once in the company of Discord, who comes from hell to ring down civil war, may be on his mind when he says,

> And Caesar's spirit, ranging for revenge,
> With Ate by his side come hot from hell,
> Shall in these confines with a monarch's voice
> Cry "Havoc!" and let slip the dogs of war.
>
> (3.1.271–74)

Antony's speech thus fuses rhetorical traditions with remarkable originality by sounding the voices of prophecy, curse, and threat all at once. Ironically, the warning of impending horrors, usually spoken by a choric observer such as Carlisle who, in *Richard II,* prophesies another Golgotha, here is spoken by the man who will bring those horrors about. The prophecy is thus self-fulfilling: not Caesar's spirit, but Antony himself, will let slip the dogs of war. Antony's language, on reflection, seems to be spoken with a self-conscious passion; and one may grow more suspicious that he is employing the heroic idiom to disguise his motives when, in the Forum scene that immediately follows, he turns revenge to political advantage and manipulates the throng with rhetorical artifice. His method is well known, so I shall cite just one overlooked allusion to revenge tradition to prove my point. Claiming that he is not disposed to "stir" the "hearts and minds" of the people "to mutiny and rage" against the "honorable men" who killed Caesar (3.2.123–26)—a disclaimer that echoes the language Brutus uses to stir the conspirators to do the deed—Antony produces Caesar's will, which, he says, "I do not mean to read":

> Let but the commons hear this testament—
> . . . .
> And they would go and kiss dead Caesar's wounds
> And dip their napkins in his sacred blood.
>
> (3.2.132–35)

Antony's lines poignantly recall the by-then-famous scenes in which Hieronimo dipped his napkin in Horatio's blood as a token of revenge and in which Margaret tormented York with the napkin dipped in the blood of his son Rutland. It is important to recognize the power of Antony's allusion. He says, in effect, that if the people knew the will of Caesar, they would all turn into Hieronimos ranging for revenge against the "honorable" assassins. He adopts, for the moment, a diction that had served him in his earlier lament and to which, after this, he need not return. The arch control of his Forum speech, in fact, employs little of such emotive language. He has no need for it. The allusion to *The Spanish Tragedie* simply is a reminder of an idiom Antony had milked and then cast off. In his shift of rhetorical gears, Shakespeare marks Antony's emergence from the role of antique revenger to the role of Machiavellian leader who recognizes, like the later Ulysses and Aufidius, that virtue lies in the interpretation of the times.

Antony's manipulation of the revenge idiom should not come as a revelation in the Forum scene. Even before his lament, he tries out different voices that serve his immediate purposes. Entering to the conspirators, uncertain of what they have in store for him, he at once adopts the conventional language of *de casibus* tragedy, moralizing in best *ubi sunt* tradition the ephemeral nature of man's greatness:

> O mighty Caesar! Dost thou lie so low?
> Are all thy conquests, glories, triumphs, spoils,
> Shrunk to this little measure? Fare thee well.—
>
> (3.1.149–51)

In this are the seeds of Hamlet's "Imperious Caesar, dead and turn'd to clay, / Might stop a hold to keep the wind away" (5.1.213–14). But Antony is canny. Recognizing that Brutus will most respect a noble response to the murder of a friend, Antony turns to the lurid vocabulary of blood tragedy to *dare* the conspirators to butcher him too:

> I do beseech ye, if you bear me hard,
> Now, whilst your purpled hands do reek and smoke,
> Fulfill your pleasure.
>
> (3.1.158–60)

The dare works: it forces Brutus to defend his deed against Antony's characterization of it as a crime and, in the process, to offer Antony an honorable love. Antony seizes the opportunity to insure his safety by ceremonially shaking hands with the conspirators—

> Let each man render me his bloody hand.
> First, Marcus Brutus, will I shake with you;
> Next, Caius Cassius, do I take your hand;
> Now, Decius Brutus, yours; now yours, Metellus;
>
> (3.1.185–88)

—and adopts thereby a traditional heroic form that Brutus had tried to surpass in claiming that inner honesty, not outward show, determined the honor of his course. Outward show stands Antony in good stead here.

Yet he fears that his credit may stand on slippery ground. By too easily embracing a heroic alliance with the enemies of Caesar, he thinks they may have cause to suspect his honesty. Cunningly, he puts the question to them: "what shall I say?" (l. 191). What he decides to say is politically shrewd: first, to beg Caesar's forgiveness for his apparent betrayal, then to lapse back into lament for greatness gone:

> Pardon me, Julius! Here wast thou bay'd, brave hart,
> Here didst thou fall, and here thy hunters stand,
> Sign'd in thy spoil, and crimson'd in thy lethe.
> O world, thou wast the forest to this hart,
> And this, indeed, O world, the heart of thee!
> How like a deer, strucken by many princes,
> Dost thou here lie!
>
> (3.1. 205–11)

To the conspirators, this sounds convincing enough to be interrupted. To us, it ought to sound like "art." The style—one Antony has not used before—is Ovidian. The pun on "heart" anticipates that of Orsino who, some one or two years later, laments that he is another Acteon hounded by his desires: this romantic context tells us something about the artifice of such verse. But Antony's pretty conceit about the hunted hart bears a more striking resemblance to Shakespeare's early narrative poetry and to the pastoral similes and crimson conceits by which Titus and Marcus prettified Lavinia's mutilation:[5]

MARCUS: O, thus I found her, straying in the park,
Seeking to hide herself, as doth the deer
That hath receiv'd some unrecuring wound.
TITUS: It was my deer, and he that wounded her
Hath hurt me more than had he kill'd me dead.

(3.1.88–92)

Even earlier, Talbot had rallied his English forces against the French "curs" by calling them "timorous deer" who ought to transform themselves into "desperate stags" and "turn on the bloody hounds with heads of steel" (*1 Henry VI:* 4.2.45–52). But by the time of *Julius Caesar,* such Ovidian metamorphosing of violence was a thing of the past, an idiom Shakespeare had experimented with, found wanting, and discarded. Antony, in reverting to it, deliberately sets Caesar's murder in an outmoded context: the language is showy enough to persuade the conspirators that he is a man of noble feeling but artificial enough to indicate that Antony is speaking from the mind, not from the heart.

The dispassionate ease with which Antony adopts expedient voices allows him inevitably to get the better of Brutus. Brutus tries manfully to identify himself by the heroic forms he enacts; he denies that there is any disparity between idiom and selfhood. Antony admits the disparity and thus is free to play on it as he sees fit. The divorce between acting and being causes no dilemma in Antony as it does in Brutus. A particular idiom does not define his character; the self-consciousness to play roles defined by the idiom does. Lest I be thought to mean that Antony is no more than an impostor, however, let me issue a caveat. The audience's awareness that Antony has a selfhood deeper than his idiom dawns only gradually. When he laments over Caesar, offers his breast to the conspirators' swords, shakes their hands, mourns the hunting of a noble hart, and swears to avenge the murder and appease Caesar's ghost, the audience may believe in the rhetorical reality of his character. Only in retrospect—and the moment of discovery will differ for each of us—will the audience appreciate that rhetoric and character are distinct from one another. Antony's idiom shifts, not for the reason York's shifts between the second and third parts of *Henry VI*—that is, to satisfy Shakespeare's rhetorical design, but because by those shifts, Shakespeare can dramatize in Antony a dynamic process of thought that psychologically justifies the choice of idiom. Motivated by political self-interest, Antony himself has both the reason and the autonomy, lacking in Shakespeare's early heroes, to manipulate rhetorical conventions: Shakespeare allows him to usurp his own prerogative to determine character by rhetorical means.[6] As one moves chronologically through the scene of Caesar's death, therefore, Shakespeare preserves conventional modes of speech as momentarily adequate to define traditional attitudes and types of heroism, as if he, in a manner of old, has applied character with rhetorical brushstrokes; but in a retrospective analysis of all such moments, we realize that he has been forging new criteria for determining heroic character.

Antony *is* the roles he plays in sequence, but the reality of his character is more than the sum of his parts.

As with Antony, so with the play. In a sense, Shakespeare satisfies conventional expectations of blood tragedy in the cosmic unrest, the ritual slaughter, the scenes of civil discord, the appearance of the ghost. He also satisfies expectations of heroic tragedy in Caesar's *de casibus* fall, the noble reconciliation of Brutus and Cassius, the stoicism of Brutus's suicide, even in the conventional elegies spoken over Cassius—"The sun of Rome is set. Our day is gone" (5.3.63)—and over Brutus—"This was the noblest Roman of them all" (5.5.68).[7] But he does so only after exposing the conventions of heroism to ironic scrutiny, occasionally (as in Caesar's bombast) to parody, and finding them inadequate to represent a heroic reality. Heroism in *Julius Caesar* becomes real when Shakespeare holds conventions at arm's length— cuts traditional heroic patterns out of well-worn cloth only so that characters, scenes, the play itself, may try them on and complain, "These don't fit. They're yesterday's fashion. Fustian! We have outgrown them."

By the time he wrote *Julius Caesar,* Shakespeare had learned to use heroic conventions not as a dead, unambiguous shorthand, but as a flexible instrument to establish contexts by which to measure a character's behavior. They could invoke a world of ideas and values that the audience, conditioned by years of play-going, would readily comprehend, and at the same time represent archaic standards against which characters could rebel to achieve a more authentic likeness of truth. To a maturing Shakespeare of the late 1590s, looking back over his earlier work, such conventions must have threatened to depersonalize heroic behavior, generalize plot to the point of mindless imitation, and militate against the individuality of character he was striving to dramatize. For this reason, in plays of this period, his treatment of heroic conventions seems detached, ironic, even satirical. He was responding to conventional authority like an adolescent, still in need of parental guidance but eager to assert his independence from it.

Shakespeare had begun to disengage himself from the tyranny of the heroic idiom as early as *Richard III.* Richard is the first of Shakespeare's ironic heroes. He measures his own villainy in direct proportion to his ability to deceive others with shows of conventional heroism. Even in the Richard of *3 Henry VI,* Shakespeare toyed with the idea of a hero who could use rhetorical forms self-consciously and thus hint at a vitality of character behind them. Richard speaks with a detachment that renders his use of the outdoing topos ironic:

> I'll play the orator as well as Nestor,
> Deceive more slily than Ulysses could,
> And, like a Sinon, take another Troy.
> I can add colors to the chameleon,
> Change shapes with Proteus for advantages,

And set the murderous Machiavel to school.
Can I do this, and cannot get a crown?

(3.2.188–94)

Richard will outdo the heroes of antiquity in *not* being himself, in exchanging the heroic "I am" for the Cartesian "I think." The heroes Richard chooses to outdo are likewise not those traditionally associated with qualities of greatness. Earlier drama had made capital of the epic fame of Achilles, Hector, Hercules, and Alexander. Richard prefers a different strain of epic hero: Nestor, who used rhetoric as artifice; Ulysses, the politic man whom Elizabethans identified as a Machiavel; Sinon, the arch-traitor who breached every code of honor. This soliloquy, then, marks a shift away from the unselfconsciousness of traditional heroes and towards a redefinition of the hero as a self-conscious ironist.

Richard reveals the theatrical artifice of his technique when he instructs Buckingham (as Hamlet later will instruct the players at Elsinore) on how to play the tragedian over Hastings's corpse.[8] How to "quake, and change thy color, / Murder thy breath in middle of a word" (*Richard III:* 3.5.1–2): they are devices Richard himself uses in his lament over Hastings, in which he plays the heroic naif to perfection, a veritable Talbot or Titus who has assumed in another a heroic constancy to match that within himself but who now suffers disillusion; and they are devices that Brutus, with less glee, will later recommend to the "Roman actors" who are about to slaughter Caesar. Richard here delights to think that he will deceive others into crediting his outward show as true feeling. His imposture is betrayed only by the skill with which he expresses the nature of that constancy.

He gets an opportunity to play the heroic role in the second scene, when he woos the widow Anne with professions of love as absolute as those Suffolk professes to Margaret:

> If thy revengeful heart cannot forgive,
> Lo, here I lend thee this sharp-pointed sword,
> Which if thou please to hide in this true breast,
> And let the soul forth that adoreth thee,
> I lay it naked to the deadly stroke
> And humbly beg the death upon my knee.
>
> (1.2.173–78)

He casts her in the role of revenger; himself, in the role of chivalric knight, doing what he has done—murder her husband—only for love of her. His ploy anticipates the one Antony uses on the conspirators: a dare, a feigned willingness to risk all he has in order to prove his constancy, a heroic challenge issued in terms of combat: "Take up the sword again, or take up me" (l. 183). Yet his is a dare that is not a dare, for he suspects Anne's will is weak. She identifies Richard's manipulation of heroic convention for what it is in her response, "Arise, dissembler" (l. 184); but in those words, he wins the point.

Ironic man has a complex literary heritage. He originates in Greek comedy as the *eiron*, a dissembler or trickster who looks at life with a wry and detached sense of humor.[9] Aristophanes makes something more of him, a kind of hero who tears away the pretenses and impostures of other comic types. Of those types, the *eiron*'s prime target is the *alazon*, a grotesquely inflated version of the tragic hero, whose bombast is the comic counterpart of tragic hubris.[10] The *eiron* and *alazon* even figure in Aristotle's *Nicomachean Ethics* (1127, a.21) as the two vicious extremes of deceit that flank the virtuous mean of truthfulness. The *alazon* pretends to be more than he is; the *eiron*, less. The *alazon* speaks a language of metaphoric overstatement *(alazoneia);* the *eiron*, of commonplace understatement *(eironeia).* The *alazon* is self-engaged; the *eiron*, detached. In his comedies Aristophanes dramatizes a meeting of the two heroic types, tragic and comic, with the intent of letting the *eiron* puncture the *alazon*'s heroic balloon as so much hot air. "The impostor comes upon the stage. We know he is doomed to exposure. We watch him moving in boundless self-assurance nearer and nearer to the moment when he shall be stripped of all his pretences."[11] In the *Acharnians*, for example, Dicaeopolis, who speaks plain Attic, confronts Euripides, the *ne plus ultra* of tragic diction, to borrow some props: Dicaeopolis winds up undermining Euripidean conventions by making them appear ludicrous in context. The relationship between the two types is developed further in Roman comedy, where the *eiron*, frequently a witty slave, makes a mockery of the *miles gloriosus*. In his relationship to the conventional hero—vaunting king or braggart soldier—the *eiron* does heroic service.

Richard does similar service. His last heroic forgery outdoes all those previous by parodying the language of Tamburlaine at his most hyperbolic. Spurred to new heights by desperation, Richard pulls out all the stops. He wants to marry Elizabeth's daughter to shore up his position; thus he urges Elizabeth to woo for him in the terms of boundless aspiration that Tamburlaine used to woo Zenocrate:

> Put in her tender heart th' aspiring flame
> Of golden sovereignty; acquaint the Princess
> With the sweet silent hours of marriage joys.
> And when this arm of mine hath chastised
> The petty rebel, dull-brain'd Buckingham,
> Bound with triumphant garlands will I come
> And lead thy daughter to a conqueror's bed;
> To whom I will retail my conquest won,
> And she shall be sole victoress, Caesar's Caesar.
>
> (4.4.328–36)

Like the *eiron* of Attic comedy, Richard exposes the conventions of conqueror drama as imposture and its idiom as *alazoneia* simply by the way he exploits them to his own mean ends. Through him, Shakespeare suggests that a sequence of heroic roles may not a true hero make; and he begins to withdraw his commitment to the heroic idiom as adequate for dramatizing, in itself, a fully fleshed tragic hero.

Shapespeare allows Richard, as no other character before him, to use the idiom with irony, sometimes mockery. But Richard's detachment from the conventional medium does not account for his tragic fall. Richard does not suffer a crisis of identity, as Brutus will a few years later, by trying on heroic roles that ill suit him. Instead, he wears those roles with unabashed revelry, almost as comic disguises; and that revelry reveals his true colors as a stage villain, itself a conventional figure sprung from the Vice and popularized more recently in Marlowe's vengefully Machiavellian Barabas.[12] Richard declares his character in the opening soliloquy—"I am determined to prove a villain" (1.1.30)—and never swerves from that course. Such self-declaration is itself a rhetorical device as old as the theater: though Richard may use irony as a means of self-advancement, he seldom if ever turns it inward to see what that "self" is. In other words, Shakespeare uses irony *through* him in a rather Aristophanic way, to expose the superficiality of a stock heroic idiom, but not to lead him to any tragic self-awareness. The language by which Richard demonstrates his most constant purpose to hate and revenge, in fact, is straightforward, untouched by circumspection; and in a language of equal self-engagement, he honors a "deep intent" (1.1.149) to get and keep the crown that likens him to traditional conqueror heroes. In a battle to defend that crown, he resorts without irony to the language of noble English warriors who preceded him in the *Henry VI* trilogy:

> A thousand hearts are great within my bosom.
> Advance our standards, set upon our foes;
> Our ancient word of courage, fair Saint George,
> Inspire us with the spleen of fiery dragons!
>
> (5.3.347–50)

If we note a certain irony in Richard's using the language of chivalry to defend an ill-gotten crown, the irony is Shakespeare's. Richard, at bottom, is as firmly bound by the conventions of historical melodrama as Shakespeare's earlier heroes were bound by the conventions of the plays that circumscribed them. He wheels and deals like a Medieval Boss Tweed, driven by lust for things of this world and finally haunted by the ghosts of victims past. His tragedy is cast in the traditional mold of the *Mirror for Magistrates,* in which death comes as a just retribution for proud and ambitious men.

Richard II is the first of Shakespeare's heroes to direct his irony inwards. His tragedy involves heroic conventions in a newly organic way (I would venture to say revolutionary: no dramatist had used them so before): despite his repeated forays into the traditional idiom, Richard fails to engage

himself with a heroic ethos, and out of that failure emerges a more profound sense of his character. If he has any traditionally heroic self-image, it
lies in the notion of a divinely sanctioned kingship, the crown inviolable.
Critics tend to believe that he is as absolute as his words:[13]

> Not all the water in the rough rude sea
> Can wash the balm off from an anointed king;
> The breath of worldly men cannot depose
> The deputy elected by the Lord.
>
> (3.2.54–57)

His self-confidence seems as unbounded as that of the monochromatic
heroes of the *Henry VI* plays. Yet he is too aware of political reality to believe
that Bolingbroke has come but for his own and too aware of his own
limitations to believe that he can contend with Bolingbroke in arms. Thus,
Richard settles into a detached contemplation of the heroic self-image that
a more traditional hero would defend without thought.

By thinking, Richard becomes the first of Shakespeare's "modern" tragic
heroes. He knows that his concept of *de jure* kingship is fragile and likely to
be shattered by Bolingbroke's presumption. That knowledge would provoke Titus, disillusioned, valiantly to attempt to preserve the integrity of
his self-image. In Richard, it provokes no such thing. He feels obliged to
defend his kingship verbally but is sorely tempted to resign himself to
Bolingbroke's *de facto* kingship as an historical inevitability: "I am sworn
brother, sweet,/To grim Necessity" (5.1.20–21). The scene in which Richard
affirms his divine kingship is structured according to this ambivalence: it
centers on a dialectic between his expressions of heroic engagement and
ironic detachment, mediated by a succession of lesser characters who bring
him news of defeat and then enjoin him to play the hero.

Richard begins the scene with an apparently conventional assertion of
heroic will, full of bellicose imagery:

> This earth shall have a feeling, and these stones
> Prove armed soldiers, ere her native king
> Shall falter under foul rebellion's arms.
>
> (3.2.24–26)

Yet Richard asserts not what he will do, but rather what will be done for
him: his lines convey not an active will, but a passive assumption. This
ambivalence is reinforced in his next speech, which begins with an epic
simile identifying Richard in traditional terms as a glorious sun whose
rising will force the night-reveling Bolingbroke to tremble at his sins, but
ends in a most unrealistic faith that God's angels, not his own soldiers, will
defend the throne from Bolingbroke's army. Richard's heroism, one suspects, is merely metaphoric. And so, when Salisbury arrives with news that
the Welsh have fled to Bolingbroke, Richard too readily dramatizes himself

as the victim of *de casibus* tragedy: "All souls that will be safe, fly from my side, / For time hath set a blot upon my pride" (ll. 80–81). Aumerle challenges him to live up to his regal image—"Remember who you are" (l. 82)—and Richard renews the language of heroic engagement:

> I had forgot myself. Am I not king?
> Awake, thou coward majesty, thou sleepest!
> Is not the king's name twenty thousand names?
> Arm, arm, my name!
>
> (3.2.83–86)

These lines echo those of Talbot and York, who without any irony defined their armies as the "substance, sinews, arms, and strength" of their heroic selfhoods. Richard is less ingenuous. His identity as king may invoke the sinews of twenty thousand men, but what he calls to arm is but his name—a title, distinct from selfhood. His vaunting is not so much a heroic self-assertion as a ceremonial *attempt* at self-assertion. As he cannot enforce a constancy between his will and his words, his words constitute a kind of heroic imposture, a hyperbolic artifice by which Richard tries to talk himself into a semblance of engagement.

In structuring the play, Shakespeare found a dramatic correlative for Richard's failure to be fully engaged with the established forms of heroism he invokes. To affirm a traditional hierarchical order of things, he borrowed for the first two acts the form of old political Morality plays. Richard dominates a sequence of ceremonial scenes, showing a public character perfectly consonant with his formal idiom (thus allowing little sympathy for him), and counseled by a number of secondary characters who, in brief scenes of their own, comment chorically on the plight of England. But as Richard loses his grip on the kingship and Bolingbroke rises to power, the Morality structure breaks apart: Shakespeare no longer confirms the centrality of Richard's role. Scenes with Bolingbroke offer a rival center of attention; and his efficient Machiavellian style sharply contrasts with Richard's epic self-indulgence. To reclaim the centrality of his position, Richard self-consciously tries to stage his own tragedy in a series of conventional topoi that Shakespeare, had he remained true to the form of the old play, would have provided for him. Surrounded by loyal followers, Richard launches into a long elegiac discourse on the vainglory of kingship. "For God's sake, let us sit upon the ground / And tell sad stories of the death of kings!" (3.2.155–56) he says, fully conscious that he is offering his own contribution to the *Fall of Princes:*

> for within the hollow crown
> That rounds the mortal temples of a king
> Keeps Death his court, and there the antic sits,
> Scoffing his state and grinning at his pomp,
> Allowing him a breath, a little scene,

> To monarchize, be fear'd, and kill with looks,
> Infusing him with self and vain conceit,
> As if this flesh which walls about our life
> Were brass impregnable.

(3.2.160–68)

The tone belittles the absoluteness with which *de jure* kings are supposed to conceive of themselves. Richard is ironically aware that his ceremonial kingship is subject, if not to Bolingbroke, then to death. In this speech's "trembling equipoise between jest and earnest,"[14] Richard seems to stand outside himself as if at a play, a spectator moralizing on a great man's fall.

He carries his histrionics further at Flint Castle. There, once again commanding the imperious language of Godhead, here affirms his inviolability and, in the well-tested terms of biblical curse, he prophesies destruction for England much as Antony does for Rome:

> God omnipotent,
> Is mustering in his clouds on our behalf
> Armies of pestilence; and they shall strike
> Your children yet unborn and unbegot;

and though Bolingbroke may "come to open / The purple testament of bleeding war," Richard threatens—again, in terms that anticipate Antony and Henry V as surely as they look back to Gorboduc and Tamburlaine—that "ten thousand bloody crowns of mothers' sons" shall change the complexion of England's face before the crown is his (3.3.85–100, passim). Yet this vaunt, delivered with such apparent conviction, yields with suspicious alacrity to a formal language of *contemptus mundi*, most apt for a king who knows his time is at its period: "I'll give my jewels for a set of beads, / My gorgeous palace for a hermitage, / My gay apparel for an almsman's gown" (ll. 147–49), and on it goes. The piling up of syntactical repetitions begins, in context, to sound sardonic, as if Richard is taking perverse delight in casting off his kingly pride to try on other-worldly garb. And coming down to meet Bolingbroke in the base court, Richard cannot resist mythologizing his fall in the heroic terms of Ovid moralisé: "Down, down I come, like glist'ring Phaeton, / Wanting the manage of unruly jades" (ll. 178–79). Like many of the set-speeches regarded as the glories of the play, this one is spoken with quotation marks around it.

Richard's ironic manipulation of tragic conventions is nowhere more evocative than in the deposition scene. There, he not only mocks the ceremonial form by which Bolingbroke hopes to acquire the rights of kingship—"Here, cousin, seize the crown" (4.1.182)—but also calls into question the whole *Mirror* tradition that had for years underlain English tragedy. By asking for a looking-glass, contemplating his face in it, then shattering it into "an hundred shivers" (l. 290), he signifies "the moral of this sport" (l.

291): conventional forms of tragedy no longer fulfill their appointed tasks. His tragedy is more real than they have the power to reflect. Playing on this conceit, Richard casts doubt on the authenticity of any traditional means of dramatizing heroic kingship. Echoing the cadences of Dr. Faustus, for whom self-knowledge came too late, he longs elegiacally for the golden age of kingship he now knows never existed:

> Was this the face
> That every day under his household roof
> Did keep ten thousand men? Was this the face
> That, like the sun, did make beholders wink?
> Is this the face which fac'd so many follies,
> And was at last out-fac'd by Bolingbroke?
>
> (4.1.282–87)

De jure kingship, Richard realizes, like Helen of Troy, lives largely in myth.

Richard II is more essentially a tragic *eiron* than Richard III. While Richard III's role-playing always looks toward a final goal and thus marks him as a traditional villain-hero in spite of himself, Richard II's does not: the self-directed irony with which he plays kingship in all its guises penetrates far deeper into the nature of tragic characterization. His dilemma springs from his failure to be engaged with the roles he plays. Shakespeare makes dramatic his very struggle to achieve some semblance of conventional tragic heroism. The simple, Morality-based assumptions of Richard's kingship are, like the brittle glory he sees reflected in the glass, shattered by his ironic self-awareness. The traditional topoi of Renaissance tragedy are, for him, too conventional a basis on which to build a heroic identity.

Shakespeare presents the *eiron* and the *alazon* more in the manner of Attic comedy in *1 Henry IV,* a play which, though it is not tragic, helps to clarify his redefinition of what constitutes tragic heroism. Hotspur is the hero of epic tradition. Quick to rage, chivalric to a fault, and absolute in his image of himself and his world, he balks at the king's injustice, denies him the prisoners of war, and presumes to take the law of the realm into his own hands:

> An if the devil come and roar for them,
> I will not send them. I will after straight
> And tell him so, for I will ease my heart,
> Albeit I make a hazard of my head.
>
> (1.3.125–28)

Such is the choleric language of a hero who dares risk all to follow the dictates of his will. His is a heart that prompts him to speak nothing but his mind, and that, bluntly. In the head lies the hazard. His will dictates that he "revenge the jeering and disdain'd contempt / Of this proud king" (ll. 183–84); and his lust for revenge kindles a chivalric hyperbole: "O, the blood more stirs / To rouse a lion than to start a hare!" (ll. 197–98). His vaunting climaxes in a famous bit of braggadocio that echoes Duke Humphrey's censure of the "dogged York, that reaches at the moon, / Whose overween-ing arm I have pluck'd back" (*2 Henry VI: 3.1.158–59*):

> By heaven, methinks it were an easy leap
> To pluck bright honor from the pale-fac'd moon,
> Or dive into the bottom of the deep,
> Where fathom-line could never touch the ground,
> And pluck up drowned honor by the locks,
> So he that doth redeem her thence might wear
> Without corrival all her dignities.
>
> (1.3.201–7)

The glance back at York is telling, for the nature of Hotspur's honor is, like York's, Achillean, devoted entirely to a private rather than to a public quarrel: an egotistical commitment to the self alone—"without corrival"—which in the context of an ordered state must be regarded as an excessive and outmoded brand of chivalry. In short, Hotspur is a composite of tradi-tional heroic types—chivalric knight and hot-headed revenger—whose heroic diction, however expressive, is clearly mocked as *alazoneia* by a chorus of chiding observers:

> He apprehends a world of figures here,
> But not the form of what he should attend.
>
> (1.3.209–10)
>
> Why, what a wasp-stung and impatient fool
> Art thou to break into this woman's mood,
> Tying thine ear to no tongue but thine own!
>
> (1.3.236–38)

Falstaff's idiom humorously counterbalances Hotspur's antique heroics. Everything he says and does deflates what Hotspur stands for: it is all directed toward base survival. Instinct, for him, means cowardice, not cour-age; and honor is a mere scutcheon. Who hath it? He that died a' Wednes-day. Sometimes, to achieve his ends, Falstaff ventures into the realm of mock-heroics. He adopts an Ovidian voice to suggest that when Hal be-comes king, his Eastcheap cronies be metamorphosed from thieves to "Diana's foresters, gentlemen of the shade, minions of the moon" (1.2.25–26); later, he stands the traditional outdoing topos on its head to defend his turning tail at Gad's Hill, a defense that would do credit to the most invet-erate *miles gloriosus*. But these reductive uses of the heroic idiom are so comic and delightful in their ingenuity that, rather like the silly pageant of the Nine Worthies in *Love's Labor's Lost* or the tragical mirth of *A Midsummer Night's Dream*, they do not in any serious way impugn the legitimate func-tioning of the idiom in the rest of the play.

Hal does impugn it. He plays *eiron* both to Hotspur and Falstaff. The son of a politician who, like Richard III, employs heroic guises to further his ambition for the crown, Hal is much more like "the skipping King" (3.2.60) than his father realizes; for like Richard II, he is detached from any conventional commitment to the roles he plays. He knows that until the time comes for him to be king, he is expected to act the role of chivalric prince: he chooses, however, to act that role among a leash of drawers in Eastcheap who, he wryly observes, "take it already upon their salvation that, though I be but Prince of Wales, yet I am the king of courtesy" (2.4.8–10). And when, in a mock-play, he tests his own mettle to stand up to his father's censure, he winds up deposing Falstaff and "King Cambyses' vein" (l. 383) in order to act the king himself in a vein more earnest and more modern. Having stripped away the layers of fat Jack's heroic imposture until he is left, as at Gad's Hill, a naked gull, Hal at last, only half in jest, banishes him.

Hal's method of exposing Hotspur's heroic excesses is more complicated because Hotspur is less obviously an *alazon* than Falstaff is. With an ironic sense of both Hotspur's virtues and vices, Hal would divorce himself from such traditional heroic self-possession and would attribute to Hotspur a fustian that his admirers might call hubris. In contemptuous parody, Hal belittles Hotspur's claim to greatness by echoing an accusation once leveled at Tamburlaine, that even in love he can utter only barbarisms.[15] Agydas attempts to talk sense to Zenocrate:

> How can you fancy one that looks so fierce,
> Only disposed to martial stratagems?
> Who, when he shall embrace you in his arms,
> Will tell how many thousand men he slew,
> And, when you look for amorous discourse,
> Will rattle forth his facts of war and blood,
> Too harsh a subject for your dainty ears.
> (*Tamburlaine: Part One*, 3.2.40–46)

Hal translates it into the prosaic comedy of direct discourse:

> I am not yet of Percy's mind, the Hotspur of the north, he that kills me some six or seven dozen of Scots at a breakfast, washes his hands, and says to his wife, "Fie upon this quiet life! I want work." "O my sweet Harry," says she, "how many hast thou kill'd today?" "Give my roan horse a drench," says he, and answers, "Some fourteen," an hour after, "a trifle, a trifle." (2.4.100–108)

Tamburlaine is acquitted of the charge by Zenocrate herself; his heroic reputation is cleared. But Hotspur stands no chance against Hal's mock-heroic jibes. They deliberately ridicule an older mode of heroic representation that cannot survive more ironic scrutiny. By using them, Shakespeare not only warns against too easy a sympathy for Hotspur. He also sheds Marlowe.

No matter how much he enjoys mocking Hotspur, Hal realizes that he must play the role of chivalric knight in earnest if he is ever to emerge as the true prince in the public eye. With due deliberation, therefore, he sets out to emulate those qualities that have made Hotspur the apple of Henry IV's eye. Even as his father challenges him with the image of Hotspur as a "Mars in swathling clothes" (3.2.112), Hal responds in the idiom now recognized as the hallmark of Shakespeare's most traditional heroes. First, he pretends to an integrity of self-image in a line that anticipates Coriolanus's belief that the hero is always author unto himself—"I shall hereafter, my thrice gracious lord, / Be more myself" (ll. 92–93)—at once affirming that there is but one self he can possibly be and fulfilling his father's expectation that shows of heroism will reflect inherent nobility. Second, he vaunts with the self-assurance of a conqueror, calling up manifold images of blood, metaphors of cruelty, and extravagant comparisons to do him service:

> For every honor sitting on his helm,
> Would they were multitudes, and on my head
> My shames redoubled! For the time will come
> That I shall make this northern youth exchange
> His glorious deeds for my indignities.
> Percy is but my factor, good my lord,
> To engross up glorious deeds on my behalf;
> And I will call him to so strict account
> That he shall render every glory up,
> Yea, even the slightest worship of his time,
> Or I will tear the reckoning from his heart.
>
> (3.2.142–52)

Third, he gives his father an oath by which he absolutely commits himself to the performance of the deed: "This is the name of God I promise here, / The which if He be pleas'd I shall perform" (ll. 153–54). The heroism Hal swears to *sounds* noble, but he is not fully committed to the rhetorical forms that express it. He draws too liberally from the stock idiom, an idiom he has previously disparaged as fustian, to let us believe fully in his metamorphosis. I am not suggesting that Hal does not mean what he says: he does mean it, and his performance bears it out. But what he *says* represents only a part of what he *is*, and that distinction gives him the edge on Hotspur.

Vernon complicates our perception further by taking Hal's reformation at face value and spreading his fame as a newborn chevalier:

> I saw young Harry, with his beaver on,
> His cushes on his thighs, gallantly arm'd,
> Rise from the ground like feathered Mercury,
> And vaulted with such ease into his seat
> As if an angel dropp'd down from the clouds
> To turn and wind a fiery Pegasus
> And witch the world with noble horsemanship.
>
> (4.1.104–10)

The speech, which gains from being spoken by one of Hal's enemies, is such a conventional heroic apotheosis that one is tempted to believe it; one is tempted, too, to believe that Hal's offer to "try fortune" with Hotspur "in a single fight" in order "to save the blood on either side" (5.1.99–100)—an offer made in the noblest tradition of epic warfare—is not heroic artifice (could Hal think the offer a chance worth taking because, like the offer of grace, "It will not be accepted"?) but a true indication that what Hal says now adequately represents what he is.

The test of mimetic truth comes when Hal and Hotspur meet. Hal overcomes Hotspur; and thus, winning his honors from him, he fulfills the requirements of conventional heroism. But in adopting Hotspur's idiom, Hal nevertheless stands ironically apart from the values the idiom conveys. Meeting Hotspur on the field, he vaunts in language that harks back to the most ardent conqueror heroes and looks forward to Julius Caesar's grandiose declaration that he is the only constant star in the firmament:

> think not, Percy,
> To share with me in glory any more.
> Two stars keep not their motion in one sphere,
> Nor can one England brook a double reign
> Of Harry Percy and the Prince of Wales.
>
> (5.4.63–67)

The vaunt does what Hal intends, it provokes Hotspur to a boast in kind; and in part for this reason, it sounds less like a genuine expression of his will than a conventional gesture calculated to appeal to Hotspur's vainglory. Hal, again, is using the idiom to define a proper context for his encounter with Hotspur, a hero who can better brook the loss of brittle life (the alliteration helps to antiquate the sentiment) than the proud titles Hal wins of him. Victorious, Hal speaks an epitaph over Hotspur's corpse that fixes his tragedy firmly in the outmoded *de casibus* tradition:

> Ill-weav'd ambition, how much art thou shrunk!
> When that this body did contain a spirit,
> A kingdom for it was too small a bound;
> But now two paces of the vilest earth
> Is room enough.
>
> (5.4.88–92)

So much for the vanity of human aspirations. By overcoming Hotspur, Hal marks the ascendence of a new heroism of self-awareness. In fact, the whole scene may be interpreted emblematically as the supplanting of the conventional hero by the heroic *eiron* as a subject fit for tragedy. Hal incorporates all the forms traditionally associated with the hero—the proud titles, the vaunt, the daring, the magnanimity—within a multiple self-consciousness that, in its theatrical flexibility, transcends the monolithic heroic ethos.

Hal's simultaneous incorporation and transcendence of this ethos helps to explain why *Henry V,* as Normal Rabkin points out, seems to some critics a testament to chivalric kingship and to others, an exposé of Machiavellian policy.[16] The problem critics have in pinning down the nature of the play may be attributed to the way Shakespeare uses heroic conventions to delineate Henry himself. Shakespeare's devices are by now familiar. In the opening scene, the bishops bear glorious witness to Hal's mythic reformation; yet their witness may be discredited because they are out to use him for their own political ends. He, in turn, speaks with traditional confidence that God's shall be the quarrel against France; but his repeated insistence on it, and his subsequent testiness when Williams suggests that the king himself must take the responsibility, renders that confidence suspect. Like Titus, all tears, Henry rues the fact of his friends' treachery in the scene at Southampton; but the tears may be half-feigned, because he stages the traitors' exposure to insure maximum public outcry against them and sympathy for himself. Like Talbot, he rallies his men 'round the English banner, bidding them to "imitate the action of the tiger" (3.1.6) in good set terms, "for Harry, England, and Saint George" (l. 34); but the forfeit of their lives is something about which, he admits in private, he has grave doubts. Before Harfleur, he vaunts like Tamburlaine, his threats outdoing those of all who came before:

> What is it then to me, if impious war,
> Array'd in flames like to the prince of fiends,
> Do with his smirch'd complexion all fell feats
> Enlink'd to waste and desolation?
> What is 't to me, when you yourselves are cause,
> If your pure maidens fall into the hand
> Of hot and forcing violation?
> What rein can hold licentious wickedness
> When down the hill he holds his fierce career?
>
> (3.3.15–23)

Yet one suspects that he is only using such *alazoneia* for political ends when he admits what no general in his right mind would, that he has no control over his rampaging soldiers, and even more when the town surrenders and he responds with clemency and perfect *gentilesse.* Throughout, he employs ceremony to enforce the justice of his kingship, while in soliloquy, he confesses doubt: "O ceremony, show me but thy worth!" (4.1.241). Shakespeare, in short, both perpetuates and repudiates the myth of Henry passed on to him in chronicle, play, and legend. It is too simple to assert either that Henry *is* the patriot king of legendary fame or that he *is* a Machiavel guilty of heroic imposture. The play validates his heroism even as it submits that any heroism is as much a matter of public show as inner worth. Henry's going in disguise to bolster the flagging spirits of his men puts the paradox in a nutshell. As he tests the idea of kingship and bristles when soldiers suspect him of ignoble behavior, the play casts doubt on the conventions by which he has tried to rally their confidence in him. But merely his going to them, his caring enough to walk among them as a soldier speaking bluntly to other soliders, is itself the stuff of which legends are made.

The whole play attempts to define Henry's true nature. All its lesser characters reflect, discuss, challenge, or argue about the cruxes of heroism that emerge from Henry's actions. The French are devoted to ostentatious chivalry, writing sonnets to their mounts, bragging about their skill at horsemanship (with whoresmanship not far behind), and contending with one another over the ornamental glory of a name: their superficiality helps to authenticate Henry's claim that the English "are but warriors for the working day" (4.3.109), rough, rude, and ready heroes. The English brand of heroism is best represented by Exeter, a man "as magnanimous as Agamemnon" (3.6.6–7) who speaks with the voice of the old order, of which Henry would fain have his followers think he is the paragon. When Exeter narrates the death of "the noble Earl of Suffolk," he recreates a world of chivalric pathos that Shakespeare seemed to have left behind in *Henry VI:*

> York, all haggled over,
> Comes to him, where in gore he lay insteep'd,
> And takes him by the beard, kisses the gashes
> That bloodily did yawn upon his face.
> He cries aloud, "Tarry, my cousin Suffolk!
> My soul shall thine keep company to heaven;
> Tarry, sweet soul, for mine, then fly abreast,
> As in this glorious and well-foughten field
> We kept together in our chivalry!"
>
> (4.6.10–19)

He paints a Virgilian scene that carries us back at least as far as the scene in which Talbot dies addressing the corpse of his son, whom he holds in his arms. But the style is antiquated now, almost comic in its repeated emphasis on passionate embraces, kisses, and tears—more appropriate for an old soldier's narration than for a scene that Shakespeare wisely chose not to dramatize. Exeter does equal justice to the old-fashioned threat Henry sends him to deliver to the French king. To relate what Henry will do, Exeter conjures up the image of an apocalyptic scourge, cruel and commanding as Tamburlaine ever was to Bajazeth:

> for if you hide the crown
> Even in your hearts, there will he rake for it.
> Therefore in fierce tempest is he coming,

> In thunder and in earthquake, like a Jove,
> That, if requiring fail, he will compel.
>
> (2.4.97–101)

A few years earlier, the language would have had the power to compel; in *Henry V,* it prompts us to smile that a well-worn trope should still sound so persuasive in the mouth of one who believes in it. Fluellen, too, in his inimitable way, would transform Henry into an epic conqueror. The strained analogies by which he would liken Henry to Alexander call unwitting attention to how dissimilar they really are: one born at Macedon, the other Monmouth; both towns lie on rivers; Alexander, in his rage, killed his friend Cleitus, while Henry, in his right wits, banished Falstaff.[17] Yet this last likeness is closest and most damaging, for it shows how much Henry has sacrificed, without the excuse of heroic rage, to become an object fit for Fluellen's worship.

Not only the death of Falstaff, but the lively presence of Henry's old Boar's Head companions, men whose heroic garb is cut from whole cloth, keeps before our eyes the seamier side of human nature. At home, Pistol and Nym have nothing nobler to do than to draw swords in defense of Mistress Quickly's honor, no sooner drawn than sheathed again in cowardice; in battle, they never do make it to the breach—"I have not a case of lives" (3.2.4)—but remain behind, like the ignominious Romans who earn Coriolanus's contempt, grabbing the spoils of war, plundering, pillaging, and finally paying for it. Pistol is the crown jewel of the play's heroic parody. His verse throughout *Henry V* and *2 Henry IV* is a patchwork of scraps, orts, and misquoted fragments from heroic drama of the previous decade. Swearing revenge on Doll, Pistol assults our ears with his most famous volley of misremembered rant:

> Shall pack-horses
> And hollow pamper'd jades of Asia,
> Which cannot go but thirty mile a day,
> Compare with Caesars, and with Cannibals,
> And Troiant Greeks? Nay, rather damn them with
> King Cerberus, and let the welkin roar.
>
> (*2 Henry IV:* 2.4.162–67)

The humor of this speech depends largely on our hearing him mangle two of Marlowe's most famous lines, both spoken by the hero Pistol would most emulate, Tamburlaine: "Holla, ye pampered jades of Asia!" (*Part Two:* 4.4.1) and "My sword struck fire from his coat of steel . . . As when a fiery exhalation . . . Fighting for passage, makes the welkin crack" (*Part One:* 4.2.41–45). But there are other gems in the crown, no doubt stolen from plays no longer extant. "Cannibals" must once have been "Hannibals"; "King Cerberus" a probable conflation, in the style of *Locrine,* of Cambyses and hell's three-headed hound. In subsequent speeches, Pistol makes raids on *The Battle of Alcazar* and *The Turkish Mahomet and Hiren the Fair Greek* as well.[18] Such fustian is a perfect vehicle for a "captain" whose bravest deed is to tear a poor whore's ruff in a bawdy house. Beyond the immediate context, moreover, it provides clear evidence of how ludicrously inflexible as a means for representing reality Shakespeare now regarded the heroic idiom of the old plays. George Hibbard summarizes Shakespeare's achievement eloquently:

> In the process of feeling his own way forward to new modes of dramatic expression he had, imperceptibly yet effectively, educated his audience, leading them to bring new expectations and new standards of judgment with them when they came to the playhouse. Pistol embodies his conscious recognition of what he had achieved, for the assumption behind the figure is that the playgoing public will not be taken in by him, as Master Justice Shallow and Mistress Quickly are, but will appreciate him for what he is—a walking parody of old techniques and outworn modes of expression. (P. 6)

In measuring how far Shakespeare's mimetic art had come, one must remember that Pistol parodies not only the language of Marlowe, Greene, and Peele, but also the language of *Titus Andronicus* and *Henry VI*.

Henry V, however, does not so much repudiate the patterns of the old plays as update them. All its ironic treatment of heroic artifice ought not to hide the fact that the play often meets our expectations of the traditional conqueror play. It dramatizes the sacking of France by a legendary English king. Its structure, consisting of parallel but distinct episodes, all organized around a heroic theme, harks back to the structure of Tudor interludes and, more directly, to the application of that structure to heroic subjects in *Tamburlaine* and *The Battle of Alcazar.* The Chorus, furthermore, encourages belief in the myth of Henry's greatness and in the epic nature of his deeds, even though actors are mere shadows incapable of bringing forth "so great an object" (Prologue, l. 11). Just as Talbot once did with the Countess of Auvergne, the Chorus challenges the imagination of his audience to piece together the imperfections in order to envisage the hero whole.[19] That he succeeds as well as Talbot will be attested to by all those critics who have called *Henry V* Shakespeare's most chauvinistic heroic exercise.

Shakespeare employs the idiom of old plays with more profound irony in *Hamlet.* In the middle of things, he offers a mirror of what *Hamlet* might have been like in its *ur*-form: a primitive revenge tragedy called *The Murder of Gonzago.* The Player King and Queen speak of their love in the static generalizations and moral abstractions that characterized set-speeches in plays of decades past; and the three rhyming couplets that Lucianus mutters identify him once and for all as the Vice-like revenger of an old play—a Horestes, perhaps, or a more recent Jew of Malta—who takes obsessive delight in villainy: "Thoughts black, hands apt, drugs fit, and time agree-ing, / Confederate season, else no creature seeing. . ." (3.2.253–54). One might rightly assume that Shakespeare incorporates this fragment as a mimetic foil, an imitation of a type of rhetorical drama that he has forsa-ken, to hold up to his audience as a lens through which they can see how far he has advanced in realism. Revenge tragedy as a genre had, after all, been démodé for at least five years. When Hamlet inflicts Lucianus's arcane plotting on his courtly audience, therefore, the playhouse audience would have appreciated his wry admission of the play's archaism: "Begin, mur-derer; leave they damnable faces, and begin. Come, the croaking raven doth bellow for revenge" (ll. 250–52). His lines echo, in a tone hovering between delight and derision, fustian from *The True Tragedy of Richard the Third,* printed seven years earlier but performed well before that: "The screeking Raven sits croking for revenge. / Whole heads of beasts comes bellowing for revenge."[20] Hamlet seems to be casting aspersions on the stock revenge idiom as incapable of expressing what he feels or delineating what he must do.

"It would be convenient," writes Howard Felperin, "to think that in mov-ing with Hamlet from the banquet hall of the play scene to his mother's closet we have also moved forward through theatrical history, left behind an archaic theaticality with its stiff and stylized postures for contemporary realism with its more intimate disclosures of deepest personality" (47–48). But such is not the case. Shakespeare's references to archaic sources play a more pervasive and complex role than critics usually acknowledge. On his way to his mother's closet, Hamlet pauses to dally with the revenge idiom, summoning images of apocalypse and blood-thirst to help him screw his courage to the sticking place:

> 'Tis now the very witching time of night,
> When churchyards yawn and hell itself breathes out
> Contagion to this world. Now could I drink hot blood,
> And do such bitter business as the day
> Would quake to look on.
>
> (3.2.387–91)

If his purpose is too easily diverted—"Soft, now to my mother" (l. 391) has the force of a nonsequitur—he at least for a moment has sounded very much like the conventional Nemesis. In the closet, furthermore, Hamlet castigates his mother in such allegorical terms as liken him to a frenzied prophet: Virtue scourging Vice.[21] He metamorphoses a suggestively psy-chological encounter into an occasion for homiletic rant until his father's ghost, a significant vestige of Senecan blood tragedies, admonishes him to get back to the business of revenge. At certain points, then, Shakespeare allows *Hamlet* to imitate the idiom and adhere to the conventions that probably informed the *Ur-Hamlet.* In daring to do so, he keeps archaic models before us as reminders of how far his deviation from those models had ushered in a mimetic revolution.

Hamlet the hero, like *Hamlet* the play, achieves theatrical authenticity in direct proportion in his failure to be contained by such archaism. The epitome of Shakespeare's tragic *eirons,* he directs his irony both outwards, to the playing of roles for public consumption, and inwards, to his mode of self-apprehension. Hamlet would like to conceive of himself as a traditional revenger, passionately committed to his heroic purpose and able to use the diction of old plays unselfconsciously. In a manner akin to that of Hieronimo or, less vengefully, Tamburlaine, he declares that he was born to "set right" the time now "out of joint" (1.5.189–90)—to purge the sins from a fallen Babylon; and yet he sees that task as loathesome both at the outset—"O cursed spite"—and later, when he identifies his role for his mother: "heaven hath pleas'd it so / To punish me with this, and this with me, / That I must be their scourge and minister" (3.4.180–82). The very unwillingness with which he accepts the archaic role signifies how short the role falls in encompassing his whole character. Try as he may, Hamlet cannot be what he would.

Hamlet tries without success to emulate an ideal hero cut in the conventional mold. Such a hero is figured primarily in his father, as both picture and ghost, whom Hamlet describes in the popular Ovidian language of mythic apotheosis:

> See, what a grace was seated on this brow:
> Hyperion's curls, the front of Jove himself,
> An eye like Mars, to threaten and command,
> A station like the herald Mercury
> New-lighted on a heaven-kissing hill—
> A combination and a form indeed.
>
> (3.4.56–61)

This formal embodiment of heroism—formal even in the ghost who, though drawn from a different tradition, is nonetheless noble—challenges Hamlet to perform a revenge for which he lacks resolve, and that challenge causes Hamlet's dilemma. He is conscious of his obligation to fulfill the revenger's role, yet his consciousness of it as "role" leaves him powerless to perform it. He initially responds to the ghost with vaunting conviction:

> My fate cries out,
> And makes each petty artery in this body
> As hardy as the Nemean lion's nerve.
>
> (1.4.80–82)

Inflamed with a hero's metaphoric daring, he vows to "sweep to [his] revenge" (1.5.32) in an absolute identification of selfhood with purpose: "I have sworn 't" (l. 113). But the opposing voice of ironic self-knowledge begins to be heard even as Hamlet asserts his heroic will. He will "put an antic disposition on" (l. 173), as if by instinct, without sensing that it may violate the vow he has just made. Hamlet's two voices lock horns throughout the play. His archaic diction achieves a level of conventional reality simply because one knows what it stands for; but coming from the lips of a character whose verisimilitude is defined by his ambivalence toward archaic convention, it sounds stagy, rather like Antony's lament over Caesar. Hamlet's contrary voice deprecates the most sacred assumptions of the heroic ethos. It is heard most strongly in the graveyard, when he contemplates the fates of the world's most ambitious heroes: "Why may not imagination trace the noble dust of Alexander, till 'a find it stopping a bung-hole?" (5.1.203–4). This reductive perspective makes Hamlet's will to be fully engaged with the heroic ethos difficult to credit.

Hamlet ponders the discrepancy between self and role when the players confront him with their painted passions. Hamlet would have the players recite "Aeneas' tale to Dido" (2.2.446),[22] and especially the section in which "the rugged Pyrrhus" (l. 450) comes to avenge himself on Troy for the death of his father Achilles. Hamlet is moved to recite the verse himself:

> Roasted in wrath and fire,
> And thus o'er-sized with coagulate gore,
> With eyes like carbuncles, the hellish Pyrrhus
> Old grandsire Priam seeks.
>
> (2.2.461–64)

Drawn by his own obsessive inaction to the figure of the antique revenger, Hamlet tries to apply the archaic ethos to himself. His imagination is ablaze with the wrath, the rage, the bloody blameful blades that characterized many old heroic narratives such as this, including Shakespeare's own sensational *Rape of Lucrece*. But the description of Pyrrhus is no more than that: a conventional bit of narrative, luridly overwrought, that bears no real likeness to Hamlet's situation. Aware of the imposture that lies at the heart of his heroic self-image, Hamlet despairs that he cannot summon up on behalf of his cause even as much passion as a player can for his fiction, "his whole function suiting / With forms to his conceit" (ll. 556–57). And there's the rub. Even an actor's "forms," outward shows, are passionate enough to convince the most skeptical audience of an inner torment, whereas Hamlet, who feels the inner torment, cannot bring himself to enact "forms" sufficient to persuade even himself, let alone an audience, that his feeling is genuine. If he could, "he would drown the stage with tears / And cleave the general ear with horrid speech / . . . and amaze indeed / The very faculties of eyes and ears" (ll. 562–63, 565–66): that is, he would suit his whole function in forms of heroic rant of the sort that amazed—verb beloved of epic poets—audiences of a decade past. But aware that such an effect is theater, not life, he "can say nothing" (l. 569). He is a victim not so much of cowardice as of too much playgoing.

To reflect on the inadequacy of his heroic engagement, Hamlet holds up as mirrors two traditional heroes. One, Fortinbras, an aspirant conqueror and a very Hotspur of honor, determines to carry out his dead father's business by repossessing a worthless piece of land. Hamlet contrasts Fortinbras's absolute resolve with his own infirmity of purpose:

> Examples gross as earth exhort me:
> Witness this army of such mass and charge
> Led by a delicate and tender prince,
> Whose spirit with divine ambition puff'd
> Makes mouths at the invisible event,
> Exposing what is mortal and unsure
> To all that fortune, death, and danger dare,
> Even for an egg-shell.
>
> (4.4.46–53)

Hamlet is ironic even in his praise; for while he inflates his image of Fortinbras to the divine proportions of a Tamburlaine who would take arms against "fortune, death, and danger," he also deflates that image in a breath by using reductive and faintly ridiculous words like "puff'd," "making mouths," and "egg-shell." Hamlet has too much respect for God-like reason to praise unqualifiedly one in whom it fusts unused. Thus his assessment of Fortinbras's heroism in tinged with an irony that sees him hovering somewhere between admirable hubris and comic *alazoneia*.

In Laertes, Hamlet sees a less distorted image of himself. Duty-bound, like Hamlet, to avenge his father's murder, Laertes nevertheless acts on his own initiative and is capable of Kydian resolve. He vaunts with the hyperbole of the stock-in-trade revenger—

> To hell, allegiance! Vows, to the blackest devil!
> Conscience and grace, to the profoundest pit!
> I dare damnation.
>
> (4.5.133–35)

—and, like Titus, he is even willing to resort to policy to attain his goal. In descending to poison rapiers, Laertes flirts with parody.

It is in response to him that Hamlet comes closest to allying himself with his heroic ideal. In an excess of grief over Ophelia's death, Laertes leaps into her grave and indulges in rant that is strictly 'Ercles' vein:

> Now pile your dust upon the quick and dead,
> Till of this flat a mountain you have made
> T' o'ertop old Pelion, or the skyish head
> Of blue Olympus.
>
> (5.1.251–54)

Vile phrase, "skyish head": the sort of pretense that gives epic diction a bad name. But there 's more in it. Laertes' lines glance back at Ovid's narration of how the giant race piled Pelion upon Olympus (*Metamorphoses,* I), and the allusion suggests that the speaker himself may boast of giant stature. Laertes would not object to the suggestion. Hamlet takes this fustian as a challenge to his own commitment to Ophelia. Leaping in after Laertes, he at last musters the will to forge a heroic identity in the hyperbolic language of self-assertion: "This is I, / Hamlet the Dane" (ll. 257–58). He proceeds to match Laertes' diction in a verbal cock-fight based on the outdoing topos:

> 'Swounds, show me what thou 't do.
> Woo 't weep? Woo 't fight? Woo 't fast? Woo 't tear thyself?
> Woo 't drink up eisel? Eat a crocodile?
> I'll do 't. Dost thou come here to whine?
> To outface me with leaping in her grave?
> Be buried quick with her, and so will I.
> And, if thou prate of mountains, let them throw
> Millions of acres on us, till our ground,
> Singeing his pate against the burning zone,
> Make Ossa like a wart!
>
> (5.1.274–83)

At first, it appears that Hamlet has finally reached the summit of a heroic passion toward which he had been struggling for four long acts. The violent excess of his imagery—drinking poison, eating crocodile, tearing one's own flesh—taunts Laertes; his determination to show his superhuman love by being buried quick with Ophelia takes up the gauntlet Laertes has cast down; and when he talks of mountains, Ovid answers Ovid—if Laertes' passion would o'ertop old Pelion, the giant scale of Hamlet's passion would *dwarf* Ossa. Line for line, Hamlet surpasses Laertes in an idiom as conventionally acceptable as that of York who, in a much earlier play, anticipates the form of Hamlet's speech:

> Bid'st thou me rage? Why, now thou hast thy wish.
> Wouldst have me weep? Why, now thou hast thy will.
>
> (*3 Henry VI:* 1.4.143–44)

But such antique diction has never fully defined Hamlet's character before; and unless one is willing to grant that he has suddenly become the hero of the old play he has so longed to be, one may suspect that he is employing the idiom as a vehicle for ironic self-expression. His repeated reference to it as rhetoric seems to bear this out. Laertes, he says, comes here "to whine," "to outface" him, to "prate"—this last, a verb that belittles such language as nonsensical boasting. His final vaunt, however, best reveals the self-consciousness with which he is outdoing Laertes: "Nay, an thou 'lt mouth, / I'll rant as well as thou" (ll. 283–84). Irving Berlin would smile to think that Shakespeare, had he been our contemporary, might have written "Anything You Can Do, I Can Do Better" as a comic duet for Hamlet and Laertes. Even when Hamlet is most passionate in defending his honor, as he is in this scene, he remains paradoxically detached, observing himself playing a Hotspurious role. And through him Shakespeare, in the very act of offering a traditional idiom to satisfy our expectations of heroic tragedy, educates us to regard that idiom as too archaic to express the complex ethos of a real hero.

Hamlet finally meets the criteria for revenge tragedy: after the ghost's injunction, the doubt and delay, the occasions missed, the madness, the accidental judgments and purposes mistook, Hamlet finally rises to the heroic fulfillment of his pledge. But it meets them only by half. Each conventional form it uses contains within itself an aspect of self-criticism that makes it less than conventionally fulfilling. Like *Henry V* and *Julius Caesar*, the other great heroic plays of Shakespeare's midcareer, *Hamlet* uses a self-conscious protagonist to keep one aware of the play's dynamic interaction between satisfaction and repudiation of generic expectations. The protagonist's attempt to find a self consistent with the demands of convention is Shakespeare's greatest contribution to heroic mimesis: the realism of a hero resides not in achievement of established goals, as in the plays of Shakespeare's predecessors, but in his attempt to align himself with a traditional role—to become the hero of the old play, chronicle, or epic poem that Shakespeare took as his source. Brutus struggles to become the honorable liberator of Rome; Hal, the chivalric king of legendary fame; Hamlet, the revenger in a play by Kyd.

Shakespeare makes it easy for us to identify with his tragic *eirons*. We may apply to all of them what Maynard Mack writes of one: "That Hamlet does not manifest the extreme engagement of Othello and the rest, but seems to stand back, withholding something, a man of multiple not single directions, is perhaps the reason that our feelings about him . . . contain no jot of patronage. He is never anyone's dupe."[23] Though not to the same degree as Hamlet, other heroes—Richard II, Hal, Brutus, Antony—share in this multiplicity. The more effort the *eiron* expends in self-examination, the more willingly we engage ourselves with him—perhaps because he saves us from making that expenditure, but more probably because his introspection, his struggle to come to terms with heroic conventions, directly illuminates *our* understanding of how the play transcends those conventions. In his self-criticism, the *eiron* absorbs the roles of those critics, such as the choric chiders of Hotspur's wrath, who guide our response to the traditional, unselfconscious hero. And as those critical voices are internalized, as they become combatants in a civil war that rages within the *eiron*, we are drawn into that warfare too, rooting for him to break the old molds and break away from the traditional expectations that restrict and limit his capacity to be himself.

The hero's struggle adumbrates Shakespeare's. He incorporates in these plays the forms and figures of past heroic drama almost as if to prove what he has left behind: antimimetic fossils. Occasionally he subjects them to ruthless parody, as in Pistol's rant or Aeneas's lamentable tale to Dido. More often, he employs them integrally as models from which the hero can detach himself in order to dramatize an unconventional reality: Brutus's administering an oath on the strength of honesty alone, Richard's self-dramatization as a Mirror of all fallen princes, Hal's vaunting assurance that Percy is but a factor to engross up glorious deeds on his behalf, and Hamlet's vow to outdo Laertes in 'Ercles' vein are just a few obvious examples. Necessary as the fossilized idiom is to provide a heroic context for his radical experiments in mimesis, Shakespeare nevertheless rejects it outright as a means of representing *tragic* heroism. When traditional heroes appear in these middle plays, they are either not tragic or so conventionally tragic that one looks on them dispassionately as representatives of an outmoded world. In the early plays one admires and sympathizes with a chivalric Talbot, an aspiring York or a vengeful Titus despite—perhaps because of—the conventions that define them. One tends to smile at similar characters in the middle plays. Shakespeare exaggerates their archaism, relegates them to the status of foils for his more self-conscious protagonists. Hotspur's chivalry is riddled with egotistical excess; Caesar's grandeur is grossly inflated; Laertes defies the gods too patly; Fortinbras makes mouths at invisible events. Shakespeare withdraws sympathy from them in direct proportion to the conventionality of their characterization. In doing so, he indicates how far, too, he has withdrawn allegiance from the traditional heroic idiom that once served him well. That withdrawal, however, should not obscure the degree to which the greatness of these middle plays is indebted to the formative figures of his youth.

4

The Matter of Troy

*I*n perhaps no play does Shakespeare allow the complex range of responses or test the traditional patterns of heroic tragedy more rigorously
than in *Troilus and Cressida,* a play that falls significantly between *Hamlet* and
the other great tragedies of Shakespeare's maturity. *Troilus* comes at a junc-
ture in Shakespeare's career: with analytic and sometimes caustic retro-
spection, it surveys his representation of heroism in the earlier plays.
Appropriately for such a survey, he turned, for his source, to the wellspring
of all heroic legend, Homer's *Iliad.* His knowledge of the *Iliad,* however,
derived not primarily from Homer, but from Homer's many redactors,
whose contradictory interpretations and romantic excrescences may have
inspired the complexity of attitudes toward the matter of Troy dramatized
in *Troilus.* Indeed, the welter of conflicting sources and the resultant impos-
sibility of assuming that an Elizabethan audience would bring fixed expectations to the legend may explain why Shakespeare was attracted to it in the
first place. It had been transmitted from Homer, Virgil and Ovid by two
spurious eye-witnesses to the Trojan War whose accounts supplanted Homer's during the Middle Ages and who, in their conflicting biases, helped to
create ambiguities in later attitudes toward Homeric heroes: Dictys, fourth-
century and pro-Greek; and Dares, sixth-century and pro-Trojan.[1] Lydgate
and Caxton, from whom Shakespeare derived much of his "siege" material,
based their accounts on those of Dares and Dictys, but they recast the
Trojan War in the age of chivalry and imbued its heroes with feudal ideals.
In their anachronistic judgments, the Trojans fared better than the
Greeks—perhaps to be expected of English writers who saw themselves as
descendants of Troy—and the most epic of heroes, such as Achilles, earned
their strongest censure.[2] With the Renaissance man's preference for classical over medieval authority, however, it is likely that Shakespeare referred
as well to some version closer to Homer's original, either Chapman's *Seauen
Bookes,* published with *Achilles Shield* in 1598, or some other translation to

which he had access.[3] Any of these would have helped to redeem Homer's heroes from their unflattering medieval accretions. That Shakespeare was as capable as Chapman of treating these heroes with high seriousness, the tapestry in *The Rape of Lucrece* amply attests.

All this spells confusion, and it is precisely this confusion that Shakespeare capitalizes on in *Troilus and Cressida*. The play is generically indeterminate. One may say of it what Falstaff uncharitably says of Mistress Quickly: a man knows not where to have her. The epistle prefatory to the 1609 Quarto calls it Shakespeare's wittiest comedy; although, unlike Cressida herself, it was "never clapperclawed with the palms of the vulger," it nevertheless was "passing full of palm comical." In the First Folio, however, it finds its place among the tragedies. And the title pages of both editions refer to it as the "History of Troilus and Cressida." The danger has always been that critics would attempt to impose generic consistency and tonal unity on the play and thereby rob it of the interplay among mimetic modes on which Shakespeare relies to educate us to more ambivalent, less conventional responses. One school of critics[4] persists in regarding the play as a serious, even sympathetic portrayal of epic love and heroic value. These critics have had to do battle with others who think the play more comic, a mock-heroic burlesque of the Troy matter in which Shakespeare "was out to show that all the paladins of antiquity and medieval romance, of Homer and Spenser . . . were 'lustful brutes and stupid bullies.' "[5]

Much of the play, of course, bears out the latter school. But much of it does not. Its dramatic core resides in Ulysses' debate with Achilles over the nature of heroic authenticity that I discussed in the first chapter. Ulysses maintains that perseverance alone keeps honor bright: Achilles must keep practicing the conventions of heroic behavior if they are to have currency and he, credibility. But Achilles argues, and Ulysses indirectly affirms, that he has an intrinsic worth, apart from convention, that chokes criticism in the utterance: if he had not, Ulysses would not be soliciting his aid. The crucial question for heroic representation—whether or not a hero's *being,* for an audience, depends exclusively on his *doing*—necessarily involves the expectations and prejudices the audience brings to the play. In one way, Shakespeare confirms the prejudice against "merrygreeks" that T. J. B. Spencer argues was prevalent in Elizabethan society. Humanists such as Erasmus and Lyly, more familiar with Latin than Greek writings, reflected the Roman attitude towards the Greeks and in particular perpetuated the allegation that Greeks were faithless: Horace had capped the tradition by interpreting the *Iliad* as Homer's condemnation of "intrigue, double-crossing, lechery, and quarrelsomeness" among the Greek heroes.[6] This helps to explain why, in Shakespeare's version, Ajax appears to be a dolt in love only with himself, why Achilles sulks in his vanity, in love only with Patroclus, and why Ulysses and the other windbag generals devote their greatest efforts to a petty and, it turns out, ineffectual intrigue. Thersites, as spokesman for this point of view, reduces the greatest of myths to mere patchery, juggling, and knavery:

> All the argument is a whore and a cuckold, a good quarrel to draw emulous factions and bleed to death upon. (2.3.71–73)

> Lechery, lechery, still wars and lechery; nothing else holds fashion. (5.2.198–99)

But if this were all, the play would be easy to categorize. It is not. Shakespeare also depends on his audience to bring more mythic expectations to the play so that he may challenge them and even, though not often, satisfy them. Agamemnon, cuckold that he is, still is capable of addressing himself to sacred questions of good governance; Nestor honors the chivalric virtues of a bygone age in a golden verse that transcends fustian; Ulysses conforms to the traditional image of him as the wise and nimble politician, even in his scheming; and Achilles, whose mean-spirited slaughter of Hector ought to confirm one's worse suspicions of his character, nevertheless assesses so acutely the way heroic reputation is made and maintained that one half admires him for practicing what he preaches. For the most part, of course, Shakespeare challenges "the assumptions and associations underlying the familiar myth" by dramatizing a disparity between what heroes say and what they do; but it is wrong to assume that even among the Greeks, whom he treats least kindly, he means only to debunk the basic tenets of epic mythology.[7] He preserves just enough of their classical dignity to demand a more complex response. He deliberately frustrates the desire for absolute confirmation of one's expectations. His treatment of Helen, the central figure of the myth, is symptomatic: she is neither a great beauty nor a great whore, the opposite shores of her reputation in the Renaissance. She is merely the subject of debate. Her value, Shakespeare seems to suggest, depends on what one brings to her.

For his main plot, Shakespeare strayed from Homer to focus on a medieval embellishment of the Troy legend, a romance derived from Benoit de Sainte-Maure's vernacular *Roman de Troie*. In it, the story of Troilus and Briseida figured as a minor episode in an enormous reworking of the *Iliad* as a chivalric poem.[8] The romance had gone through several metamorphoses, of which Shakespeare was most familiar with Chaucer's *Troilus and Criseyde* and Henryson's *Testament*. The complexity of Chaucer's narrative, which provided Shakespeare with the substance of his main plot, yields something of the ambivalence in attitude that characterizes the sources of the Greek plot.[9] Troilus is, on the one hand, an admirable hero, a great prince who suffers a *de casibus* fall from fortune because he places too much faith in things of this world such as Criseyde, and not enough in providence. His constancy in love and marvelous feats in battle lend pathos to his tragedy. Yet as a courtly lover, Troilus is callow, self-indulgent, histrionic. His naiveté stands in marked contrast to Criseyde's worldliness. He allows Pandarus to direct his wooing; he feigns sickness to win Criseyde's sympathy, invades her chamber with the trepidation of an Andrew Aguecheek, and offers his own sister to Pandarus as payment for services rendered. His methods make a travesty of the conventions of courtly love. Furthermore, his neglect to rescue Criseyde from the clutches of her Greek hosts and his excessive lamentation after she is gone suggest that in him Chaucer was parodying chivalric heroism as well. Thus this great poem— for some, the epitome of tragic romance—is too riddled with self-mockery to take itself seriously; and Troilus, like the poem, is at once tragic and comic, admirable and ridiculous.[10]

Something in him caught Shakespeare's imagination. I venture it was the ambivalence with which Chaucer presented him—on the one hand as a legitimate chivalric hero; on the other, as a figure whose very pretensions to chivalric heroism point out the illegitimacy of the whole code. If Shakespeare was looking for a legendary figure in whom to test the residual power of myth against the pressures of psychological realism as a means for establishing character, he could not have found a better one than Troilus. While subsequent versions of the legend, especially after Henryson, sullied the reputations of Criseyde and Pandarus as fish monger and fish, Troilus's reputation for idealism grew until the three became household words for the qualities they were thought to typify. They anticipate their own reputations with ironic accuracy in Shakespeare's play: "Let all constant men be Troiluses, all false women Cressids, and all brokers-between Pandars!" (3. 2. 200–202). In becoming a Renaissance type for constancy, Troilus must have presented himself to Shakespeare as all the more likely a subject in whom to explore the tensions among the various and contradictory ways of representing heroism. For if Troilus was becoming cemented in legend, a character whose reality was as confined by reputation as Talbot's was, the very process of *becoming* cemented must have suggested to Shakespeare that Troilus had exercised choice and was *willing* to be self-deceived in the face of Cressida's growing reputation for inconstancy—such willingness as would mark in him, as in the more self-conscious of Shakespeare's heroes, a tragic split between self and role.

Shakespeare's representation of Troilus as hero, then, focuses the problems of tone and genre that keep the play's critics in dubious battle. Troilus espouses the chivalric codes and speaks the impassioned verse of Shakespeare's early, conventionally drawn heroes: he is a Talbot or a Titus in war, a Suffolk or a Romeo in love. In his fight to preserve Helen, he asks a rhetorical question that the Trojan council adopts as its main creed: "What's aught but as 'tis valued?" (2. 2. 52). The question of value for the Trojans at large, whether or not Helen is worth fighting for, evokes from him an argument for complete subjectivity:

Were it not glory that we more affected
Than the performance of our heaving spleens,
I would not wish a drop of Troyan blood
Spent more in her defense.

(2.2.195–98)

Helen is the formal, not the final, cause of war. She is but a symbol for whatever the Trojans ascribe to her. For Troilus, "she is a theme of honor and renown" (l. 199), the abstract of a chivalric glory like the glory Hotspur hankers for; and she is "a spur to valiant and magnanimous deeds" (l. 200), such proofs as will enhance Trojan reputations until "fame . . . come canonize us" (l. 202). Troilus apparently has no doubt that public approbation is the promised end of brave deeds and that fame and glory—public approbation in perpetuity—will justly determine heroic value. In his faith that others' evaluation of him will be consonant with his heroic selfhood, he declares a conventional reciprocity between audience and actor that Achilles at first challenges and later, with cold-blooded calculation, turns to advantage.

Troilus thus seems to embody the monolithic ethos that characterized Shakespeare's early heroes. The world, he thinks, mirrors his own values: when he looks into it, his own image smiles back and assures him of his inviolable heroic identity. The representative of the world in whom he is most desirous to see that image reflected is Cressida. By investing his own values in her, he is able to regard her as the perfect lover, apt repository for his romantic idealism. He presumes in her a "constancy in plight and youth," an "integrity and truth" that is "the match and weight" of his: she, as his alter-ego, will "feed for aye her lamp and flames of love" (3. 2. 157–64, passim). Heroism such as this, of course, is willful, stubborn, blind. Shakespeare had ridiculed it before in Hotspur, perhaps Fortinbras, as too outmoded and self-referential to survive in a political context; and Ulysses, in his speech on degree, warns that such egotism, untempered by social considerations or unsoftened by morality, will do itself in, for

Then every thing includes itself in power,
Power into will, will into appetite;
And appetite, an universal wolf,
So doubly seconded with will and power,
Must make perforce an universal prey,
And last eat up himself.

(1.3.119–24)

Including himself in power, of course, is precisely what Troilus does when he insists that only subjective value can give meaning to life. He refuses to temper his will with reason. If need be, he will become passion's slave; and yet the force with which he commits himself to that passion, the simple and unswerving conviction to match that of Hotspur, allows us to admire him as a pattern of heroism—someone Sidney would have deemed worthy of emulation:

> Nay, if we talk of reason,
> Let's shut our gates and sleep. Manhood and honor
> Should have hare-hearts, would they but fat their thoughts
> With this cramm'd reason. Reason and respect
> Make livers pale and lustihood deject.
>
> (2.2.46–50)

This is the very stuff of traditional chivalric heroism. If it smells musty in this play, if it seems anachronistically to summon an idiom that Shakespeare had last used with serious intent in his early histories, it nevertheless has convinced some critics that Troilus *is* the hero he claims to be. Reuben Brower, for example, finds him "both 'a true knight' and an ancient hero in whom word and deed are in harmonious correspondence."[11] Ulysses' assessment of Troilus—the more reliable, perhaps, because spoken by a Greek—tends to verify Brower's evaluation:

> The youngest son of Priam, a true knight,
> Not yet mature, yet matchless, firm of word,
> Speaking in deeds and deedless in his tongue,
> Not soon provok'd, nor being provok'd soon calm'd;
> His heart and hand both open and both free,
> For what he has he gives, what thinks he shows.
>
> (4.5.96–101)

This last line distills the essence of both Troilus's reputation and, analogously, the conventional mode in which his character (according to Brower) is represented. Just as the chivalric hero, by tradition, gives frankly what he has, so, we are to assume, what the actor shows onstage represents fully what he is. Ulysses pictures the Troilus that legend would lead us to expect and that Brower thinks he finds. But this is not exactly the Troilus Shakespeare provides.

He presumes on the conventional evaluation of Troilus in order to serve up something more complex that will make us distrust our preconceptions and engage us actively in the process of mimetic discovery. For Troilus is neither so constant in love nor so idealistic in battle as he would lead us, and himself, to believe. A strain of skepticism in him creates a tension with his self-willed idealism so strong as to suggest that "he is one who has himself seen half-way through the fictions of romantic love."[12] Even at the outset, he acknowledges a possible disparity between Helen's intrinsic value and the value that so many men thrust upon her:

> Fools on both sides! Helen must needs be fair,
> When with your blood you daily paint her thus.

I cannot fight upon this argument;
It is too starv'd a subject for my sword.

(1.1.93–96)

In this condemnation of chivalric folly, Troilus separates his own valuation from that of the collective will. His sarcasm anticipates the more considered judgments of Hector and Diomedes that Helen is not worth the keeping. Even in the heat of his passion for Cressida, too—in their love-tryst, which ought to be full of romantic affirmations, as it is in Chaucer—Troilus betrays a surprising detachment from the traditional heroic ethos he would attribute to himself. Though conceiving of himself as a Romeo, absolute in love, he mocks the hyperbolic claims of the chivalric lover. The only "monster" in love, he assures Cressida, is its inflated diction,

when we vow to weep seas, live in fire, eat rocks, tame tigers, thinking it harder for our mistress to devise imposition enough than for us to undergo any difficulty impos'd. (3.2.76–79)

The echo of Hamlet's heroic claims of what he will do to prove his love for Ophelia only adds to the parody of conventional expressions of love in old plays. Troilus shows that Shakespeare has surpassed them. Yet insofar as he shares in these fictions, as many critics argue he does, he stands self-condemned. He goes on to note a disparity between the will's desire and the limits to performance:

This is the monstrosity in love, lady, that the will is infinite and the execution confin'd, that the desire is boundless and the act a slave to limit. (3.2.80–82)

The assertion of heroic potential is tempered here by an awareness of human limitation: one hears in Troilus the voice of the Chorus in *Henry V,* acknowledging that only the audience's willing suspension of disbelief can transform paltry actors and a bare stage into a representation of heroic greatness. In their immediate context, of course, these lines have narrower sexual connotations, as Cressida makes clear in her challenge to Troilus's potency: "They say all lovers swear more performance than they are able" (ll. 83–84). But beyond that, Troilus recognizes that if "act" is "a slave to limit," it cannot realistically bear the weight of value that he would have it bear. He implicitly admits a possible error in his profession that the will can create absolute value. The voice of skepticism thus wages perpetual war on the voice of belief and argues that Troilus is not quite the constant hero he professes himself to be: "I am as true as truth's simplicity, / And simpler than the infancy of truth" (ll. 167–68). By so defining himself, he aims to preserve the conventional reality of his legendary character; but the very self-consciousness inherent in such an admission qualifies that reality and encourages us to apply to Troilus the criteria by which we measure the verisimilitude of Shakespeare's more ironic heroes—Hal, Antony, Hamlet.

These cracks in Troilus's seemingly unified perception of himself and his world become schismatic in his persistent pleas that Cressida "be true" when they part from one another. At each "be true" Cressida takes umbrage, until Troilus's final rationalization betrays that his real fear is not so much of her inconstancy as of his own:

> But something may be done that we will not;
> And sometimes we are devils to ourselves,
> When we will tempt the frailty of our powers,
> Presuming on their changeful potency.
>
> (4.4.94–97)

The "changeful potency" he would deny expresses, in a sense, his fear that character may be something more (or less) than fixed. The possibility of change over time, for him, implies a kind of autonomy that he suspects would ruin the traditional assumptions and inflexible beliefs—in other words, the conventions of epic characterization—by which he has circumscribed his world. This is a suspicion that none of his protestations of faith can erase, no fine poetry can purge. And the suspicion he projects onto Cressida grows all the stronger because he simultaneously insists on regarding himself as a paragon of truth. "Who, I? Alas, it is my vice, my fault," he claims with legendary certainty; "Whiles others fish with craft for great opinion, / I with great truth catch mere simplicity" (ll. 102–04). But the self-consciousness of the claim betrays a mind far less certain. When he first characterized himself as the very type of truth and simplicity (in a speech I have already discussed), he challenged her to do the same: he presumed in her a constancy, integrity, and truth that were "the match and weight" of his. Even in that challenge, however, he expressed doubt of her ability or willingness to live up to his expectation, for it began, "O that I thought it could be in a woman" (3.2.156). In their scene of farewell, that doubt works a subtle divorce between his claim of self-constancy and the potential for inconstancy he sees in her—a barely conscious split between I and Thou that, when he peers into it, makes him recoil in horror.

All this evidence calls into question the nature of Troilus's heroism. If he can doubt Cressida's faith, can he be as trusting as he claims? Can he be the pattern of chivalric heroism and, at the same time, fully cognizant of the conventionality of his role? Shakespeare throughout displays an ambiguity in the nature of Troilus's mimetic reality; and it is striking that our awareness of that ambiguity is most acute in the scenes where Troilus most insistently voices his chivalric idealism. I have magnified the ambiguity because it is too often overlooked, and Troilus taken absolutely at his word. But the ambiguity is nonetheless present. In fact, Shakespeare seems to dramatize in Troilus the evolution of heroic mimesis itself from the traditional unity of character and convention that he relied on in his early histories to a more dynamic opposition of character and convention by which his more recent heroes achieved their authenticity. This evolutionary aspect of Troilus's character allows us to accept him (as Brower does) as a perfectly traditional hero; but it also, paradoxically, requires us to expect that he will, like Hamlet, mature to a self-knowledge that both subsumes and transcends heroic convention.

Troilus's character is complex enough for us to entertain the possibility that he will grow to such tragic maturity. He endures a subliminal tension between idealism and skepticism, between what he would like to believe and what he recognizes to be true, that increasingly fights its way to the surface of his awareness; and when it does, we assume that Troilus will have the autonomy, the dramatic reality, to choose what to do with it. Once Shakespeare invites us to measure Troilus by the criteria of psychological verisimilitude that we applied to his heroic *eirons*, we expect him, like them, finally to see through the fictions and follies of traditional forms of heroism: any attempt on his part to resist enlightenment and remain a slave of form will perforce discredit his claim to tragic heroism.

Troilus moves to the brink of mimetic maturity at Calchas' tent. There, he weighs his belief against his doubt in the sort of soliloquy that ought, according to Shakespearean practice, to lead to self-discovery. He wrestles with the fact of Cressida's betrayal in a paradox:

> Bi-fold authority, where reason can revolt
> Without perdition, and loss assume all reason
> Without revolt! This is, and is not, Cressid.
>
> (5.2.148–50)

In order to resolve the paradox, he must use reason; but reason is bound to disillusion him. Instinctively, he shies away from it and trusts to "a credence in my heart, / An esperance so obstinately strong, / That doth invert th' attest of eyes and ears" (ll. 123–25). This is the very perversity of his romantic creed. In the council scene, Troilus invoked his eyes and ears as witnesses partial to his cause, reliable allies in creating constant value. Here, they tend to disprove what he wants proven; and so, caught between his habitual dependence on them and his reluctance to believe them now, he concludes that they were "created only to calumniate" (l. 127)—the word by which Ulysses has cast aspersions on Time, an equally fickle agency. Ulysses linked eyes with time in a terse image of inconstancy—"The present eye praises the present object" (3.3.180)—that contradicts Troilus's faith that eyes will assist him in creating constant value. Now, the eyes provide empirical proof that Troilus cannot entirely ignore, and so his recourse is to place Cressida's integrity among those seemingly inviolable universal laws enumerated by Ulysses in the degree speech:

> If beauty have a soul, this is not she;
> If souls guide vows, if vows be sanctimonies,
> If sanctimony be the gods' delight,
> If there be rule in unity itself,
> This was not she.
>
> (5.2.142–46)

These universals also define the unity of the traditional hero. For Troilus to preserve a faith in his own unity of being, he must continue to regard them as absolutes. But, in the words of A. P. Rossiter, "what Troilus has seen appears to him as the refutation of those principles. . . . Those *ifs* turn into negative propositions. For since this *is* she, there *is* no 'rule in unity itself,' no principle of integrity. . . . The absolutes are myths."[13] And so, one might add, is the legend of a most absolute Troilus.

The tragic *eiron*, with his multiplicity of perspectives, would recognize the legitimacy of both sides; and Shakespeare prepares Troilus for just such a recognition by permitting him to use the *eiron*'s customary metaphor of internal warfare:

> Within my soul there doth conduce a fight
> Of this strange nature, that a thing inseparate
> Divides more wider than the sky and earth.
>
> (5.2.151–53)

The old heroic unity begins to crack under the pressure of contradiction. But Troilus halts the combat when it has barely begun. Instead of suffering it to go on until it is resolved by his own tragic awakening, he falls back into his solipsistic sleep. As Robert Ornstein observes, he "projects his inner confusion into a law of universal chaos and would have us believe that because *his* vanity is stricken the bonds of heaven are slipped":[14] "Cressid is mine, tied with the bonds of heaven" yields to "the bonds of heaven are slipp'd, dissolv'd, and loos'd" (ll. 158, 160). Troilus is doing what he has always done, finding it easier to see in the world at large a reflection of himself than to come to grips with a world that threatens to destroy his heroic integrity. Ulysses underscores Troilus's willful retreat by asking a question much like those asked of Hotspur and Caesar: "May worthy Troilus be half attach'd / With that which here his passion doth express?" (ll. 165–66). On the surface, the question mocks the excess of Troilus's self-engagement. But underneath, it recalls the Troilus who once was characterized by an ambivalent sense of his legendary self and who might have grown to be only "half attach'd" indeed.

Had Ulysses asked the question of a Richard II, a Hal, an Antony or a Hamlet, the answer would have been different; for they use the language of heroic engagement always with some parodic (even if serious) intent. They are, in fact, "half attach'd" with what their "passion doth express"; the other half is imposture. But that is not the case with Troilus. His answer assures Ulysses that he has cast off all introspection and has instead—classic case of transference—latched onto another cause to divert his will: revenge on Diomed. In an instant he converts his courtly love into epic hate. The shift of idiom comes naturally and unselfconsciously:

> Ay, Greek; and that shall be divulged well
> In characters as red as Mars his heart
> Inflam'd with Venus. Never did young man fancy
> With so eternal and so fix'd a soul.
> Hark, Greek: as much as I do Cressid love,
> So much by weight hate I her Diomed.
>
> (5.2.167–72)

In trading love for hate, opposite extremes on the scale of absolute value, Troilus stagnates. He has turned his back on discovery; determined to be a constant lover before, he is equally determined to be a vengeful warrior now. Shakespeare marks his reversion to heroic adolescence by allowing him to brandish the outmoded, faintly ridiculous rant of a Senecan revenger:

>   Not the dreadful spout
> Which shipmen do the hurricano call,
> Constring'd in mass by the almighty sun,
> Shall dizzy with more clamor Neptune's ear
> In his descent than shall my prompted sword
> Falling on Diomed.
>
> (5.2.175–80)

These lines recall the antique diction of the speech on Pyrrhus that the Player speaks for Hamlet; more damningly, they echo the kind of verse mutilated by Pistol. Shakespeare uses such fustian with a sure hand: here, it depersonalizes the authenticity of character toward which Troilus has been building and returns him to type. It diminishes him. Not the promised Hamlet, Troilus comes to have no more tragic merit than a Hotspur or a Laertes. Without pause for reflection, he does "mad and fantastic execution" on the Greeks (5.5.38). He is a warrior in whom passion has conquered all reason. He ends in a satirical stasis, an intensification of the thing he was, essentially unchanged.[15] We are jolted by having to reapply to Troilus the conventional criteria for heroic character that we thought Shakespeare had forsaken.

As a further disappointment to our tragic expectations, Troilus is denied what medieval sources grant him: death at Achilles' hands. Had Shakespeare granted him death, he would have defiled the criteria for tragic heroism that he encourages us to apply to Troilus; for he focuses so singly on Troilus's psychological dilemma that we are obliged to measure his tragedy not by the elementary *de casibus* criteria of, say, Chaucer, for whom

Troilus was simply Fortune's fool, "wrecche of wrecches, / out of honour falle / Into miserie," but by the criteria used to measure the tragedies of Shakespeare's more recent reflective heroes. Here as elsewhere, Shakespeare raises and thwarts our expectations. He keeps us restless in the search for tonal consistency and generic definition.

Hector is another matter. Shakespeare's audience would have come with another set of expectations for him. Medieval writers had transformed Homer's Hector into a paragon of chivalric virtue. Chaucer considered such virtue to be above might in this "parfit knight":

> Of Ector nedeth it namore for to telle:
> In all this world ther nys a bettre knyght
> Than he, that is of worthynesse welle;
> And he wel moore vertu hath than myght.
> This knoweth many a wis and worthi wight.
>
> (*Troilus and Criseyde:* 2.176–80)[16]

Lydgate more classically, perhaps because more closely following Homer, emphasized Hector's prowess; but his imagery of light, redolent of Christian texts, tempered such prowess with a more medieval concept of virtue as well:

> This Priamus hadde childre many on,
> Worthi pryncis, & off ful gret myht;
> But Ector was among hem euerichon
> Callid off prowesse the lanterne & the lyht;
> For ther was neuer born a bettir knyht.
>
> (*Fall of Princes:* 1.5930–34)[17]

This tradition enabled Shakespeare to invoke Hector in his earliest plays as an exemplary blend of manly strength and Christian courtesy. The Countess of Auvergne, we remember, taunts Talbot with a diminutive comparison:"I thought I should have seen some Hercules, / A second Hector, for his grim aspect / And large proportion of his strong-knit limbs" (*1 Henry VI:* 2.3.19–21). If the comparison raises Talbot to a pinnacle of legendary heroism, it also puts Hector in the company of a demigod and indicates what company he kept in the Renaissance imagination. King Henry imagines Hector as the supreme defender as he apotheosizes a departing Warwick: "Farewell, my Hector, and my Troy's true hope" (*3 Henry VI:* 4.8.25); and it is as a city's champion, too, that Marcus conceives of Titus Andronicus as "the Roman Hector" (4.1.90). So secure was Hector's reputation, in fact, that Shakespeare could easily afford to parody his achievements in the pageant of the Nine Worthies in *Love's Labor's Lost* where, as played by the braggart Armado in wretched rhyme, Hector—

the heir of Ilion;
A man so breathed, that certain he would fight, yea
From morn till night, out of his pavilion.

(5.2.649–51)

—challenges Costard-Pompey to a duel, ostensibly to defend the honor of
his lady, the pregnant Jaquenetta, but in fact to defend himself from the
charge of having gotten her with child. The burlesque of chivalry implicit
here demonstrates to what extent Hector had been transformed into a
medieval knight.

In *Troilus,* critics usually assume, Shakespeare treats Hector no more
seriously than he treats the other heroes. Just as, in dramatizing them, he
creates a tension between traditional expectations and actual performance,
so, in Hector, he creates an epic warrior whose death is not tragic in any
real sense, but a spoof of the deaths of those blindly heroic knights who
trod the boards in earlier, popular plays. Hector, after all, keeps company
with fools on both sides—as much with an effeminate Paris, whose knightly
mount only Helen can appreciate, as with a doltish Ajax, with whom Hector squares off for a maiden battle. In Hector, it would follow, Shakespeare
ridicules chivalric excess, as though he were little changed from Armado's
lampoon. The chief evidence for this interpretation lies in the contradictory stands Hector takes during the Trojan council scene. To Troilus's claim
that "particular will" determines value, Hector rejoins, "'Tis mad idolatry /
To make the service greater than the god" (2.2.56–57); and he refers instead to the "moral laws / Of nature and of nations" (ll. 184–85) to fix a
more absolute value. Helen, he argues, must be returned: reason refutes
the romantic claim that commitment can make a worthless object worthy.

Yet the truth of such reasoning is something to which Hector cannot
subscribe. In a sudden and, to some critics, a satirically devastating about-
face, he forsakes reason to embrace Troilus's subjective idealism:

> Hector's opinion
> Is this in way of truth; yet ne'ertheless,
> My spritely brethren, I propend to you
> In resolution to keep Helen still,
> For 'tis a cause that hath no mean dependence
> Upon our joint and several dignities.

(2.2.188–93)

Hector admits to having already sent a "roisting challenge" among the
Greeks in the name of his lady (Andromache this time, not Jaquenetta), a
challenge that undermines the basis of his argument that Helen is not
worth fighting for. Fighting in the name of woman is exactly what Hector
commits himself to, and in the most chivalric of terms. Aeneas's formal
delivery only heightens their anachronistic absurdity:

> If there be one among the fair'st of Greece
> That holds his honor higher than his ease
> And feeds his praise more than he fears his peril,
> That knows his valor, and knows not his fear,
> That loves his mistress more than in confession
> With truant vows to her own lips he loves,
> And dare avow her beauty and her worth
> In other arms than hers—to him this challenge.
>
> (1.3.25–72)

Hector's choice of particular will over truth, then, is deliberately wrong-headed. We search in vain for a credible motive. Some critics have leveled against him a charge of dissembling, of playing the role of devil's advocate; others have found in him a consistent love of sport, as much on the field of intellect as on the field of war.[18] Both views impose a rational consistency on his character, but neither satisfactorily explains his behavior. If we expect psychological verisimilitude of the sort that the play encourages us to assess in characters such as Troilus, Cressida, Achilles and others—if we weigh Hector's actions in light of the "reason" he has acknowledged to be "truth"—we are stymied. It is easy, then, to resort to the explanation that Hector is another butt, a caricature of errant chivalry.

Shakespeare may have had something else in mind. Hector may defy conventional expectations because he acts not according to the logic of the individual psyche, but according to the symbolic logic of the play's broader concerns. Douglas Cole vigorously defends Hector's reversal against those critics who cry "Satire!" "On a dialectical level," he writes, "it confirms the impotence of ethical truth in the face of a seductive and destructive myth of honor and dignity."[19] Alan Dessen, identifying a Morality-like structure in the council scene, suggests that Hector's reversal represents reason's inability to "stand up against the siren call of Honor," its psychological motivation subordinated to its function in the Trojan psychomachia.[20] Both critics, then, understand Hector as a figure drawn from a more allegorical mode of drama. In the fashion of earlier dramatists, Shakespeare externalizes Hector's character so that it is a function of idea, not psychology. Hector has no inner life: he is insensible to contradiction, suffers no internal warfare, fails to engage in reflective soliloquy as Shakespeare's thinking heroes do. The mimetic mode Shakespeare employs to convey his heroism is far simpler and more conventional than that he employs for, say, Troilus: and if we understand the requirements of that mode—its affinity with allegory—then our expectation of psychological verisimilitude fades.

Hector becomes the emblem for constancy to an ideal that Troilus longs to be. Going off to battle despite the prophetic dreams and warnings of his family, he embraces Troilus's romantic creed—

> Life every man holds dear, but the dear man
> Holds honor far more precious-dear than life.
>
> (5.3.27–28)

—and takes a vow to fight that is as sacred to him as Troilus's vow to love Cressida: "The gods have heard me swear" (l. 15); "I must not break my faith" (l. 71). Revealingly, Hector manifests his constancy in devotion not to another character, for that would have required some potential for psychological growth and change, but to a code of behavior inherent in knighthood—courtesy.

Like Troilus's love for Cressida, Hector's devotion is self-referential. He tends to project his courtesy onto others and assume that they will abide by its rules. Realizing that he is to be pitted against his own cousin Ajax, son to Hesione, he declares that theirs will be only a maiden battle and refuses to shed family blood. Unlike Caxton, who harshly concludes that Hector's courtesy to Ajax cost Troy the war, Shakespeare does not suggest that this encounter is in any way decisive. In fact, he treats Hector's courtesy with delicacy and admiration. Even the Greeks, who scorn chivalry, praise Hector's courtesy. Ajax transcends his own boorishness to say, "Thou art too gentle and too free a man" (4.5.139); and if there is a tinge of criticism here, there is none in Nestor's apotheosis of Hector as a "Jupiter" who deals life, not death, in battle (l. 191): "I would my arms could match thee in contention, / As they contend with thee in courtesy" (ll. 205–6).

The context of the Trojan War, to be sure, makes such courtesy a bit preposterous. In act 5 a disillusioned Troilus, even while admiring his brother's clemency in the abstract, condemns it as "fool's play" in practice (5.3.43). Troilus takes his cue from Caxton, who, echoing Virgil, inveighs against Hector's offer to do Ajax's pleasure: "Non est misericordia in bello That is to saye ther is no mercy in bataill A man ought not to take misericorde / But take the victorye who may gete hit."[21] Troilus finds in Hector's courtesy a kind of hamartia: "Brother, you have a vice of mercy in you, / Which better fits a lion than a man" (ll. 37–38), an analogy that ennobles Hector's character even as it disparages his wisdom. When, in the alliterative verse of the antique revenger that Troilus will shortly become, he urges Hector to "leave the hermit Pity" and to let "the venom'd vengeance ride upon our swords, / Spur them to ruthful work, rein them from ruth" (ll. 45, 47–48), Hector calls him "savage." Troilus defends himself with the realist's answer, an answer that Hector, whose reality extends no farther than his emblematic function permits, of course cannot understand: "Hector, then 'tis wars" (l. 49).

Our response to Hector's courtesy, then, is ambivalent. Although it is shown to be a foolish way to deal with Greek perfidy, it nevertheless is a valiant attempt to create constant value. Achilles, in his discourteous vaunting, has given Hector fair warning that he will not subscribe to the chivalric code; yet Hector, true to the code, allows Achilles to escape when he has him down. Achilles insults him: "I do disdain thy courtesy, proud Troyan" (5.6.15). Hector's ethos thus appears the more inflexible when he assumes shortly thereafter that Achilles will offer him a courtesy in kind: "I am unarm'd. Forego this vantage, Greek" (5.8.9). This assumption epitomizes Hector's faith that the world will conform to his standard of conduct, a faith more naive than Troilus's faith that Cressida will be true. Yet the faith is a part of chivalric convention; there is dignity in its formal simplicity; and when Shakespeare gives us no reason to expect that Hector should move beyond the bounds of that convention, we would be wrong to ridicule him for staying within it.

By the time Troilus accuses Hector of having a "vice of mercy," Hector has assumed the mantle of idealism that Troilus in despair has cast off:

> No, faith, young Troilus, doff thy harness, youth;
> I am today i' th' vein of chivalry.
> Let grow thy sinews till their knots be strong,
> And tempt not yet the brushes of the war.
> Unarm thee, go, and doubt thou not, brave boy,
> I'll stand today for thee and me and Troy.
>
> (5.3.31–36)

The language could not be clearer. Hector is moving further and further into the realm of allegory, carrying the significance of both Troy and Troilus on his shoulders. He is their prince, their champion, who in defying augury for the sake of worldly honor is ripe for a fall in the *de casibus* tradition of Lydgate's *Fall of Princes.*

The context of Hector's death reinforces that tradition. With the economy of medieval conventions, Shakespeare turns the famous scene into a moral exemplum and encourages us to evaluate it symbolically, as he did the deaths of Talbot and York in *Henry VI,* rather than realistically. Not long after he spares Achilles' life, Hector sets his mark on a Greek in sumptuous armor:

> I'll be master of it. Wilt thou not, beast, abide?
> Why, then fly on, I'll hunt thee for thy hide.
>
> (5.6.30–31)

This passage is disputed by critics. Caxton and Lydgate alike attribute to Hector a certain covetousness, and more than one modern critic have agreed that Shakespeare, too, meant to debase Hector for "yielding to the impulse for loot."[22] But such debasement would be inconsistent with Shakespeare's depiction of Hector as the representative of courtesy. Hector's lines, if regarded from a realistic point of view, may prove his greed: "Most putrefied core, so fair without, / Thy goodly armor thus hath cost thy life" (5.8.1–2); but their epigrammatic quality begs for allegorical interpretation, wherein they signify not greed, but the Trojan pursuit of worldly beauties, such as honor and glory, that may have no intrinsic value.[23]

The idiom places Hector in the world of the early chronicle plays, in which the hero could die simply by falling from his high place without having to suffer any psychological dilemma or growth to knowledge. Hector's death—which had, in medieval redactions of the Troy legend, come to represent the fall of chivalry—served as a model for the death of York narrated in *3 Henry VI*:

> Environed he was with many foes,
> And stood against them, as the hope of Troy
> Against the Greeks that would have ent'red Troy.
>
> (2.1.50–52)

Rhyming couplets give a formality to Hector's death that underscores its function as an emblem, like Talbot's or Hotspur's, for the fall of an antique world. This formality parodies the mode of tragic expression Shakespeare had used in his early histories. In a more comic context, Hector's lines might have been spoken by Bottom's Pyramus:

> Now is my day's work done; I'll take good breath.
> Rest, sword; thou hast thy fill of blood and death.
>
> (5.8.3–4)

The context of *Troilus*, however, is not comic; and if the archaic style tends to detach us from the substance, it does not discredit the substance any more than it would in a chronicle play. Achilles adds to the formality by personifying Troy as the corpse of her fallen hero:

> So, Ilion, fall thou next! Come, Troy, sink down!
> Here lies thy heart, thy sinews, and thy bone.
>
> (5.8.11–12)

We may recall a Talbot who, in defining his heroic identity as an emblem for England's might, invokes the army as "his substance, sinews, arms, and strength" (*1 Henry VI*: 2.3.63). In both cases, the representative of chivalry is swept up in the grip of forces greater, if less courteous, than himself.

In Hector's death, Shakespeare creates an enclave of medievalism that is tonally inconsistent with other events of the play and that requires us to confront conventional heroism head-on. It is tempting, of course, to try to smooth out the play's troublesome tonal shifts by appying uniform naturalistic criteria to all the heroes: such a view necessarily assumes that Shakespeare exaggerated and deformed conventions to make Hector a butt of satire and his death, heroic burlesque. An alertness to how Shakespeare employs conventions in context, however, suggests that Hector's chivalry, though insufficient to hold its place in the relative world of Greekish warfare, may not be as ridiculous as critical opinion has judged it to be. These conventions are an acceptable dramatic means of representing a legendary heroism that, even if displaced by more complex modes of mimesis, could still function legitimately on the Elizabethan stage. Hector's death is tragic according to the values that its Morality-like formalism of presentation permits us to accept. It does not contradict, but rather complicates, the play's assessment of those values as inadequate to define a tragic heroism such as we look to find in a more psychologically developed character such as Troilus. And herein resides its importance. By offering it "straight" as *de casibus* tragedy, without the excesses or choric derision that would have accompanied it in the great middle plays, Shakespeare demonstrates that he has achieved artistic maturity and intellectual balance: he may revert to a more primitive idiom of heroic representation without having to put it down, mock it, feel threatened by it. It can stand side by side with the far more sophisticated idiom of Troilus's failed tragedy (one in which conventions *are* used with derision) and not suffer on that account. Shakespeare, in *Troilus*, embraces as legitimate a far greater *range* of mimetic alternatives than he has ever done; and this fact is of signal importance to his development as a tragic dramatist.

Troilus encapsulates Shakespeare's decade-long evolution of a strikingly varied heroic idiom that causes us to shift expectations and responses from play to play. In it, Shakespeare pauses to reflect on heroic mimesis in all its forms before turning to his mature tragedies. But *Troilus* does more than provide a locus for mimetic experimentation and evaluation; it serves also as a repository of legendary heroes on whom, and on whose mode of representation, those later tragedies can draw in their effort to achieve a convincing heroic reality.

A brief look at the allusion to the matter of Troy in *Coriolanus* will illustrate Shakespeare's method. When Volumnia brags that she is a Hecuba to her son's Hector—

> The breasts of Hecuba,
> When she did suckle Hector, look'd not lovelier
> Than Hector's forehead when it spit forth blood
> At Grecian sword, contemning.
>
> (1.3.40–43)

—an audience would at once have understood her to mean that Coriolanus embodied the virtues of valor, constancy and fortitude belonging to the noblest Trojan of them all. But she raises problems, for Coriolanus is far from the medieval knight that Hector, in the Elizabethan imagination, had become; and his isolation, pride, and wrath—the manifold descriptions of his metallic hardness and his almost godlike strength to run reeking o'er the lives of men (most unlike the Hector of *Troilus*, who deals life)—have prompted one critic to identify him instead with Homer's Achilles.[24] There is little reason, however, to think that at the end of his career, Shakespeare would suddenly have traded a medieval for a more classical conception of Homer's heroes. On the contrary, I find evidence that he distinctly recalled

scenes from his own *Troilus* when writing *Coriolanus,* and an examination of
these recollections may help to clarify the way in which Shakespeare
created Coriolanus's heroic authenticity.

Though his stoic fortitude puts him in a world apart from chivalry,
Coriolanus shares Hector's concept of honor as an absolute commitment to
one's purpose. His trust in a bond of friendship with his fellow warriors,
and in particular his fraternal vows with Cominius, owe something to the
courtesy that knights honored in one another:

> I do beseech you,
> By all the battles wherein we have fought,
> By th' blood we have shed together, by th' vows we have made
> To endure friends, that you directly set me
> Against Aufidius. . . .
>
> (1.6.55–59)

Coriolanus may not talk of pavilions and entering the lists, but his desire to
fight only the bravest man is analogous to Hector's challenge, broadcast
among the Greeks to rouse Achilles from his torpor, and to his blunter
request of Achilles: "I pray you, let us see you in the field. / We have had
pelting wars, since you refus'd / The Grecians' cause" (4.5.266–68).

Coriolanus, of course, does not tilt with lips or fight in the name of his
lady, unless that lady be his mother. But he does look on Aufidius, as
Hector looks on Achilles, as someone with whom he shares a community of
heroic values that transcend party lines. He sins in envying Aufidius's nobility: "And, were I anything but what I am, / I would wish me only he" (1.1.
231–32). Coriolanus's praise of his enemy grows more hyperbolic, perhaps
more chivalric, when he thinks, as Hector does, of war as a sport:

> Were half to half the world by th' ears and he
> Upon my party, I'd revolt, to make
> Only my wars with him. He is a lion
> That I am proud to hunt.
>
> (1.1. 233–36)

It is natural, then, that when banished from Rome, Coriolanus seek his
world elsewhere in a union with Aufidius and, out of courtesy, offer him
either his throat or his service. Aufidius responds with a courtesy that
would have delighted Hector. His heart "dances" at the sight of Coriolanus
more "than when I first my wedded mistress saw / Bestride my threshold"
(4.5.121–23):

> Let me twine
> Mine arms about that body, whereagainst
> My grained ash an hundred times hath broke,
> And scarr'd the moon with splinters. Here I clip
> The anvil of my sword, and do contest

> As hotly and as nobly with thy love
> As ever in ambitious strength I did
> Contend against thy valor.
>
> (4.5.111–18)

Courtly love achieves heroic expression in this odd coupling.

In time, Aufidius will fail to honor the love he here professes—a breach of courtesy much like Achilles', that will dissever bonds of heroism that Coriolanus thought had wedded them forever. Echoes of *Troilus and Cressida* point up Coriolanus's inability to come to terms with such inconstancy in a fellow warrior. Aufidius himself, when they fight, casts him in an antique role—"Wert thou the Hector / That was the whip of your bragg'd progeny, / Thou shouldst not scape me here" (1. 8. 12–14)—and by implication, he casts himself as Achilles. Herein lies the importance of knowing not just Homer, but Shakespeare's own revision of the Troy legend as well, because he patterns Coriolanus's relationship with Aufidius after his own, not Homer's, conception of Hector's relationship with Achilles; the death of Coriolanus after his own conception of the death of Hector.

In the selfsame moment he calls Coriolanus a Hector, Aufidius identifies in himself a motivation that makes him kin to Achilles. "Not Afric owns a serpent I abhor / More than thy fame and envy" (ll. 3–4), he confesses; and we recall Achilles' similar concern for his suffering reputation, "My fame is shrewdly gor'd" (3.3.228), when he hears that Hector will fight with Ajax, not him. Each one is motivated less by faith in intrinsic value than by desire to win fortune in men's eyes, for which the tangible signs of success, whether or not they represent true heroic achievement, are a *sine qua non.*

It takes just this one additional defeat at Coriolanus's hands to convince Aufidius that an *appearance* of honor counts for more than the thing itself. Weighing the Achillean option, wrath or craft, he marks his own fall to policy:

> Mine emulation
> Hath not that honor in 't it had; for where
> I thought to crush him in an equal force,
> True sword to sword, I'll potch at him some way
> Or wrath or craft may get him.
>
> (1.10.12–16)

Even this early in the play, he warns that, like Achilles, he will disdain courtesy—in this case, the laws of hospitality; decidedly medieval laws for a Volscian—to indulge a private revenge:

> Where I find him, were it
> At home, upon my brother's guard, even there,
> Against the hospitable canon, would I
> Wash my fierce hand in 's heart.
>
> (1.10.24–27)

It looks suspicious, then, when he embraces Coriolanus like a bride on his threshold. He may recognize in Coriolanus an absolute merit, a "sovereignty of nature" (4.7.35) that remains constant despite the whims of popular judgment; but he recognizes, too, that such sovereignty is worth little if the people elect not to honor it. His questioning why Rome refused to acknowledge Coriolanus's merit is similar to Achilles' questioning why the generals passed him by without deference; and his answer echoes Ulysses' observation that all value is relative, all reputation subject to envious and calumniating time:

> So our virtues
> Lie in th' interpretation of the time;
> And power, unto itself most commendable,
> Hath not a tomb so evident as a chair
> T' extol what it hath done.
>
> (4.7.49–53)

Praise for past deeds, as Ulysses warns Achilles, will not keep honor bright. Aufidius applies this wisdom to his envy of Coriolanus: just as the tribunes have done, so will he twist the interpretation of Coriolanus's virtues in the public eye, divorce his heroic achievements from their conventional significance, in order to sully his reputation. Thus, the paradox that "most absolute" Coriolanus could never fathom: "When, Caius, Rome is thine, / Thou art poor'st of all" (ll. 56–57). What ought to signify most clearly his heroic worth will instead signify nothing.

Achilles stops at nothing to win Hector's honors from him. Even the act of feasting, which traditionally signifies a community of heroism, will be turned to advantage:

> I'll heat his blood with Greekish wine tonight,
> Which with my scimitar I'll cool tomorrow.
> Patroclus, let us feast him to the height.
>
> (5.1.1–3)

Shakespeare marks the disjunction between reputation and performance most jarringly when Achilles arms to do battle with Hector. Ulysses voices the traditional expectation of Achilles in conventional hyperbole: "O, courage, courage, princes! Great Achilles / Is arming, weeping, cursing, vowing vengeance" (5.5.30–31). But Achilles meets that expectation in the least chivalric way possible. He calls his Myrmidons about him, as Al Capone might have called his hit-men, to instruct them in the art of a gangland slaying:

> And when I have the bloody Hector found,
> Empale him with your weapons round about;
> In fellest manner execute your aims.

> Follow me, sirs, and my proceedings eye.
> It is decreed Hector the great must die.
>
> (5.7.4–8)

Once they perpetrate this bit of mayhem, taking Hector most discourteously, his helmet and shield off, Achilles instructs them to report the deed falsely and thereby to maintain his legendary fame: "On, Myrmidons, and cry you all amain, / 'Achilles hath the mighty Hector slain'" (5.8.13–14). Then, to satisfy Homeric tradition, he determines to tie Hector's "body to my horse's tail; / Along the field I will the Troyan trail" (ll. 21–22). By thus displaying "proof" of a deed he has never done, Achilles attempts to reconstitute the myth of his own heroic virtue.

Just so, Aufidius attempts to "work / Myself a former fortune" out of Coriolanus's death (5.3.201–2). Calling his conspirators together much as Achilles called his Myrmidons, he demonstrates first how he will persuade the people to withdraw their confirmation of Coriolanus's heroic value by making the Roman compromise appear to be an instance of treachery; second, how such treachery must be paid with death; third, how Coriolanus's death will result in the rebirth of his own fame:

> At a few drops of women's rheum, which are
> As cheap as lies, he sold the blood and labor
> Of our great action. Therefore shall he die,
> And I'll renew me in his fall.
>
> (5.6.45–48)

Public recognition, Aufidius agrees with Achilles, can make the man.

Coriolanus enters the scene like Hector, all innocent in his heroic certainty—"Hail, lords! I am return'd your soldier" (l. 72); and thus unsuspecting, he is provoked to rage when Aufidius taunts him with "breaking his oath and resolution" (l. 97), anathema to a hero. His rage is all the pretext Aufidius needs to set his conspirators upon Coriolanus for what looks like an unpremeditated murder. The strategy works. One lord judges that Coriolanus's "own impatience / Takes from Aufidius a great part of blame" (ll. 149–50); and as Aufidius delivers an epitaph on Coriolanus's "noble memory" (l. 158), a magnanimous act that recalls his earlier embrace of Coriolanus, he is once again securely the heroic idol of his tribe. By manipulating conventions in order to win a fame that fact will not support, he, like Achilles, cheapens the significance that customarily accrues to heroic tradition. The death of Coriolanus, therefore, like the death of Hector, raises the question of how to evaluate convention's role in heroic mimesis: whether the outward and visible signs may be trusted to represent an inward and spiritual strength.

If *Coriolanus* refers so pervasively to *Troilus*, to what end? Shakespeare's purpose, we may assume, was subtler than my catalogue of echoes suggests. One answer may lie in the mimetic distinctions Auerbach draws between history and legend. History achieves its reality by recreating a sense of the past with a richness of context and fulness of detail that legend does not require. When Shakespeare turned to Plutarch for his source, and in particular drew from that source a figure about whom Elizabethans knew little, he had no choice but to strive for historical verisimilitude. Coriolanus was not the stuff of legend, because little-known soldiers never are. He was, on the contrary, a real Roman, and Shakespeare painstakingly recreated the cultural traditions and political situations in which Plutarch placed him.[25] Those details that make act 1 seem needlessly complicated for an audience—the political haggling between senators and tribunes over the corn laws, the republican tensions between patricians and tribunes, Coriolanus's intolerance of the increasingly democratic turn of events—all reinforce the impression of historical authenticity; and Coriolanus's relationship with others, especially with his mother, is developed with a psychological complexity that compels us to apply naturalistic criteria to the play.

Legend, however, makes no such demands on us. Criteria for judging it are far more elementary. We do not expect from it the historical details, cross-currents, and uncertainties that contaminate the purity of action and confuse the simple orientation of characters. What Auerbach writes of Homer's method may be applied to Shakespeare's treatment of Hector and Achilles' relationship, if not to the whole of *Troilus and Cressida:*

> Legend arranges its material in a simple and straightforward way; it detaches it from its contemporary historical context, so that the latter will not confuse it; it knows only clearly outlined men who act from few and simple motives and the continuity of whose feelings and actions remains uninterrupted.[26]

Whereas Coriolanus's isolation results from a psychological and political struggle, Hector's isolation is symbolic. His relationship with his wife and mother matters little; for Coriolanus, it matters a great deal. Troy, for Hector, exists as but a spur to glorious deeds; Rome, for Coriolanus, is a city of mortal consequence. Similarly, whereas Achilles may in bold metaphoric strokes fell Hector in order to preserve his own reputation, Aufidius, to achieve the same goal, must justify a public motive for slaying Coriolanus, frame a scene for appearance's sake to provoke Coriolanus, and then consider the political consequences of his action. Legend is unencumbered by such considerations.

When Shakespeare alludes in *Coriolanus* to the matter of Troy as he had dramatized it in *Troilus,* he establishes mimetic points of reference that ally history with legend to create a dramatic counterpoint. The death of Hector in particular provides a legendary model on which the death of Coriolanus may be constructed so as to test convention against historical verisimilitude. Such a model, while establishing by contrast the relative realism of Coriolanus's tragedy, also clarifies the conflicting forces that cause his tragedy, imbues them with legendary significance and, ultimately, raises the action to almost mythic status. Shakespeare in this way does for a little-known history what already had been done for him in sources for his English history plays and others such as *Julius Caesar, King Lear,* and *Antony and Cleopatra:* review history through the clarifying lens of legend.

Like the other tragedies of Shakespeare's maturity, *Coriolanus* presumes in its audience a foundation in heroic tradition that can be tapped to create a rich network of associations. But in studies of Shakespeare's reworking of sources, perhaps not enough has been made of how his reference to his own earlier work contributes to the mimetic sophistication of his later plays. Just as a proper understanding of the Hector and Achilles scenes in *Troilus* may depend more on a knowledge of Shakespeare's early chronicle plays than of Homer or his medieval redactors, so an understanding of *Coriolanus* may be enhanced if one realizes that Shakespeare modeled the relationship between Coriolanus and Aufidius at least in part on the relationship between Hector and Achilles as he had developed it in *Troilus.* It is not necessary to assume that Shakespeare's audience was aware of the allusions to his own earlier work: even a modern audience with less access to heroic traditions will perceive shifts of idiom and tensions between history and legend in a given play without cross-reference to other plays in the canon.[27] Nor is it necessary to assume that Shakespeare himself was fully conscious of the extent of his self-reference. Echoes and transformations of his early work may play an important part in Shakespeare's art without his explicit intent. Such self-reference does, however, allow insight into the creative process, conscious or unconscious, by which Shakespeare chiseled heroic tragedy out of the intractable stuff of history.

5

The Integrity of the Noble Moor

*I*t may be unsafe to say that if Shakespeare had not tested the potentials of traditional heroic mimesis in *Troilus and Cressida,* he probably would not have written *Othello;* but I believe it is true. For in *Othello* he reverts to the tragedy of a conventional hero, a hero he had not dared to take as his central subject since the days of Talbot and Titus: one whose deeds, diction, and absolute being are kin to those of the epic warriors, chivalric knights, and blood revengers who had long possessed the Elizabethan imagination. Othello is the sort of hero Shakespeare would have ridiculed in his middle plays as an *alazon,* made pompous by the same archaic idiom he had mocked in Caesar and Hotspur, Laertes and Fortinbras, and, more acerbically, in the Ancient Pistol. Shakespeare had treated such heroes less predictably in *Troilus:* some, like Ajax, he subjected to devastating satire; but others, most notably Hector, he cast in a deliberately antique mode so that one could accept their heroic reality with quotation marks around it. There are no quotation marks around Othello.

He is the "real McCoy": a man of action, confident, decisive, bold. His tragedy is not cerebral: it does not require him to be conscious of the disparity between selfhood and the demands of traditional heroic character, as Hamlet is, and Hal, and Richard II, and Brutus, and Antony. Where they achieve dramatic reality by wrestling with their failure to live up to conventional expectations, Othello is real because he *does* live up to them. His credibility as a character does not depend, as Troilus's does, on his coming to terms with a latent skepticism. It depends instead on Shakespeare's adoption, in good faith, of an idiom that he for years had been repudiating as insufficient to establish authentic heroism on stage. He turns the clock back to a conception of heroic mimesis such as he had relied on in his earliest tragedies, wherein heroes are heroes because they do and say what heroes have always done and said. But ten years had made a difference in Shakespeare's approach to character. Whereas the heroic idiom fully determined the reality (such as it was) of characters in the early plays, and they had to bend with it to suit the exigencies of plot, Othello determines his own use of the idiom: it serves him; it flexes when he does; he lends *it* credibility. When he acts and speaks in the heroic vein, he does so as a man who thinks like a hero, not merely as one who is bound to convention; and as such, he breathes new life into a moribund theatrical ethos. This is Shakespeare's boldest achievement in *Othello*. By picking up where he left off in *Titus Andronicus* and forging a *psychology* of heroic character to give purpose to an otherwise archaic idiom, he redeemed the traditional hero from years of condescension and brought him of age.

Working from a suggestion in Cinthio, Shakespeare created in Othello a model warrior: valiant and unsuspicious, self-confident and yet unselfconscious enough to define himself without boasting by the conventional assertion of heroic selfhood:

> My parts, my title, and my perfect soul
> Shall manifest me rightly.
>
> (1.2.31–32)

Othello declares that he is nothing if not himself: he assures us that his inner being and his outward expressions of heroism are in harmonious correspondence, that all we need to know of him is what we see. This integrity marks him as a kind of chivalric hero for whom the universe is constant and all values unquestioned, for whom honor, as it did for Troilus and other traditional heroes before him, means abiding by the election of one's particular will, no matter what the consequences. Shakespeare in his middle plays had mocked the absolutism of such heroic self-assurance; but in *Othello*, mockery is overcome by admiration.

Othello's language in particular has a chivalric cast, like that of a knight of romance. With the bewitching tongue of a hero who has encountered things not of this world, he strings out before the senators, as he has already done before Desdemona, his feats of derring-do, exotic adventures, and miraculous escapes in a verse that G. Wilson Knight has aptly called the "Othello music":[1]

> I spoke of most disastrous chances,
> Of moving accidents by flood and field,
> Of hair-breadth scapes i' th' imminent deadly breach,
> Of being taken by the insolent foe
> And sold to slavery, of my redemption thence,
> And portance in my travels' history,
> Wherein of antres vast and deserts idle,
> Rough quarries, rocks, and hills whose heads touch heaven,
> It was my hint to speak—such was my process—
> And of the Cannibals that each other eat,

The Anthropophagi, and men whose heads
Do grow beneath their shoulders.

(1.3.136–47)

Othello is very much aware that in his narrative he is not only defending himself, but also creating an ethos: the formal balance of the syntax suggests it, and his admission—"It was my hint to speak—such was my process"—confirms it. The style of his speech is thus stately, clear, and serene, but it is also studied. As Knight observes, it does not have the compression of dramatic metaphor. It has instead the leisure of picturesque simile; it luxuriates in the romantic fantasies of high adventure. The images, concrete and magnificent in themselves, never fully express the passions of Othello's character: they remain descriptive ornaments, objects for aesthetic contemplation, artful amalgams of a rich literary tradition. Othello creates his ethos with an almost Miltonic eclecticism, in fact. The martial phrases such as "imminent deadly breech" and "being taken by the insolent foe" recall Homeric warfare and place him in the company of Shakespeare's War-of-the-Roses generals such as Talbot and York. But the Latinate diction and the sense of wonder it evokes ally it more closely with the literary Virgil and Ovid than the formulaic Homer. Even more, Othello's insistence on exotic trials and far-away places—on slavery and redemption, on "antres vast and deserts idle," and on monstrous figures who inhabit such worlds—ally it more closely with contemporary romance than with Homer, Virgil, *or* Ovid. The whole narrative, in fact, bears the influence of popular romances such as *Amadis de Gaule* that were the daily escapist fare of sensation-seeking Elizabethans. Even though Shakespeare's handling of his sources, both epic and romance, yields an exceptional verse style to characterize a hero who is *not* therefore confined to any *particular* heroic tradition, it is nevertheless important to recognize that the Othello music has conventional origins. Its eclecticism defines Othello's literary ancestry: we would be wrong to criticize it by modern standards as histrionic rodomontade.[2]

Like most of Shakespeare's earlier conventional heroes, Othello projects his own heroic qualities onto the world and then prizes the world for possessing those qualities. If the egotism implicit in this world-view is a limitation, it is a limitation that falls within the conventions of heroic character. As Arthur Sewell suggests, Othello's egotism is a primal innocence not yet tainted with self-interest.[3] As if by nature, the traditional hero worships, in the object of his love, a recreated image of himself. Troilus idealizes Cressida as an image of constancy in love. Timon lauds his Athenian flatterers as examplars of classical friendship. And Othello worships Desdemona as a "fair warrior" whose visage images his "soul's joy" and brings him a "content so absolute" that he cannot possibly divorce his own being from hers (2.1.180, 182, 189).[4] The solipsism inherent in Othello's love is made more explicit in his explanation to the Senate that "She love'd me for the dangers I had pass'd, / And I love'd her that she did pity them" (1.3.169–70). She loves him, in other words, for the very qualities by which he has defined himself for her in his romantic narration; and he loves her because she loves them and takes them as models for her own behavior.

As, in Cinthio, Disdemona pleads with the Moor to allow her to join him in the soldier's life, so, in Shakespeare, she pleads with the Senate. Her language is as absolute as Othello's:

> That I did love the Moor to live with him,
> My downright violence and storm of fortunes
> May trumpet to the world.

Her images conjure up the martial glory, disastrous chances, and moving accidents that she so admired in Othello's narration. She continues:

> I saw Othello's visage in his mind,
> And to his honors and his valiant parts
> Did I my soul and fortunes consecrate.
> ....
> Let me go with him.
> (1.3.251–53; 255–57; 262)

In consecrating herself to Othello in war, Desdemona makes herself one with his heroic image. Thereby she reinforces the legitimacy of that image by offering him a true reflection. I cannot agree with those detractors who suggest that Othello's first love is to war, the second to her;[5] for as Othello projects everything he holds of value onto her, his love for and faith in her necessarily give him heroic self-definition. It is for this reason that he pleads that she be granted a hero's freedom of choice: "Let her have your voice. / . . . I therefore beg it not / To please the palate of my appetite, / . . . But to be free and bounteous to her mind" (ll. 263–68, passim). His own will has had its way and has elected her; now he wishes hers, whose constancy he trusts absolutely, to have its way as well. Free and bounteous: his vocabulary is tinged with heroic magnanimity.

Thus Othello and Desdemona both speak the language of heroic engagement, of vows irrevocable, of giving up worlds for what they believe in: she for her chastity—"Beshrew me if I would do such a wrong / For the whole world" (4.3.80–81)—and he for her—"If heaven would make me such another world / Of one entire and perfect chrysolite, / I'd not have sold her for it" (5.2.149–51). This is a kind of commitment that lesser men cannot understand. Othello can preserve his integrity only by maintaining his faith in the object that mirrors all his value. He speaks true when he affirms, "My life upon her faith" (1.3.297). If his love for her be self-love, then, like

Troilus's love for Cressida, it is a self-love from which he cannot possibly extricate her without losing himself in the process:

> But there where I have garner'd up my heart,
> Where either I must live or bear no life,
> The fountain from the which my current runs
> Or else dries up—to be discarded thence!
>
> (4.2.57–60)

If she fails to sustain the value he has assigned to her, he will no longer be able to define himself by that value. Such an investiture of heroic selfhood in another, by its very nature, leaves that selfhood open to tragic disintegration.

That disintegration, when it comes, is characterized not by the almost comically instantaneous shift to the language of revenge as it is in Troilus, but by a stammer, a syntactical breakdown, a failure of the Othello music to come to terms with experience. Critics have long noticed that Othello's language begins to echo the reductive vocabulary and syntax of Iago, a language riddled with images of appetite and bestiality by which Iago has reduced traditional heroic values to baseness.[6] "Damn her, lewd minx! O, damn her, damn her!" Othello cries (3.3.479); and later, "Lie with her? Lie on her?. . . Pish! Noses, ears, and lips.—Is 't possible? —Confess—handkerchief!—O devil! . . . I will chop her into messes. Cuckold me?" (4.1.35, 42–43, 199). His choppy syntax reflects the new disorder within him caused by his loss of her and, consequently, his loss of occupation. Gone are the luxuriant cadences of the romantic warrior; gone, the strong rhythms of self-assured heroism. In their place are halting phrases, awkward stops, nonsequiturs—"You are welcome, sir, to Cyprus.—Goats and monkeys!" (l. 264)—all of which attest to the vile success of Iago's method.

But the apparent ease with which Iago is able to exchange Othello for a goat has prompted an ever-increasing group of critics to find, deep within Othello's being, an element responsive to Iago's cynicism. Iago, they suggest, far from being a wily villain who alters Othello's nature, is merely a catalyst who brings to the surface impulses latent in Othello from the start. They attribute less to Iago's skill than to Othello's weakness and are inclined to interpret that weakness not as heroic naiveté, but as a predilection for monstrous thought.

Maud Bodkin was the first to impute baser, "primordial images" to Othello's heroism in her application of Jung to literary interpretation:[7]

> Iago seems to Othello so honest, so wise beyond himself in human dealings, possessed of a terrible power of seeing and speaking truth, because into what he speaks are projected the half truths that Othello's romantic vision ignored, but of which his mind held secret knowledge.

F. R. Leavis seized upon this idea to attack Bradley's sentimental reading of Othello's character and made popular the idea of Othello's innate responsiveness to evil:[8]

> . . . it is plain that what we should see in Iago's prompt success is not so much Iago's diabolic intellect as Othello's readiness to respond. Iago's power, in fact, in the temptation-scene is that he represents something that is in Othello—in Othello the husband of Desdemona: the essential traitor is within the gates.

Among the disciples of Bodkin one may count Robert Heilman, who acknowledges his extensive debt; G. R. Elliott, who does not; J. I. M. Stewart, who entertains the notions that "Othello hears an inner voice that he would fain hear and fain deny"; Matthew Proser, who asserts that Iago simply provides Othello with "a set of images which make concrete and demonstrable feelings and attitudes already latent in him"; H. A. Mason, who thinks Othello uses Iago "to give himself permission to go even lower in his suspicions"; and Derek Traversi, who lends all his critical acumen to an affirmation that Othello has a "peculiar vulnerability to the irrational forces of animal feeling."[9]

The most recent exponent of Bodkinism, Bernard McElroy, finds in Othello "a predisposition to believe" Iago, "and that predisposition is not merely an unsettling dream but his world-view itself."[10] This last is disturbing. Predisposition goes further than Leavis's theory of responsiveness and borders on a consciousness—emphasized by the words "world-view"—that would put Othello in the company of Shakespeare's tragic *eirons* like Hamlet, who are aware of a disparity between self and self-image and capable of maintaining multiple perspectives on the world. In Othello, McElroy writes, "we have a man whose consciousness is balanced upon a fine edge between a tragic awareness of life as a process of suffering and disaster, and an awareness of the transcendent, joyful powers of love" (126), but who "ceases to believe that love has such powers because he never did fully believe it in the first place" (125). A man, in short, whose mind is far from absolute; a man who belies all the heroic traditions in which Shakespeare has taken pains (with ironic futility, it would seem) to immerse him.

That such a reading violates Shakespeare's conception of Othello by making him too much the *eiron*, too much kin to Hal and Hamlet, will become clearer, I think, if one compares him with the hero in whom Shakespeare had most recently tested the power of a traditional heroic ethos to stand up to the pressures of self-consciousness, Troilus. He, as I have shown, strives to maintain a perfect faith in Cressida but is so riven by doubts that he falls short of the absoluteness requisite to do so. He would be a complete legendary hero; but as the first of such heroes to whom Shakespeare granted any potential to grow into something more than that, and close to Hamlet in both spirit and age, he preserves a distinct trace of the *eironeia* that characterized heroes just prior to him.

On numerous occasions Troilus expresses doubt that his heroic will can create absolute value. Though he would presume in Cressida a constancy to match his own, he nevertheless fears the power of mutability—what he calls "changeful potency." Troilus's fear is genuine, different from Othello's "fear" of that "unknown fate" that rhetorically enriches the value of Desdemona's love. Yet Bodkinists find in that passage from *Othello* the strongest evidence to support their contention that Othello has a tragic awareness of life:

> If it were now to die,
> 'Twere now to be most happy; for, I fear,
> My soul hath her content so absolute
> That not another comfort like to this
> Succeeds in unknown fate.
>
> (2.1.187–91)

These lines, argue Bodkinists, attest to a fatalism in Othello that rivals his belief in Desdemona's power to rescue him from it. Riddled with "discords sensed by his prophetic soul,"[11] Othello predicts for himself a miserable end—a prediction he reaffirms in his most ardent declaration of love:

> Excellent wretch! Perdition catch my soul
> But I do love thee! And when I love thee not,
> Chaos is come again.
>
> (3.3.92–94)

The prophetic soul, I would suggest, is the reader's, not Othello's. Othello's language does indeed presage death and discord, but hyperbolic expressions of perfect happiness often yoke the extremes of love and death together conventionally: Romeo and Juliet, after all, are allowed to speak of death in love in the full flush of Petrarchan fancy without having critics claim that they, at their tender age, are haunted by an awareness of life's horrors. The same, I suggest, holds true for Othello. He may (I would not deny) have more knowledge than they, at his mature years, of fate and mutability. But in the imagery with which he here attempts to express the inexpressible, fear of an unknown fate functions largely as a rhetorical device by which we can take the measure of his ultimate joy. If *we* are made aware, through those images, of a possible impending tragedy, so much the better for Shakespeare's art, but it does not necessarily follow that Othello is aware of it or that he must be held accountable for the resonance of every image he uses.

Troilus, on the contrary, is fully aware of the power that "injurious time" and the "injury of chance" may wield to mock his achievements and "strangle our dear vows"; he is fully aware that there is "no remedy." He has a skepticism that runs parallel to his romantic innocence in a paradoxical tension. Next to it, Othello's most pessimistic statement—

> 'tis the plague of great ones;
> Prerogativ'd are they less than the base.
> 'Tis destiny unshunnable, like death.

> (3.3.279–81)

—sounds sententious and impersonal, and implies not so much a tragic self-awareness as a momentary despair, voiced with his customary hyperbole. It is followed, in fact, by a retraction: "If she be false, O, then heaven mocks itself! / I'll not believe 't" (ll. 284–85). Unlike Troilus, Othello rejects all doubt, all suspicion, out of hand, because he has no capacity, as Troilus does, for ironic introspection. *Deny*

The difference between Troilus and Othello is crystallized in the eaves-dropping scenes common to both plays, in which the heroes become disillusioned with the women in whose fidelity they have staked their own integrity as heroes. Troilus, outside Calchas's tent, witnesses Cressida's fall in her symbolic forfeiture of the sleeve Troilus had given her as a parting token of love. "He that takes that doth take my heart withal," she confesses to Diomedes (5.2.85). Othello witnesses what he takes to be an equally symbolic act in Cassio's flaunting of the handkerchief that Othello had given to Desdemona and that Iago, having stolen, has made to signify nothing less than Desdemona's heart. Both heroes are confronted with a paradoxical knowledge that two truths seem to be told, each contradicting the other. Troilus expresses the paradox with syntactical precision:

> Bi-fold authority, where reason can revolt
> Without perdition, and loss assume all reason
> Without revolt! This is, and is not, Cressid.

> (5.2.148–50)

Less analytic than Troilus, Othello expresses the paradox with far more passionate involvement, alternating statements of belief and disbelief, praise and damnation:[12]

> A fine woman! A fair woman! A sweet woman! . . . Ay, let her rot, and perish, and be damn'd tonight; for she shall not live. No, my heart is turn'd to stone; I strike it, and it hurts my hand. O, the world hath not a sweeter creature! She might lie by an emperor's side and command him tasks. (4.1.177–78; 180–84)

The bifold authority of which Troilus is aware but which Othello only feels destroys the unity of heroic character that both of them had claimed for themselves.

There is this difference between them: Troilus recognizes in that bifold authority a tragic dilemma, and although he avoids it by substituting adolescent rage for growth to self-knowledge, his mere recognition of it places him squarely in the province of Shakespeare's *eironic* heroes and demands that we measure him by their yardstick. Othello, however, is not (to use the cuckold's phrase) caught on the horns of a dilemma. His tragedy is not one of conflicting world views, but one of erroneous choice, the flaw of less introspective heroes. His awareness of paradox exists on a much more rudimentary level than Troilus's and, furthermore, allows of resolution. As early as the temptation scene, he has clarified that paradox for himself by confiding to Iago,

> I think my wife be honest and think she is not;
> I think that thou art just and think thou art not.
>
> (3.3.389–90)

Only in the tension beteen these paradoxes does Othello, unable to reconcile his faith in both Desdemona and Iago, lose his heroic integrity. Either Desdemona is honest and Iago unjust, or Desdemona dishonest and Iago just. If only he could know for certain that one of the two alternatives was valid, he could alleviate all doubt and become whole again. It is on this desire for certainty that Iago capitalizes. He would convince Othello that the second alternative is valid; and by doing so, he would offer to preserve Othello's heroic ethos, though in a radically different form.

The question arises, If Othello is not predisposed to regard himself as a tragic victim, why does Iago succeed in making him one? How does Iago's cynicism infect him? Othello's credulous nature—a characteristic of many heroes; most recently, Hector—is something Iago can easily play upon. Iago all along has set himself up as Desdemona's rival for Othello's love;[13] and Othello, unsuspicious of Iago's malignant purpose, has been as willing to project his own heroic virtues onto Iago as onto Desdemona. Othello is confident that Iago possesses the great soul, honest heart and innate sense of justice that are his own best qualities; and with unconscious irony he contrasts this heroic image of Iago with the knavish image that in fact characterizes Iago best:

> And, for I know thou 'rt full of love and honesty,
> And weigh'st thy words before thou giv'st them breath,
> Therefore these stops of thine fright me the more;
> For such things in a false disloyal knave
> Are tricks of custom, but in a man that's just
> They're close dilations, working from the heart
> That passion cannot rule.
>
> (3.3.123–29)

Othello affirms Iago's honesty so often that he resembles Timon persis-

tently defending his Athenian parasites as honest men. At one point in the
first act, he mentions his rival loves in juxtaposition:

> A man he is of honesty and trust.
> To his conveyance I assign my wife,
> ································
> My life upon her faith! Honest Iago,
> My Desdemona must I leave to thee.
>
> (1.3.287–88; 297–98)

These lines foreshadow what will in fact occur. Presuming on Othello's
gullibility, Iago will "convey" Desdemona from him by stealing her honor
and then will offer himself in place of her as a man of perfect faith, a
mirror in whom Othello may see his true reflection.

Iago functions much like the *eiron* of Attic comedy. He would strip
Othello of all heroic pretense and expose him as a naked gull. From the
outset, he ridicules Othello as an *alazon*, "loving his own pride and purposes," full of "a bombast circumstance," and "horribly stuff'd with
epithets of war" (1.1.13–15). Othello and his fantastical style belong, he
suggests, to the comic tradition of *miles gloriosus:* Desdemona first loved him
"for bragging and telling her fantastical lies. And will she love him still for
prating?" (2.1.223–24). Furthermore, Iago perceives him to be a dupe who
"will as tenderly be led by th' nose / As asses are" (1.3.402–3); and to lead
him on, Iago will say anything that Othello may think credible, without
regard to its truth or falsity:

> And what's he then that says I play the villain?
> When this advice is free I give and honest,
> Probal to thinking . . . ?
>
> (2.3.330–32)

> I told him what I thought, and told no more
> Than what he found himself was apt and true.
>
> (5.2.183–84)

For one who plays nothing but *eironic* roles, "honesty" and "what I thought"
are relative, even unknowable, commodities. Iago in fact draws no distinction between what is apt and what is true. What is "probal to thinking,"
susceptible of proof, becomes for him an acceptable substitute for truth.
His is the truth of the theater: it assumes that an audience can judge the
legitimacy of character only on the basis of outward show—the only
"proofs" an audience has to go on—but it also acknowledges how erroneous and illusory such judgments can be. Othello is one who, unlike Iago,
puts his whole trust in a more traditional conception of mimesis. Like one
of Marvin Rosenberg's naive audience, he counts on the absolute correspondence of outward show and inner being: what he sees and hears cir-

cumscribes, for him, all that *is*. He thus plays right into the hands of Iago, who can easily deceive him with dramatic *shows* of truth.

Iago's remarks on reputation indicate how relative a thing dramatic truth can be. To Cassio, who has lost his reputation, Iago speaks a consolation that disparages the idea of heroic fame and assures him (ironically, for one who stakes his being on appearances alone) that true merit has a reality that mere words have no power to grant or to take away:

> Reputation is an idle and most false imposition; oft got without merit, and lost without deserving. You have lost no reputation at all, unless you repute yourself such a loser. (2.3.263–65)

Good sentences, and well chosen for his particular audience. Behind them lies the belief (whether or not it is Iago's is impossible to surmise) that character may have within itself that which contradicts public fame. But Othello believes that character and fame are inextricable, just as they were in Talbot years before; and so, in speaking to him, Iago forsakes his prosaic skepticism and adopts instead the traditional certainties of heroic verse:

> Good name in man and woman, dear my lord,
> Is the immediate jewel of their souls.
> . . . .
> But he that filches from me my good name
> Robs me of that which not enriches him
> And makes me poor indeed.
>
> (3.3.160–66, passim)

Again, the lines reveal something about the deceptive nature of theatrical truth: appearance—how one is viewed by the audience—is tantamount to reality. Iago has already suggested to Cassio that reality depends on more than that; but here he contradicts himself, and for good reason. For it is on Othello's simple faith in the congruity of appearance and reality that Iago builds his case against Desdemona. He will ensnare Othello with a show.[14]

Othello opens the way for Iago by telling him that he requires ocular proof of Desdemona's infidelity before he will believe it. Proof alone, he says, will enable him to overcome all doubt and to sustain his heroic integrity:

> I'll see before I doubt; when I doubt, prove;
> And on the proof, there is no more but this—
> Away at once with love or jealousy!
>
> (3.3.196–98)

Although his insistence on ocular proof appears to have a rational basis, in fact it betrays in him, as it did in Troilus, a blindness to the fallibility of the senses. Sensory evidence has always been sufficient proof for him. He has never had reason to doubt it. But his dependence on it makes him highly susceptible to Iago's method, which invests ocular evidence with false significance and thus provides the "proof" to contradict Othello's expectations:

IAGO: Ha! I like not that.
OTHELLO: What dost thou say?
IAGO: Nothing, my lord; or if—I know not what.
OTHELLO: Was not that Cassio parted from my wife?
IAGO: Cassio, my lord? No, sure, I cannot think it,
          That he would steal away so guilty-like,
          Seeing you coming.

                                                      (3.3.35–40)

There is nothing inherently suspicious in what Othello has seen. Iago makes it so by the construction he puts on it. Cassio is an honest man; an honest man would not sneak guiltily away; therefore this was not Cassio. But Othello knows that it was Cassio and thus must rework the syllogism to account for Cassio's guilty appearance. He makes Iago's task the easier by actually inviting him to supply those proofs by which he will confirm appearance as reality.

Those proofs are a long time coming. Iago in the interval urges Othello to entertain doubts that he knows will destroy him:

                    I speak not yet of proof.
    Look to your wife; observe her well with Cassio.
    Wear your eye thus, not jealous nor secure.
    I would not have your free and noble nature,
    Out of self-bounty, be abus'd.

                                                      (3.3.202–6)

These words themselves abuse that free and noble nature that Iago swears he is trying to protect. He dictates how Othello's eye should see, "not jealous nor secure": an ambivalence that Othello, in his insistence on certainty, is incapable of handling. Iago warns Othello against himself even more ironically by admitting that he is inciting Othello to that very suspicion which he has said would damn a man. "But, O, what damned minutes tells he o'er / Who dotes, yet doubts, suspects, yet strongly loves!" (ll. 174–75), he cunningly generalizes; and within a minute, he narrows the case to Othello's particular:

    I am to pray you not to strain my speech
    To grosser issues nor to larger reach
    Than to suspicion.

                                                      (3.3.225–27)

The suspicion, not the deed, confounds Othello. For when he suspects, doubts, and loses faith in the woman by whom he has affirmed his heroic identity, he must call into question that identity and, in effect, cease to be

Othello. With all the romantic imagery of chivalric warfare by which he once had defined himself for her, he divests himself of heroic definition and gives himself over to the chaos of doubt:

> Farewell the tranquil mind! Farewell content!
> Farewell the plumed troop, and the big wars
> That makes ambition virtue! O, farewell!
> Farewell the neighing steed, and the shrill trump,
> The spirit-stirring drum, th' ear-piercing fife,
> The royal banner, and all quality,
> Pride, pomp, and circumstance of glorious war!
> And, O you mortal engines, whose rude throats
> Th' immortal Jove's dread clamors counterfeit,
> Farewell! Othello's occupation's gone.
>
> (3.3.353–62)

In this last aria of his heroic career, Othello bids farewell to the Othello music. He recapitulates, much as Richard II does when he ritually divests himself of all the pomp and ceremony that made him king, a lifetime of faith in heroic absolutes, now "proved" untenable.

The ocular proof of Desdemona's infidelity that Iago provides, far from allowing Othello to preserve his heroic integrity by stifling doubt (as Othello fondly hoped it would do), succeeds only in deepening his uncertainty. He learns too late that doubt does not always lead to easy resolution; he hopes only that *more* proof will bring with it the resolution that will define his course of action. More proof, of course, comes in the form of a handkerchief. But the proof itself is superfluous. At issue is Othello's demand for it, by which he compounds his initial error. For while evidence, if its significance is filtered through false syllogisms, can prove Desdemona's guilt, no evidence can possibly erase Othello's suspicion of her guilt. As Winifred Nowottny suggests, "it is useless for Othello to say 'I'll see before I doubt, when I doubt, prove,' since infidelity does not necessarily produce evidence of itself and fidelity cannot be put to the proof."[15] Proof of Desdemona's fidelity would require of Othello a leap of faith for which the ocular evidence he has sworn to believe is irrelevant. He creates the conditions for his own disintegration:

> Villain, be sure thou prove my love a whore!
> Be sure of it. Give me the ocular proof,
> ....
> Make me to see 't, or, at the least, so prove it
> That the probation bear no hinge nor loop
> To hang a doubt on. . . .
>
> (3.3.364–65; 369–71)

Othello here forsakes a love based on intuitive faith for a rational process, a relativism that defies his heroic nature. If ocular evidence can prove only

Desdemona's guilt, then he would have her proven guilty, so long as the proof allows him to erase all doubt. For an absolute truth he would substitute a proof so apt, so probal to thinking (Othello's "probation" echoes Iago's phrase) that it cannot be logically disputed. Nothing indicates more clearly how Othello's heroism disintegrates under the pressure of Iago's *eironeia*.

Cinthio's Ensign "cloaked the vileness hidden in his heart with high sounding and noble words, and . . . showed himself in the likeness of a Hector or an Achilles."[16] Iago never disguises his malice in the mask of epic heroism; but when Othello's faith in Desdemona is shattered, Iago offers him an alternative heroic role to play, one that will enable him to reintegrate his monolithic ethos without having to come to terms with paradox. Othello, true to form, retreats to certainty rather than advance to self-knowledge. He tragically misplaces his will's election—transfers all his faith to a man who shows him the way to regain his heroic "occupation"— without suspecting that the nature of that occupation has been diabolically perverted. His embrace of Iago's alternative heroic role is apparent at once in his return from the fractured syntax and bestial imagery that characterized his loss of selfhood to a more expansive heroic diction that is the product of composure. At first, he uses an incantatory diction of revenge that parodies the language of *The Spanish Tragedie* and all its bloody progeny:

> Arise, black vengeance, from the hollow hell!
> Yield up, O love, thy crown and hearted throne
> To tyrannous hate! Swell, bosom, with thy fraught,
> For 'tis of aspics' tongues!
>
> (3.3.451–54)

The Othello music bears more than a trace of Kyd's Revenge at this point; but if it sounds archaic, we must remember that Othello is feeling his way toward a restored sense of heroic selfhood. After a few "blood, blood, blood's" he gains enough confidence to supplant such fustian with a style of his own that, like the earlier Othello music, is distinguished by its richly allusive quality:

> Like to the Pontic Sea,
> Whose icy current and compulsive course
> Nev'r feels retiring ebb, but keeps due on
> To the Propontic and the Hellespont,
> Even so my bloody thoughts, with violent pace,
> Shall nev'r look back, nev'r ebb to humble love,
> Till that a capable and wide revenge
> Swallow them up. Now, by yond marble heaven,
> In due reverence of a sacred vow,
> I here engage my words.
>
> (3.3.457–66)

The personifications that so often turned revenge plays into allegories of blood still lurk: revenge is a monster to swallow up bloody thoughts, and those thoughts themselves move like murder, with Tarquin's ravishing strides, toward their design. But these gleanings from the allegorical tradition are tucked between a wonderful epic simile, replete with "abstruse geographical references" (the words are Knight's, 101) such as are found in Othello's early narrative, and an irrevocable vow to a pagan heaven such as might have been spoken by the noblest of ancient heroes. This eclecticism makes it a far more authentic revenge idiom than that of Troilus who merely resorts to the hackneyed hyperbole of Senecan imitators. Othello's speech bears the stamp of his earlier marmoreal style: splendid, remote, and allusive. His final line, "I here engage my words," reveals what force these words have for him: they allow him to reintegrate his heroic identity on the basis of a conventional idiom that has, for him, always been the only true reality.

Othello does not picture himself as a blood revenger of the old school. More like Brutus, he would disavow all private motive and transform the act of murder into a sacrifice of state, made in the name of justice for the general cause. Thereby he would all the more constantly maintain his image as a heroic idealist. But his attempt to reconstruct that image on such a basis lapses; his resolve wavers; his faith in Desdemona reasserts itself and would demand more proof before giving o'er; and that proof, when Iago provides it, provokes him to a bloodlust that is far from his heroic ideal:

> Get me some poison, Iago; this night. I'll not expostulate with her, lest her body and beauty unprovide my mind again. This night, Iago. (4.1.203–5)

Only in act 5 does he settle into the judgmental calm that marked his heroism in act 1 and that permits him to regard his murder of Desdemona in the same way Brutus regarded his murder of Caesar, as a sacrifice, motivated by his desire to uphold standards of public morality rather than by his desire for private retribution:

> It is the cause, it is the cause, my soul.
> Let me not name it to you, you chaste stars!
> It is the cause. Yet I'll not shed her blood,
> Nor scar that whiter skin of hers than snow,
> And smooth as monumental alabaster.
> Yet she must die, else she'll betray more men.
>
> (5.2.1–6)

Here in full measure are exotic, aloof, often classical (he mentions a "Promethean heat" a few lines later) images that suggest Othello is once again in full command of his idiom. But in the studied equanimity of his verse, he disguises from himself the fact that his heroism is not of a piece with what it once was, is tainted with a narrow egotism and moral relativism that once were alien to him. He thinks that in sacrificing Desdemona he is finally reinstating his old heroic absolutism. He is unaware how much that sacrifice is, in fact, a self-sacrifice.

In Othello, Shakespeare portrays a man desperately trying to preserve the mold of traditional heroism in a world that would wrench him from it. For such self-preservation Othello would pay any price: swallow Iago's "proofs" whole, accept Iago's proffered friendship as genuine, adopt Iago's values as his own. If critics find Shakespeare's reversion to an archaic heroic type as subject fit for tragedy unpalatable, and if they therefore try to discover in Othello some latent skepticism, some traitor within the gates, to explain his tragedy, that is perfectly understandable. It is difficult, especially in our psychoanalytic age, to fathom the conventionally heroic mind as Shakespeare fathomed it, even to conceive that a hero so governed by outmoded codes of behavior as Othello is *could* be tragic. Shakespeare, after all, had already educated us to expect tragic issue from intellectual and unconventionally heroic men such as Hamlet; he had, and recently, laughed conventional heroes to scorn. But that only enhances the stature of *Othello*. In so far as Shakespeare *does* revert in it to a more conventional and thus less accessible heroic type, so much the greater is his achievement in making the Moor credible as a noble, sympathetic, and—even most skeptics would agree—tragic hero.

Othello's recognition of error, when it comes, is itself conventional, more like a classical anagnorisis than a final awakening to a cynicism that has always lain in him subliminally. Troilus, for all his obstinacy, was far more capable of tragic apprehension than Othello; and because of that, we judge his tragedy by the criteria of Shakespeare's more knowing heroes, and it fails. Othello's does not. Our expectations of him are different, less demanding, because he has never been on the verge of self-awareness. Indeed, Othello has to have the truth thrust upon him in all capital letters: "O gull! O dolt! / As ignorant as dirt! Thou hast done a deed—" (ll. 170–71). But what he learns from it, however minimal a recognition it may seem, has enormous moral import for a monolithic mind like his. Iago has lied to him. Othello knows that he has restored his identity in the image of a false heroism; knows, too, that he must endure for the second time the pain of disintegration. It will be made all the more painful by his realization that if only he had kept faith in Desdemona, he would be Othello still. In killing her, he has killed himself. It is a recognition that says everything. For at last he is aware of a radical deficiency in his heroic concept of life: his one certainty—the only one that counts—is that all his old certainties were not strong enough to endure.

Even in his apprehension of truth, Othello behaves as absolutely as he has throughout. Just as Coriolanus, on leaving Rome, swears to his friends and family,

> While I remain above the ground, you shall
> Hear from me still, and never of me aught
> But what is like me formerly.
>
> (4.1.51–53)

so Othello, with just as constant a mind, moves swiftly to shore up his heroic image by resorting to the self-dramatizing language of his first romantic narration, full of exotic adventure and ornate, almost Miltonic images that tend to detach us, as they do him, from the passion of the moment:

> Speak of me as I am; nothing extenuate,
> Nor set down aught in malice. Then must you speak
> Of one that lov'd not wisely but too well;
> Of one not easily jealous, but, being wrought,
> Perplex'd in the extreme; of one whose hand,
> Like the base Indian, threw a pearl away
> Richer than all his tribe; of one whose subdu'd eyes,
> Albeit unused to the melting mood,
> Drops tears as fast as the Arabian trees
> Their medicinable gum.
>
> (5.2.351–60)

If Othello simplifies the nature of his culpability and prompts us to question whether he in fact loved too well and was not easily jealous, he nevertheless reasserts the imagery of absolute value by which he once characterized his love for Desdemona. She is a pearl, an object of incalculable value. We may recall that Troilus described both Cressida and Helen as pearls in whose names the Trojans forged their heroic identities. So it is for Othello who, in throwing his pearl away, confesses that the enormity of his sin against romantic value is ultimately a sin against himself.

T. S. Eliot argued that in this speech, Othello gave way to self-pitying histrionics—"bovarysme," he called it.[17] Those who agree with Eliot think that the speech evinces in Othello an awareness of the disparity between self and role that constitutes the tragic vision of Shakespeare's *eironic* heroes. But the evidence is slim. If we were to apply to Othello's final scene the criteria for judgment that we learned to apply to self-conscious heroes such as Hamlet, then Othello's tragedy would be a conspicuous failure. Clearly, Shakespeare does not encourage us to do that. We expect Othello to remain true to his heroic character, and the mimetic credibility of his tragedy depends heavily on his self-constancy. Such, Shakespeare has educated us to believe, is the nature of the heroic mind: rather than suffer self-knowledge, it will close and be itself.

In the context of the play, it makes far more sense to regard Othello's last speech as his conventional bid for a public fame to acknowledge what he is, has been, and wishes to be remembered as; for public fame, he has believed all along, is the final determinant of a hero's reality. Helen Gardner relates speeches such as this to an historical phenomenon:

> Mr. Eliot's general complaint about the death-scenes of Elizabethan tragic heroes, whose *apologias* he ascribes to the influence of Seneca, ignores the historical fact that this was an age of public executions in which men were judged by the courage and dignity with which they met public death, and when it was thought proper that at this supreme moment of their lives they should submit their case to the judgement of their fellow-men.[18]

For a Shakespearean confirmation of this precedent, one has only to look ahead to the testimony of an anonymous witness to Cawdor's death in *Macbeth:*

> Nothing in his life
> Became him like the leaving it. He died
> As one that had been studied in his death
> To throw away the dearest thing he ow'd,
> As 'twere a careless trifle.
>
> (1.4.7–11)

One might see Othello figured in this eulogy: in it, we return once again to the importance of audience perception in establishing a credible heroic mimesis.

Othello, as sensitive to the need for dramatic persuasion here as he was when he pleaded his case before the Senate, publicly recreates his former identity as a noble warrior in this speech in order to do one last heroic deed: to sacrifice that identity honorably to death rather than dishonorably to Iago. Evoking a scene of past glory with all the detail by which he described his conquests to an admiring Desdemona, he divides the images of heroism by which he has defined himself—Desdemona's true and Iago's false—in order to grant the true image a final victory:

> And say besides, that in Aleppo once,
> Where a malignant and a turban'd Turk
> Beat a Venetian and traduc'd the state,
> I took by th' throat the circumcised dog,
> And smote him, thus.
>
> (5.2.361–65)

The "circumcised dog," customarily identified as Othello (who, in murdering Desdemona, has in fact beaten a Venetian and traduced the state), may further signify the false heroic image with which Iago has infected Othello's nature. By purging himself of it, Othello restores to its rightful place the heroic image that Desdemona has supremely embodied. This imaginative act thus rids Othello of the internal division that once reduced his heroic integrity to naught and that now threatens him again. If it be "bovarysme," it nevertheless is not akin to the play-acting of Shakespeare's more self-conscious heroes who try, never successfully, to ally themselves with the heroic roles they play. Othello here keeps perfect faith with his heroic ethos; his words and deed are engaged in an absolute alliance; sign and significance are one. The stage direction reads *Stabs himself:* it denotes an act consonant with his whole being. In it, Shakespeare dramatizes how a hero drawn in an unfashionable idiom can come of age, wrest archaic values from the ridicule of critics such as Iago, Bodkin, and Leavis, and— not despite, but because of, his conventionality—achieve a magnificently credible tragic pathos.

6

Timon and the Ethics of Heroism

Timon of Athens is a notoriously difficult play to pin down. Is the hero too flawed for his tragedy, or is the tragedy too flawed for its hero? Timon's misanthropic rant in the last two acts contains an imaginative vision of heroic proportions, but the first three acts have the quality of parable, not heroic tragedy. It is a play of apparently disjunctive halves in which the mimetic modes are not successfully integrated. For most critics, Timon's stature in the first half, *in* Athens, is of insufficient magnitude to justify the force of his invective in the second half, *outside* Athens. Una Ellis-Fermor complained years ago that Timon is not adequately "built into his society on the grand scale"; and Norman Rabkin more recently accused the play of failing to deal with the "unresolvable conflicts" typical of Shakespearean tragedy because in it, "Shakespeare seems to assume a simple moral position."[1] It has been tempting, therefore, to explain *Timon* in terms of the Morality tradition—to assume that Shakespeare was suppressing the individual characterization necessary for tragic heroism and working instead with the bold, flat, and general strokes of medieval allegory. Timon thus becomes an Everyman who goes unrepentant to death. He is an exemplum of Reckless Prodigality or, antithetically, Ideal Bounty; the play itself, a sweeping indictment of contemporary usury or (depending on the critic's political orientation) a satire on the "raging waste" of Elizabethan aristocrats.[2] Tyrone Guthrie, who produced the most influential *Timon* of recent history, summarizes this bias succinctly. "In our view, it is not a tragedy but a satire, directed against the Deceitfulness of Riches," he writes; and note the allegorical capital letters. It satirizes materialism exemplified by Athens, he continues, "and more particularly, as exemplified by Timon." In juding the play, Guthrie dismisses Aristotelian criteria:

> Timon is not a hero in whose sufferings we are supposed to share with pity and with terror. He is the spoiled Darling of Fortune, whom Fortune

suddenly spurns—the allegory of the Poet in the first scene of the play is intended as an extremely literal clue to the course of the story. In misfortune Timon shows unmistakably that he is not of heroic stature. He is peevish, hysterical; he adopts the cynicism of Apemantus not from intellectual or moral conviction but as a kind of compensatory gesture against society.[3]

Such a perspective makes of Timon little more than Lucian's Misanthrope, a cardboard prodigal whose tirades are the tantrums of a boy of tears, furious with his friends for refusing to play his game.

The trouble is, this view of the play as social satire exacerbates its disjunction by making sense of the first half, the fable of Timon's fall, at the expense of the second, in which anything less than a heroic Timon will not be able to carry the poetry to its tragic heights. For the fact is, Timon of the last two acts has a certain grandeur, is admirable in his unswerving hate, and cannot be dismissed merely as The Misanthrope. His declaration, "I am Misanthropos, and hate mankind" (4.3.54) is no more adequate to define his dramatic nature than Pandarus's labeling of Troilus as "truth," Cressida as "inconstancy," and himself as "go-between" is adequate to define theirs. Timon is far too eloquent, too driven, to remain a two-dimensional figure. His voice of tragic disillusion betrays a vision of society no satirical prodigal ever had. The condition that forces him to such a vision is similar to Lear's: poverty, a stripping away of the superfluities by which he, like Lear with his hundred knights, has defined himself. Just as Lear must test his ideal of kingship or Othello his love for Desdemona, so Timon must, in the first half of the play, test his ideal of friendship against reality and suffer knowledge. In him, as in them, the loss of a perfect faith justifies the conversion to righteous rage and imbues it with tragic pathos. Only his refusal to move beyond rage toward enlightened self-awareness has prompted critics to refer to him as an incomplete tragic hero, a stillborn twin of Lear.

I do not propose to claim that the play is, after all, a well-wrought tragedy and all its critics benighted. But I shall try to demonstrate that Guthrie and others of his ilk take too restrictive a view of it: the play is more than allegorical satire, and its protagonist more than a "peevish, hysterical" "Darling of Fortune" who "is not of heroic stature." Shakespeare took pains to invest Timon with certain heroic conceptions—largely alien to us, in our century—that are consonant with those of his later tragic heroes and that need to be understood in order to grasp Timon's heroic nature and, consequently, the nature of his tragedy. That the first half of *Timon* needs to be regarded in light of these conceptions will become clearer if we examine Shakespeare's transformation of his sources.

Timon actually lived in the fifth century B.C. and was referred to in Old and Middle Greek comedy as a hater of men and gods. His legend was transmitted in two classical works, one of which Shakespeare undoubtedly knew (Plutarch's brief account of his misanthropy and death in the Lives of Antony and Alcibiades) and the other of which he may have known (Lucian's more satirical account of his prodigality and hostility towards flatterers in the comic dialogue *Misanthropos*).[4] In the various Renaissance manifestations of the legend, Timon became an emblem of bestial humanity. Accusing his fellow men of beastliness, he became the thing itself. But Shakespeare's main source, as I have argued elsewhere, was the comical satire drawn primarily from Lucian and probably staged at one of the Inns of Court in or about 1602.[5] The *Timon* comedy makes explicit the *de casibus* pattern implicit in the legend and presents Timon in prosperity as well as in exile, thus achieving a pyramidal structure that Shakespeare adopts, with modification. In the comedy, Timon's reversal occurs at the end of act 3, just as he reaches the pinnacle of fortune: his wedding celebration, thus interrupted, ends in broken vows; he duns his friends and finds them wanting; he entertains them to a mock banquet, at which he pelts them with stones; he curses; he rails; he banishes himself from Athens.

For the first time in the history of the legend, Timon is allowed an immoderate rage in response to his flatterers' ingratitude, and this may have inspired Shakespeare to create a Timon of more heroic proportions:

> ffire water sworde confounde yee, let the crowes
> ffeede on your peckt out entrailes, and your bones
> Wante a sepulchre: worthy, o worthy yee
> That thus haue, falsifi'd your faith to mee.
> To dwell in Phlegeton. rushe on me heau'n
> Soe that on them it rushe, mount Caucasus
> ffall on my shoulders, soe on them it fall
>
> (4.1.1656–62)[6]

One may object that this is mock-heroic rant of the worst sort: a confusion of tags from famous curses of tragedies past, from Faustus's call to mountains and hills to come fall on him to Lucius's command that Tamora be thrown forth to beasts and birds of prey. It is the sort of fustian Hamlet parodies when he calls on millions of acres to bury him and Laertes till their ground make Ossa like a wart. Things get worse when the anonymous playwright digs into his bag of Senecan tags and allows Timon to lament in the underworld imagery of ghosts, Erebus, and the river Styx, then to swear revenge against the city: "Tysiphone, / Bring here thy flames, I am to mischiefe bente" (4.3.1863–64). But all this is pretty stock stuff for a second-rate dramatist. That we are to admire it as apt expression of Timon's rage and not smile condescendingly at it as Ercles' vein is apparent, I think, from his steward's choric observation,

> His tongue doth threaten & his hearte doth sighe
> The greatnes of his spirit will not downe.
>
> (4.3.1912–13)

Never before had Timon been ascribed such Aristotelian greatness. He becomes a prophet of hate, terrible in his wrath, and magnificent to the point of godliness, as the comedy's repeated allusions to his Jove-like nature attest. The comic Timon, therefore, no matter how ridiculous a figure he may cut, suggested to Shakespeare a heroic Timon in whom misanthropic excess could be paradoxically noble.

Heroic verse alone, however, does not make a man tragic. If it did, this comic Timon would be a match for any number of Elizabethan railers. Yet critics often write as if they discover in the railing of Shakespeare's Timon the moral dilemma to make him a tragic hero. The last two acts are, I would not deny, overpowering in their effect. But it should be apparent, simply from the fact that Shakespeare's Timon speaks a verse not substantially different (though different in quality) from that of his comic predecessor, that the tragic dilemma lies elsewhere, in the first three acts, in the conflicts that ultimately bring Timon to his misanthropic vision. In these acts, more than in the later acts, Shakespeare imaginatively transforms the comedy and weaves from the fabric of Timon's moral nature a complex ethical dialectic that makes Timon far more noble than the legendary prodigal.

Lucian probably originated the idea that prodigality caused Timon's fall from fortune.[7] In the bickering between Timon and Plutus, god of gold, he implies a history of excessive generosity for Timon. Timon lays all the blame for his fall on Plutus:

> He brought me countless troubles long ago—put me in the power of flatterers, set designing persons on me, stirred up ill-feeling, corrupted me with indulgence, exposed me to envy, and wound up treacherously deserting me at a moment's notice.[8]

Plutus counters these accusations by asserting that Timon is no different than any other squanderer. The fault lies in himself, not in his wealth:

> It is I who should rather complain; you prostituted me vilely to scoundrels, whose laudations and cajolery of you were only samples of their designs upon me. As to your saying that I wound up betraying you, you have things topsy-turvy; *I* may complain; you took every method of estrange me, and finally kicked me out neck and crop. (P. 45)

Though subsequent redactors of the legend simplified Lucian's moral as a warning against prodigality, it was left to the author of the anonymous comedy to fill out Timon's prodigal past by depicting him, in three acts, as the amoral center of his merrygreek world.

The comic Timon fits the Elizabethan stereotype of the merrygreek: a man who dedicates himself to liquor and lust and spends entire days in idleness, a word Timon uses to commend his style of living. Timon is a realist in love who knows that women will do anything for gold, a cynic about fidelity who expatiates on the art of cuckoldry, a reveler who presides over his cronies' bacchanalia, and an epicurean by nature:

> Ile vse my treasure and possesse my wealth
> and spend my dayes in pleasure whil'st I lyue.
> Wee shall goe naked to o.^r sepulchers
> and carry not one groat away w.th vs
>
> (1.5.422–25)

There is nothing particularly beneficent or noble about this *carpe diem* philosophy: it smacks of Epicure Mammon's fantasies about sensual gratification and typifies a character far more Jonsonian than Shakespearean. The author of the comedy in fact drew heavily upon Jonson's comical satires of 1599–1601 for both substance and tone.[9] Timon's boon companions are a panoply of Jonsonian humours who urge him to squander his gold on their pleasure: the fawning musician, the "lying trauailo^r," the "dissolate young man," the "cuntrey clowne." Each carries his satirical weight in Timon's entourage of turn-of-the-century London voluptuaries in an Athenian setting.

Timon presides over them and their intrigues for three acts. His bounty, far from being charitably motivated, is calculated for fame and jaded with the expectation of return:

> It is to me a Tryumph and a glorye
> that people fynger poynt at me and saye
> this, this is he, that his lardge wealth and store
> scatters among the Comons & the poore.
> ·····································
> *The* noyse ascend's to heau'n; *Timons* greate name
> In the *Gods* eares resounds, to his greate fame.
> ·····································
> I magnified by the peoples crye
> shall mount in glorye to the heauens high.
>
> (1.1.40–57, passim)

Timon here ludicrously exaggerates the idea of fame or reputation that heroes so hungered for, as if (Ulysses would argue with Achilles) a man could only know his true worth by such public estimation. Timon's hubris makes a mockery of that notion. And worse. For his very concept of friendship, the belief in which is supposed to render his friends' ingratitude reprehensible to him, is suspect: he freely admits that he bestows wealth on them not from a "good and gracious nature" as Shakespeare's Timon does (1.1.60), but with the goal of buying slaves to serve his vanity:

> A gratefull minde, thats all that I require.
> I putte my talents to strange vsury
> To gaine mee freinds, that they may followe mee
>
> (2.4.858–60)

The comic Timon, then, knows how the world goes. Although he is outraged by his friends' breach of faith, he is not really surprised or disillusioned by it. He is too much a cynic to be a gull; and as such, he is unlike Shakespeare's more credulous Timon. His "tragic" reversal is not so much a loss of faith as a loss of fortune; and fortune, crassly equated with gold, can come and go, where cynicism remains unchanged, only intensified by experience. This lack of a grand, idealistic vision to substantiate his later curses ultimately diminishes his potential for tragic heroism.

In transforming Timon into a hero who can compel admiration as well as earn censure, Shakespeare defied the legendary image of Timon as a self-indulgent merrygreek. Although the comedy inspired him to shape a world and a past for Timon, he nevertheless created a Timon who stands at a wide moral distance from the center of his world as a lord bounteous to his friends, but never their boon companion. He looks upon his wealth not as a means for self-glorification but as a means to create an ideal community of friends wherein affections are shared as liberally as gold. In "true friendship," he rejoices, "More welcome are ye to my fortunes / Than my fortunes to me" (1.2.19–21). The paradox of Timon's moral excellence is Shakespeare's major addition to his source. He defied the legend's simplistic moral and dramatized a noble struggle to preserve idealism.

Of all Shakespeare's tragedies, *Timon* most closely adheres to an Aristotelian moral scheme.[10] Timon's concept of friendship is one that Aristotle, in his *Nicomachean Ethics,* calls the most noble: the need of a rich man to have recipients for his beneficence. "Rich men," writes Aristotle, "are thought especially to require friends, since what would be the good of their prosperity without an outlet for beneficence, which is displayed in its fullest and most praiseworthy form towards friends?"[11] These are the very ethics Timon espouses:

> We are born to do benefits; and what better or properer can we call our own than the riches of our friends? O, what a precious comfort 'tis to have so many, like brothers, commanding one another's fortunes! (1.2.101–5)

Seneca defines *beneficium,* or benefit, as "the act of a well-wisher who bestows joy and derives joy from the bestowal of it, and is inclined to do what he does from the prompting of his own will. . . . A benefit consists, not in what is done or given, but in the intention of the giver or doer."[12] By intention, Timon is a benefactor to his friends.

His concept of beneficence is close to the Christian concept of charity. Indeed, numerous critics have regarded Timon as a Christ-figure, symbol for universal love betrayed by fallen man:[13] charity would thus qualify Timon for sainthood rather than heroism, to use Brower's distinction. The play does make use of Christian imagery now and then, especially in the flatterers' denials of Timon. But to claim that Timon's ethics are specifically

Christian is misleading. They are analogous, but not the same. Even in the most suggestive of lines, "there's none / Can truly say he gives, if he receives" (11. 11–12), Timon expresses no more than a classical precept of friendship (cf. *Ethics:* 8.8.3). Whereas Christianity rejects wealth for the heavenly kingdom, Timon, following Aristotle, accepts it as the necessary means for creating a perfect community on earth. It is legitimate to have wealth in order to dispense worldly gifts: "happiness also requires external goods . . . for it is impossible, or at least not easy, to play a noble part unless furnished with the necessary equipment" (*Ethics:* 1.8.15). The classical toleration of worldly "equipment" is outside the scope of Christian doctrine. It has a place, however, in the more secular heroism of medieval romance, where it crops up as *largesse,* a virtue for which heroes such as Alexander were noted and which was passed on to Renaissance heroes as a vestige of chivalric idealism. Shakespeare's portrait of Timon is suffused with this heroic conception.

Shakespeare was steeped in moral philosophy at school.[14] As a student at one of the better grammar schools, and perhaps as a teacher, he undoubtedly would have read Aristotle, Cicero, and—the Elizabethans' favorite stoic—Seneca. His familiarity with the subject informs the gentle gibe in *Troilus,* in which Hector with schoolmasterly aplomb derides Troilus and Paris as "not much / Unlike young men, whom Aristotle thought / Unfit to hear moral philosophy" (2.2.165–67). It was inevitable that at the core of *Timon* he should concern himself with the dichotomy between liberality and prodigality—the one being the mean, the other the excess. In line with Aristotle, Cicero defined liberality as the golden mean of giving discriminately to the worthy, and within one's means; prodigality as the extravagance of giving indiscriminately to the unworthy, and beyond one's means.[15] Discrimination was crucial; for to be liberal, one had to be careful not to sacrifice the fortune that was the very means of future liberality.

There was a real danger that the liberal man might spend to excess, "for it is the mark of the liberal nature to be regardless of itself" (*Ethics:* 4.1.18). The line of demarcation was faint, and all the harder to decipher because prodigality tended to err on the side of virtue. The Timon legend addressed itself to this very problem. In Lucian's dialogue Plutus, comparing himself with a bride who is abused by both jealousy and indifference in a husband, advocates Aristotle's mean: "My beau ideal is the man who steers a middle course, as far from complete abstention as from utter profusion" (Fowler, 37).

The legendary Timon steered a course of utter profusion; and Timon of the anonymous comedy, as we have seen, often betrays this characteristic flaw in his ostentatious commands:

> *Laches* bestrowe
> the streetes wth gould, and lett the people knowe
> How bountifull the hands of *Timon* are.

                                                                    (1.1.47–49)

Obviously aware of this tradition, Shakespeare plays with the dichotomy in passages that come back-to-back. Timon's faithful servants lament that his plight "is all a *liberal* course allows" (3.3.42), whereas the usurers' dunning servants retort "that a *prodigal* course / Is like the sun's, / But not, like his, recoverable" (3.4.12–14, my italics). Shakespeare lets us have it both ways and thereby creates an ambiguity in our perception of Timon's beneficence that critics have taken pains to simplify or to deny altogether.

A more romantic school of criticism, led by G. Wilson Knight, has tended to idealize Timon's behavior as perfect humanism. This accords with Timon's view of himself. Before we dismiss it out of hand, we ought to consider how close Timon in fact comes to Cicero's description of the liberal man. Unlike prodigals, who squander their money on public show, liberal men "are those who employ their own means to ransom captives from brigands, or who assume their friends' debts or help in providing dowries for their daughters" (*De Officiis:* 2.16.56); those who, moreover, are hospitable to their fellow man (2.18.64). Shakespeare's Timon, in emblematic sequence upon his entrance in the first act, redeems Ventidius's debt, enables his servant to marry by allocating him a generous dowry, and, above all, is hospitable to his friends.

As if this introductory sequence were not enough to define Timon's liberal nature, Shakespeare directs our appreciation further by using an unprecedented amount of choric commentary. Much of it is spoken by Timon's flatterers: "The noblest mind he carries / That ever govern'd man" (1.1.293–94). But even if one discounts such estimates as coming from the mouths of unreliable spokesmen, there is praise from impartial figures that is not so easy to dismiss. The choric scene in which "three Strangers" comment on the action indicates clearly that Shakespeare wants his audience to admire Timon's bounteous nature as a heroic virtue:

> I never tasted Timon in my life,
> Nor came any of his bounties over me
> To mark me for his friend; yet I protest,
> For his right noble mind, illustrious virtue,
> And honorable carriage,
> Had his necessity made use of me,
> I would have put my wealth into donation
> And the best half should have return'd to him,
> So much I love his heart.
>
> (3.2.80–88)

The term *bounty,* here and throughout, is synonymous with *benefit* and marks Timon's nature as liberal rather than prodigal.[16] A. S. Collins, in fact, has allegorized Timon as Ideal Bounty; and while the label too overtly suggests the Morality tradition, it nevertheless points to an important quality of Timon's characterization—its social definition—that allows him to acquire a kind of symbolic value as "the very soul of bounty" (1.2.209), the embodiment of a chivalric idealism that was succumbing in a capitalist age.[17]

Another school of criticism, led by O. J. Campbell, insists that Timon is no more noble than his comic counterpart and attributes to him "not generosity, but self-satisfaction at the display of his own munificence."[18] The ascription of Reckless Prodigality[19] to Timon errs in one direction just as far as Ideal Bounty errs in the other. But ever the fence-straddler, Shakespeare supplies enough choric commentary critical of Timon to allow the cynics to do battle with the romantics. Far from the temperate liberality of classical tradition, Timon's spending is "raging waste":

> If I want gold, steal but a beggar's dog
> And give it Timon, why, the dog coins gold.
> If I would sell my horse, and buy twenty moe
> Better than he, why, give my horse to Timon,
> Ask nothing, give it him, it foals me straight
> And able horses. No porter at his gate,
> But rather one that smiles and still invites
> All that pass by.
>
> (2.1.4–12)

Much of Timon's behavior bears out these observations. His expenditure is lavish and often idle. The masque of Amazons acknowledges him the patron of the five senses (1.2.122–23); he bestows rare jewels as if they were trinkets; and he boasts with grand indiscrimination, "'tis not enough to give. / Methinks I could deal kingdoms to my friends, / And ne'er be weary" (ll. 220–22). The boast indicates a deficiency in Timon's concept of friendship that underlies all his vain show: there is no sense of reciprocity. He delights in his friends only as an artist delights in his own creations (cf. *Ethics:* 9.7).

Timon actually abuses the ideal of hospitality by inviting "all that pass by." He lacks the discrimination requisite for true liberality and thus by default may be considered prodigal. He spends far beyond his means, borrows on credit, neglects to test the worthiness of his friends. Flavius, his steward, agonizes over such fiscal indiscretion:

> No care, no stop! So senseless of expense,
> That he will neither know how to maintain it,
> Nor cease his flow of riot. . . .
>
> (2.2.1–3)

Apemantus the cynic chastises Timon less directly by identifying outward signs of friendship, such as those that have fooled Timon, as false show:

> Friendship's full of dregs.
> Methinks false hearts should never have sound legs.
> Thus honest fools lay out their wealth on curt'sies.
>
> (1.2.238–40)

In fact, as Apemantus points out, Timon's friends are but trencher friends, time's flies—what Aristotle called "friends of utility," impermanent and parasitic (*Ethics:* 8.3.)—who, according to Plutarch, deliberately foster their benefactor's "dream of friendship" in order to further their own interests.[20] Plutarch insists that self-knowledge, an awareness of one's own susceptibility to flattery, is the only way to combat it. The trouble with Timon is that he, like Lear, only slenderly knows himself. He falls easily for the false sense of fellowship that his flatterers create. He defends himself with an admission that ironically echoes Aristotle's censure of prodigality, "to exceed in giving without getting is foolish rather than evil or ignoble" (*Ethics:* 4.1.31–32). "No villainous bounty yet hath pass'd my heart," Timon assures Flavius; "Unwisely, not ignobly, have I given" (2.2.178–79). But the line also echoes Othello's admission that he loved not wisely, but too well. It is an admission of error, of course, but such error contains not a jot of calculation. It has, as heroic flaws always do, come from the heart. Timon's failing, like Othello's, has been an excess of feeling, even of passion: Shakespeare causes us to admire its heroic intemperance even as we censure its folly.

Timon's inability to distinguish friends from flatterers is symptomatic of a deeper flaw in his character: his naive assumption that an ideal community is possible at all. He believes in a fixed world of classical values when Athens shows him daily that there is no support for that belief. His adherence to it, though, is at once his heroic strength and his tragic limitation: it causes him to err, but to err magnificently. If good intentions were to count as deeds, Timon would indeed be the soul of bounty. But there is a big gap between what Timon is and what he thinks he is, what he does and what he thinks he does. Like Troilus, he would see himself as "truth's simplicity" and interpret his own behavior as consistent with the humanism he espouses. He totally lacks the introspection by which he would recognize that he is guilty, in Samuel Johnson's words, of "that ostentatious liberality, which scatters bounty, but confers no benefits, and buys flattery, but not friendship."[21]

Like the noblest of Shakespeare's heroes, Timon projects his own values onto the world and assumes that the world will abide by them. Like Hector, who believes that even Achilles will honor the chivalric code; like Othello, who sees in Desdemona a "fair warrior" and thinks all men honest who but seem so; or like Lear, who trusts that it is natural for his daughters to love him "all"; so Timon believes that his friends will conform to his valuation of them. He measures every man's virtue by his own and finds none wanting. As Flavius says of bounty, "Being free itself, it thinks all others so" (l. 240). In his "dream of friendship" (4.2.35), Timon bestows benefits without ever inquiring into his own motives, satisfied that the ideal of friendship is the same in every heart:

O, no doubt, my good friends, but the gods themselves have provided that I shall have much help from you. How had you been my friends else? Why have you that charitable title from thousands, did not you chiefly belong to my heart? I have told more of you to myself than you can with modesty speak in your own behalf; and thus far I confirm you. (1.2.88–94)

Timon answers his own question. Why are they his friends? Because he has conceived them in his own image and cannot see beyond himself: what he confirms is his own delusion. His ideal community is a projection of his will: it betrays in him a solipsism akin to Troilus's and Othello's and Lear's. What makes Timon different from them, however, and more difficult to accept as a heroic figure, is the *object* of his projection. He does not invest himself in a private relationship, such as Othello's to Desdemona, or in a familial relationship, such as Lear's to his daughters, but in a more broadly *social* relationship. He gains his identity from his relationship to the group: his heroic ethos must be understood, as the ethos of no other Shakespearean hero must, in the context of social ethics. Such a context appears at first glance to diminish heroic stature: it is the province of comedy or satire, not tragedy. Tragic heroes must transcend the group, and their greatness be measured by standards that make social norms look paltry. Timon, it is often claimed, is strictly *of* the group; and when he rails against it, he has no more stature than Malvolio. This is, I think, a fundamental misreading of his character. Though social ethics lie at the heart of the play, they may be seen to ennoble rather than diminish him: comedy has no exclusive claim on them, nor must a hero be conceived in traditions apart from them. Aristotle, at least, found nothing inconsistent between a rich man's bounty and greatness of soul. The ideals that motivate Timon to act as he does are no less passionately felt than the love that motivates Othello, the kingly pride that motivates Lear, and the martial wrath that kindles Coriolanus to perform daring deeds; nor is his flaw—the ignorance of self that plagues all great ones—less significant than theirs. At every turn, Shakespeare metamorphosed the comic prodigal of legendary fame into a hero cast in the mold of other heroes of this period in his career. If the fact that Timon's heroic idealism is circumscribed by a world of sycophants and cheats makes us pigeonhole him as one of them—a self-serving prodigal, no better than his comic predecessor—then we reveal a bias that does not do justice to the complexity of Shakespeare's design.

In the speech I just quoted, the most ardent expression of heroic reciprocity in the play, Timon assures his friends, "Why, I have often wish'd myself poorer, that I might come nearer to you" (ll. 100–1). At a corresponding point in the comedy and in the tragedy, his wish comes true: for the first time he can test his ethical ideal against reality. The transformation Shakespeare wrought on the comic prodigal can best be demonstrated by juxtaposing the exchanges between the two Timons and their faithful stewards. First, the comedy:

LACH: Comfort yourselfe, you haue some friends yet lefte
TIM: Is't possible a poore man should haue friends?
LACH: Aduersitie cannot parte faithefull friends
TIM: Hee is deceau'd that lookes for faithe on earthe
       ffaithe is in heauen, & scornes mortall men.
       I am compelled by necessity
       To proue my friends: thus poore & destitute
       I goe to seeke reliefe from other men.

                                        (4.3.1605–12)

Next, the tragedy:

TIMON: Why dost thou weep? Canst thou the conscience lack
          To think I shall lack friends? Secure thy heart;
          If I would broach the vessels of my love,
          And try the argument of hearts by borrowing,
          Men and men's fortunes could I frankly use
          As I can bid thee speak.
FLAVIUS: Assurance bless your thoughts!
TIMON: And in some sort these wants of mine are crown'd,
          That I account them blessings; for by these
          Shall I try my friends. You shall perceive how you
          Mistake my fortunes; I am wealthy in my friends.

                                        (2.2.180–90)

The tone of the first exchange is skeptical; the second, confident. In the comedy, Timon plays cynical antagonist to Laches's trust in human nature. In *Timon of Athens,* the roles are reversed. This brief exchange between Timon and Flavius reiterates at a critical point Timon's overriding faith in mankind, a faith stated here so simply that one is bound to remember it during the ensuing disappearance of Timon from the scenes in which his friends are tried and found wanting; bound to remember it when Timon appears again at the end of act 3, a raging misanthrope.

Loss of such perfect faith imbues Timon's rage in acts 4 and 5 with a great moral force—enough to justify the heroic extremity of his conversion—whereas cynicism would have reduced that righteous rage to sour grapes. The comic Timon, though he achieves a kind of grand theatricality by railing against hypocrisy, ultimately is diminished by lack of this moral force. He is indeed closer to Macilente in Jonson's *Every Man Out,* an agent of satirical exposure who, governed by an envious humour, tears away at hypocritical disguises more out of spite than disillusion. As he lies down onstage, like Macilente, and from that position rails, he becomes monotonous, self-indulgent, ridiculous; so much so that when one of his flatterers laughs derisively, "Ha ha he how tragicall hee is" (4.1.1638), we can only laugh with him. Shakespeare, however, saw the tragic potential of those curses and provided for them a basis in faith disillusioned and innocence betrayed, such awakenings as alone can charge outrage with tragic pathos.

To insure that basis, Shakespeare transformed the prodigal merrygreek who stood at the amoral center of his world into an idealist who stands a world apart. It is the nobility of that idealism, missing in the legendary Timon, that lends to the misanthropy of Shakespeare's Timon such moral intensity.

Shakespeare was interested in how a traditional hero—a man of monolithic sensibilities—would respond to disillusion. Troilus had turned his back on discovery and displaced his rage; Othello had cracked under the pressure of discovery and was quick to restore his identity under a new rubric, that of heroic justicer. But Timon, once he discovers his error, lives with that knowledge: he reacts to it violently and never tries to accommodate himself to it or, as Lear will, transcend it. Our guide to Timon's misanthropy is often said to be Apemantus. A cynic in the mold of Diogenes, he defines his own occupation as "plain-dealing" (1.1.221) and adopts the voice of the Juvenalian satirist to condemn Timon's parasites:

> Aches contract
> And starve your supple joints! That there should be
> Small love amongest these sweet knaves, and all
> This courtesy! The strain of man's bred out
> Into baboon and monkey.
>
> (1.1.259–63)

Apemantus's avowed purpose is to be Timon's tutor: to teach him, in accordance with Plutarch, that self-knowledge is the only sure way to recognize flattery for what it is. It is Timon's honesty that Apemantus finds attractive. It is the fool whom he would presume to educate. He knows that idealism, however admirable in itself, makes a man a gull. But Timon is an unwilling pupil who thwarts Apemantus's best intentions: "O, that men's ears should be / To counsel deaf, but not to flattery!" (1.2.255–56).

When Timon finally learns that he has been mistaken in his friends, he expresses his disillusion in terms similar to those Apemantus has used in his earlier observations. They are "fools of fortune, trencher-friends, time's flies" (3.6.96); and his description of man's fallen nature harks back to the Poet's description of men on Fortune's hill, an allegory that Apemantus has fondly embellished:

> Who dares, who dares
> In purity of manhood stand upright
> And say "This man's a flatterer"? If one be,
> So are they all; for every grize of fortune
> Is smooth'd by that below. The learned pate
> Ducks to the golden fool. All's obliquy;
> There's nothing level in our cursed natures
> But direct villainy.
>
> (4.3.13–20)

But if Apemantus provides a language in which Timon condemns flattery, he is not a catalyst for Timon's conversion.[22] Not all his counsel, but the actual experience of ingratitude itself, rings down the change in Timon. When, after a long absence from the stage, Apemantus appears again to confront Timon, Shakespeare differentiates their characters sharply and by this contrast emphasizes the profundity of the change in Timon.

Realizing that Timon has come to believe in man's "direct villainy" without the aid of his tutelage, Apemantus grows jealous of his role as cynic. Perhaps fearing that he will be supplanted by Timon, he accuses him of imitation—"Men report / Thou dost affect my manners, and dost use them" (ll. 200–1)—and warns him against it—"Do not assume my likeness" (l. 220). He thinks Timon is usurping his role "by putting on the cunning of a carper" (l. 211); and he would not have there be another Apemantus. Yours is but "a poor unmanly melancholy sprung / From change of fortune," he chides Timon (11. 205–6); "thou / Dost it enforcedly. Thou 'dst courtier be again, / Wert thou not beggar" (11. 243–45). He advises Timon, with typical cynicism, to return to Athens and play the flatterer himself.

These accusations might be warranted by the comic Timon, who, having lost no philanthropic vision, is too jaded by the merrygreek mentality to be justified in his misanthropy. The comic Timon is, indeed, a disgruntled carper of Apemantean cynicism. But for Shakespeare's Timon, these accusations are singularly inappropriate. In them, Apemantus reveals how little he knows about the nature nof Timon's conversion. His ignorance is underscored most ironically by the fact that Timon has already discovered gold and never given a thought to returning to Athens. Gold, in fact, has only hardened his misanthropic resolve. Apemantus's superficial assessment of Timon makes us question in what way Timon is different from Apemantus's idea of him.

For years, critics have been inclined to accept Apemantus's assessment and to regard Timon as different from Apemantus not in nature, but only in degree. Theodore Spencer, for example, thinks that Apemantus in act 1 "has already reached the stage at which Timon is to arrive later, though his snarling and spitting is a much smaller thing than the all-inclusive storm of cursing and denunciation which comes from the bitterness of Timon's disillusionment."[23] Harry Levin likewise sees Apemantus as having this unifying function and contrasts him with Timon as the "natural misanthrope" against the "conditioned misanthrope," the causes being different, the results about the same.[24] William Empson thinks that Timon becomes, like Apemantus, a cynic (I suspect he would make no distinction between cynicism and misanthropy), and suggests that although they differ in degree— Timon is noble; Apemantus, mean—they do not differ in kind.[25] Even Robert Elliott, in the process of drawing valid distinctions between them, unwarily allows that Apemantus "is the poor man's misanthrope."[26] Alice Birney is less concerned with cynicism and misanthropy than with satire, and in Apemantus and Timon she finds two variations on the satirist persona—the one a "natural-born, constant, stable satirist"; the other, a "satirist of circumstances."[27] And in his eccentric interpretation of *Timon* as a comedy, Northrop Frye suggests that Apemantus and Timon do no more than exchange the role of *idiotes*—the misfit who is isolated from society—in the course of the play.[28]

Of all recent critics, Willard Farnham alone has recognized that Timon and Apemantus are intrinsically different. He cites a passage from Montaigne's *Essais*, which Shakespeare may have known, in which the professional cynicism of Diogenes, who did not consider mankind worthy of his scorn, is preferred to the misanthropy of Timon, who took things too much to heart.[29] Cynicism requires detachment; misanthropy, engagement. The one is philosophical; the other, passionate. Shakespeare allows Timon to distinguish between himself and Apemantus in something of the manner of Montaigne (though, unlike Montaigne, Timon favors misanthropy over cynicism). I have, says Timon, "had the world as my confectionary, / The mouths, the tongues, the eyes, and hearts of men / At duty" (ll. 263–65), a situation that protected his innocence and fostered his idealism. In such a situation, one does not anticipate having to walk, like contempt, alone. "I to bear this, / That never knew but better, is some burden" (ll. 269–70). Idealism contains within itself the seeds of disillusion; and conversely, disillusion implies a previous idealism. As Alvin Kernan suggests, the moral force of Timon's hate is caused by his having glimpsed the human potential.[30] In both his love and his hate, Timon displays moral absolutism. They are the opposite extremes of heroic engagement, closer to each other than either is to indifference. The engagement implicit in misanthropy is lacking in the cynic's detached philosophy.

The cynic, as Timon observes of Apemantus, has never known the auspicious conditions that encourage idealism and therefore has no cause to be disillusioned, no cause to hate:

> Thou art a slave, whom Fortune's tender arm
> With favor never clasp'd, but bred a dog.
> ·································
> Thy nature did commence in sufferance, time
> Hath made thee hard in 't. Why shouldst thou hate men?
> (4.3.253–54; 271–72)

Apemantus, in fact, is too genial to hate. Cynicism is by nature a constant way of regarding mankind, never tempted to heroic extremes. It keeps its own *eironic* middle ground and is tainted with nothing greater than envy.

Apemantus, then, knows but ultimately accepts mankind for what it is. His occupation is to be its attendant railer: human vices are his daily bread, and so he tolerates them. Shakespeare makes this clear in Apemantus's conversation with Timon about the beastliness of human nature.

TIMON: What wouldst thou do with the world, Apemantus, if it lay
              in thy power?
APEMANTUS: Give it the beasts, to be rid of the men.
TIMON: Wouldst thou have thyself fall in the confusion of men, and
              remain a beast with the beasts?
APEMANTUS: Ay, Timon.
TIMON: A beastly ambition, which the gods grant thee t' attain to!
                                                        (4.3.326–33)

Despite the dangers Timon proceeds to outline for him, Apemantus would
remain within Athens, a beast vulnerable to other beasts, whose kinship
with the Athenians Timon has accurately pinpointed in an earlier passage:

> If thou hadst not been born the worst of men,
> Thou hadst been a knave and flatterer.
>   (4.3.278–79)

Apemantus has a kind of complaisance reminiscent of Thersites's, an acceptance of himself as a part of the society he condemns, a self-
centeredness evident from the beginning—"Immortal gods, I crave no
pelf; / I pray for no man but myself" (1.2.62–63)—which is indigenous to
cynicism but outside the scope of misanthropy.

Misanthropy is a universal hatred that demands commitment to the
point of self-inclusion. Timon is appalled by Apemantus's tacit acceptance
of human failing. He would divorce himself from mankind, not be its
attendant. To Alcibiades's question, "What art thou there?" (4.3.49), he
answers, "A beast, as thou art" (l. 50). Thus, when he denounces Athens as
a realm of beasts full of guile, he implicitly condemns himself. In rejecting
the beast within himself, he wills a self-destruction that inevitably culmi-
nates in his death: misanthropy carried to the extreme of tragic engagement. As Apemantus observes with typical detachment, "The middle of
humanity thou never knewest, but the extremity of both ends" (ll. 305–6).
The extremity of disillusion that leads to Timon's death is a form of
heroism that Apemantus has no power to comprehend.

Apemantus's charge of "imitation," then, forces us to grapple with the
profundity of Timon's conversion. In the course of their confrontation in
act 4, Apemantus makes a palpable hit: Timon, in his misanthropy, indulges in an excess that borders on folly. But to assess Timon's stature
solely through Apemantus's eyes, as O. J. Campbell and his numerous
followers have done, is to be guilty of a cynic's perspective and do the play
an artistic disservice. For Timon's absolutism is far nobler than Apemantus's compromise. By contrasting them, Shakespeare directs attention to
the ways in which Timon is built on the scale of an Othello, a Lear, a
Coriolanus.

But Timon achieves his greatest stature through the magnificence of his
verse. It is in ringing down maledictions upon mankind and in vowing

revenge against a world he now sees is making a mockery of the old order that he most resembles Othello, Lear, and Coriolanus. His heroic idiom differs from and surpasses the conventional rant of the comic Timon. His outrage, like Achilles' rage, gives a heroic momentum to his verse that no mere cynic ever had. As Robert Elliott writes, "He tries to preempt the full power of the archaic curse, calling on the gods, the heavens, the earth— and, as it were, the demonic power within himself—to confound the hated creature man."[31] Like Troilus's squaring of the general sex by Cressid's rule, Timon's impulse is to generalize from the particulars of his own experience. As he turns his back on Athens, he invokes a universal malediction that inverts the ideals expressed in Ulysses' speech on degree. He begins— as have Henry V, Talbot, Tamburlaine, and others before him—by cursing an enemy wall: "O thou wall, / That girdles in those wolves, dive in the earth, / And fence not Athens!" (4.1.1–3). But as he continues, his topos changes. He adopts the language of Senecan lamentation, in which all the forces of nature are called upon to rain down their wrath upon the world and leave it chaos:

> Piety, and fear,
> Religion to the gods, peace, justice, truth,
> Domestic awe, night-rest, and neighborhood,
> Instruction, manners, mysteries, and trades,
> Degrees, observances, customs, and laws,
> Decline to your confounding contraries,
> And yet confusion live!
>
> (4.1.15–21)

We hear in this curse the hyperbole of an early Titus, lamenting the injustices done to his family; behind it, the laments of Medea, Hercules, Thyestes. What gives it a special character, however, is the satirical application of the curse to specific social relationships. Matrons are bid to turn incontinent; children, disobedient; slaves and fools, to supplant senators; maids, to visit their masters' beds; sons of sixteen, to beat out their limping sires' brains with a crutch. Details such as these ground Timon's curse in the matrix of bourgeois Athenian culture and distinguish it from the rant of more orthodox heroes.

In revenge, Timon vividly imagines the grotesque cruelties he would inflict upon the Athenians: the images he musters recall and put to shame those by which Henry V threatens the governor of Harfleur. He exhorts Alcibiades to take Athens as ruthlessly as Tamburlaine took Damascus: "Be as a planetary plague, when Jove / Will o'er some high-vic'd city hang his poison / In the sick air. Let not thy sword skip one" (4.3.111–13). The language is decidedly Marlovian. And the ensuing threat may make explicit reference to Tamburlaine's taking the Virgins of Damascus:

> Let not the virgin's cheek
> Make soft thy trenchant sword: for those milk paps,
> That through the window-bars bore at men's eyes,
> Are not within the leaf of pity writ,
> But set them down horrible traitors. Spare not the babe,
> Whose dimpled smiles from fools exhaust their mercy;
> Think it a bastard, whom the oracle
> Hath doubtfully pronounc'd thy throat shall cut,
> And mince it sans remorse.
>
> (4.3.117–25)

Shakespeare had not put such horrors in verse since Henry V had warned that Harfleur might see his soldiers

> Defile the locks of your shrill-shrieking daughters,
> Your fathers taken by the silver beards,
> And their most reverend heads dash'd to the walls,
> Your naked infants spitted upon pikes. . . .
>
> (3.3.35–38)

If Timon outdoes the barbarism of these conventional threats, it may be because he is, unlike Henry, totally engaged with his idiom. Henry uses such language to effect his ends; it does not define his character. But it does define Timon's, and that makes the cruelty of it all the more devastating.

Timon's vaunts are never translated into action, however. He is a hero in word but not in deed. In him, the will to active revenge stutters; and Shakespeare chooses instead to focus on heroic frustration, on a man for whom language is the only instrument of revenge. He thus deepens his probe into the mind of the traditional hero and reflects on how knowledge can reduce the hero to impotence. Timon's mind turns images of gold, beasts, and plague into metaphors for action: they do their work on a purely imaginative level. Although this internalization of revenge does not resolve his rage, it nevertheless moves a step beyond Troilus and Othello, who found ways to deny knowledge and thereby to preserve their heroic integrity, and a step closer to Lear, whose rage is purged entirely within the compass of his own wits.

Timon is in many ways like Lear. Alike as victims of ingratitude, alike in banishing themselves to a wilderness, they both beseech nature to be the agent of their revenge on mankind. "Common mother," Timon addresses nature,

> thou
> Whose womb unmeasurable and infinite breast
> Teems and feeds all; whose self-same mettle,
> Whereof thy proud child, arrogant man, is puff'd,
> . . . .

Ensear thy fertile and conceptious womb,
Let it no more bring out ingrateful man!

(4.3.179–90 passim)

As R. P. Draper notes, Timon's supplication in both form and substance is much like Lear's more famous supplication to the "all-shaking thunder":[32]

Strike flat the thick rotundity o' th' world!
Crack nature's molds, all germains spill at once,
That makes ingrateful man!

(3.2.6–9)

If Timon is like Lear in the general sweep of his invective, he is unlike him in never being able to transcend it. He never looks within himself for the source of reaccommodation with mankind, as Lear does, nor does he achieve Lear's insight into his own participation in the human condition. He remains to the end a detractor, cursing mankind with heroic force but without enlightenment, stunted in his capacity for the introspection that would move him beyond the conventional idiom of wrath.

As if to justify the stasis of his misanthropy, Shakespeare keeps the satirical world of Athens before Timon's and our eyes during the last two acts. In a parade that recalls the ceremonial procession of act 1 comes marching an array of figures from the world Timon left behind, each one a foil for his misanthropic humour. Alcibiades and his gold-digging whores, the three banditti who try to pass themselves off as soldiers, even the faithful Flavius who almost turns Timon's dangerous nature mild: Timon plies all of them with gold to "Hate all, curse all, show charity to none" (l. 532). Next comes Apemantus to flyte with him, in a scene I have already discussed, like "scurrae" in the conventional wit-combat described by Horace in his "Journey to Brundisium."[33] And finally the flatterers come flocking back to him, hoping once again to cash in on his generosity: the Poet and the Painter up to their old artifices, the senators begging contritely for Timon's assistance in a war against Alcibiades. In the absence of any central dramatic conflict, these brief encounters keep the play in motion. But as there is no progress within them, their cumulative effect is satiric rather than dramatic: a series of exposés punctuated by curses in the tradition of formal verse satire.[34]

To each intruder Timon gives the same acrimonious response. The repetition makes Timon a more fitting character for comedy than tragedy. What he has advised Alcibiades to do at the beginning of act 4 he virtually repeats to the senators in act 5. As before, his verse is strongly reminiscent of the Marlovian vaunt of Henry V; but despite the familiar idiom, its tone is less that of conqueror drama than of satire:

But if he [Alcibiades] sack fair Athens,
And take our goodly aged men by th' beards,
Giving our holy virgins to the stain

Of contumelious, beastly, mad-brain'd war,
. . . .
I cannot choose but tell him that I care not,
And let him take 't at worst—for their knives care not,
While you have throats to answer.

                                        (5.1.170–78, passim)

The constant stimulus of Athenians during the course of the two acts produces no visible change in Timon. Nothing has altered the immorality of Athens: the flatterers are as Greek as ever; gold determines faith as much as it did before. And because Athens has not changed, the cause of Timon's rage remains unchanged. His curses are as warranted at the end of act 5 as they are at the end of act 3. Apart from Flavius's demonstration of love and honesty, Shakespeare provides Timon with no dramatic incentive to reaccommodate himself to society.

Ever since G. Wilson Knight rhapsodized that Timon imaginatively progresses through "the breast of nature . . . the solar fire mated to earth or sea . . . the planetary spaces of the night" and unto "the wide sea of eternal darkness," however, there has been a tendency among critics to award Timon a metaphoric reconciliation with the elements, if not with man, far beyond the structural confines of the play.[35] In the course of cursing, Timon indeed projects such social phenomena as usurpation, cheating, and robbery onto the elements to a point at which he sees sun, moon, earth, and sea all as natural thieves; and from this metaphoric equation of nature with society, his later admission, "My long sickness / Of health and living now begins to mend, / And nothing brings me all things" (ll. 185–87), may in fact seem to suggest that the poetry of the play holds "the symbolic promise of purification, as the barren prospect of man's greed is blotted out in the healing waters of oblivion."[36] M. C. Bradbrook applies this idea most extremely in her theory that the play is a "tragic pageant" in which Timon figures as "solar man" who runs his course through earth, air, fire, and sea, to be finally reconciled with "the elemental powers"—a reconciliation that fulfills the expectations of court allegory even where it fails the expectations of drama.[37]

There is a problem here. No matter how much evidence can be adduced to demonstrate Timon's reconciliation, the dramatic action nowhere indicates that he grows to a more comprehensive vision of or reaccommodation to the world. The episodic structure of the last two acts is, as I have shown, static; and stasis vindicates the absoluteness of Timon's misanthropy and the resoluteness of his rant. Nevertheless, Shakespeare seems to have felt the tragedian's inevitable impulse to resolve his hero's dilemma. He strove, through the imagery of nature, to convey a movement towards reconciliation for Timon like that of his other tragic heroes, most notably Lear; strove all the harder, perhaps, because the structure of the play so stubbornly refused him the opportunity to reconcile Timon with society in dramatic terms. Unlike Lear's poetry of elemental purgation, however, which is integrated with his growth as a tragic hero, Timon's poetry reflects, in the words of Wolfgang Clemen, "a perceptible loosening of the firm guidance of the dramatic action; these debates which Timon holds with the general and universal powers and elements often appear to us as digressions and parentheses."[38] Timon's death, as a result, does not satisfactorily resolve the action: it is merely the ultimate expression of despair. The images with which Timon himself dramatizes it suggest extrinsically that he has achieved a resolution: "Timon hath made his everlasting mansion, / Upon the beached verge of the salt flood, / Who once a day with his embossed froth / The turbulent surge shall cover" (ll. 214–17); yet his final curse gainsays that suggestion and proves that intrinsically, he is unaccommodated man still: "Lips, let sour words go by and language end! / What is amiss, plague and infection mend!" (ll. 219–20). Words have been Timon's weapons; language, his power. When he dispenses with them here, he does so not as one who, like Prospero, has seen his book effect a magical regeneration of mankind, but as one who has decided at last that words are powerless to quell unregeneracy. His death affirms nothing.

The poetry of tragic resolution in *Timon* thus exists in a tension with a confining and unresolved structural form. That form, like the absolute nature of Timon himself, was inherent in the legend as it was passed down from Lucian through the comedy. Shakespeare must have been willing to adhere to it, at least to a degree, or he would not have been drawn to the legend in the first place. He knew that Timon's culpable excesses were not the best stuff from which to fashion an admirable tragic hero. A great man whose liberality may be construed as foolish profligacy and whose heroic rage stagnates in misanthropic curses cannot easily lay claim to admiration or sympathy. Perhaps, as in the case of *Troilus,* the potential ambivalence toward Timon in the sources was the very thing Shakespeare found attractive about them and suitable for his dramatic purposes. It permitted him to test our admiration of the traditional heroic ethos by straining it to the limits—by subjecting that ethos to the perils of satirical form, wherein the hero fails to grow to enlightenment or self-knowledge and instead repeats his strident hyperbole over and over again for two acts, like an Othello who never gets over the first flush of anger against Desdemona or a Lear who never comes in from the storm. If history has shown that neither admiration nor censure has won complete control of critical opinion of Timon, that does credit to the circumspection of Shakespeare's design; for the heroic ethos that informs Timon, and that Shakespeare scrutinizes in him more closely than in Othello, Lear, or Coriolanus, may preserve its simple dignity and tragic grandeur even when it is satirized for inflexibility, ignorance, and excess.

7

Persistence of the "Old" Lear

*I*t is difficult to place *King Lear* in the traditions of Shakespeare's heroic plays because Lear's heroism seems of a different sort, biblical rather than pagan. It involves more suffering than bold action, more self-doubt than self-assurance. These qualities may befit a Job, but they are not easily conveyed by the idiom Shakespeare had developed for his "worldly" heroes. Many critics have come to regard Lear not as a traditional hero at all, but as a tyrant who errs, endures humiliation, and earns redemption in much the same pattern as Morality play tyrants do.[1] The traditions of such homiletic drama, of course, are a world apart from the traditions Shakespeare invoked to create Antony and Othello, Titus and Timon. Reuben Brower, in fact, calls Lear not a hero, but a saint; and if he exaggerates, most would nevertheless concur that the *emphasis* of *Lear* falls on patience rather than defiance.

Lear's response to his world, though, depends a great deal on the heroic traditions I have discussed in previous chapters. In the first two acts, the old idiom establishes values that Lear must transcend if he is to survive. Even when he does transcend them—suffers knowledge, accepts accountability, learns patience—the heroic idiom persists. It creates a counterpoint with the homiletic idiom to keep Lear defiantly regal even when he turns humble, and the tension between idioms accounts in part for the complexity of Lear and for what we most admire in him: his assertion of selfhood in the face of horrors that laugh such assertion to scorn.

At the outset, Lear bestrides the stage like a colossus. He is Shakespeare's most imperious hero. With complete fidelity to the heroic type on which he is modeled, he claims to have absolute sway—to control not only worlds, but affections. He conceives of himself much as Julius Caesar does in Shakespeare's earlier play as a generous, magnanimous, and great-souled leader, living proof that there is a constancy in man to match that of the gods. With a theatrical show to equal Caesar's, Lear at once declares his "fast intent" to give up imperial sway and his "constant will" to publish his daughters' dowers (1.1.38, 43). But if he gives up the substance of his power, he is intent upon keeping the form and prerogatives for himself. "Only we shall retain / The name, and all th' addition to a king" (ll. 135–36), he declares to his public; and it is obvious that he, unlike Coriolanus, thinks that the name and outward shows of kingship—and public recognition of those forms, which is something Lear never questions—are tantamount to kingship itself. He dispenses crowns to his sons-in-law as confidently as Tamburlaine does to his generals; for, as he tells Kent, nothing has ever dared come between his sentence and his power. His language, in other words, has always served adequately to define his character; he has never had reason to doubt that he is what he says. Words, to him, are as good as deeds; he treats them "as entities, which carry their own truth within them."[2] The hyperbolic idiom of traditional heroism has cast him in its mold; and in it he would remain, content.

But in the Lear of act 1, Shakespeare parodies the idiom of the old conqueror plays as tellingly as he does in the bombast of Julius Caesar, as if to show that anyone who dares to use such vaunt without a sense of irony, or role-playing, is destined for a fall: the ethos implied by such vaunt is unacceptable to society, and society will root it out. Lear falls as surely as Caesar. The love-test he stages is designed, like Caesar's thrice refusing the crown offered him, for public acclaim and affirmation of his heroic identity. "Tell me, my daughters," he bids,

> Which of you shall we say doth love us most,
> That we our largest bounty may extend
> Where nature doth with merit challenge?
>
> (1.1.48; 51–53)

Lear's claim to be bounteous allies him with Timon and other figures of *largesse;* but Lear is not so nobly bountiful as Timon. Timon would deal kingdoms to his friends for mere gratitude. Lear, who has already divided up the kingdom, attaches strings to it: his daughters must perform rhetorical shows of affection, like dogs do tricks, to get their shares. Timon never put such demands on his beneficiaries. Holding up the promised kingdom as bait, Lear angles for a response that will glorify his kingship and attest that he is "all." He is certain that his daughters' rhetoric will signify, as absolutely as his own, what is and always has been true—that he is every inch a king; or if, as some claim, he is not so certain, at least bribery will allow him to maintain his illusion. When he learns otherwise, that words are mere words, the absoluteness of his character is rent asunder and his faith in the heroic idiom dissolves.

The heroic prototype of Lear's challenge to his daughters, it seems to me, is Tamburlaine's challenge to his three sons to prove their mettle. "Be all a scourge and terror to the world, / Or else you are not sons of Tamburlaine" (*Part 2:* 1.4.63–64). Tamburlaine accuses them of lacking the courage and steel needed to be sons of his: "methinks their looks are amorous . . . Their fingers made to quaver on a lute, / Their arms to hang about a lady's neck" (ll. 21, 29–30). He taunts them into expressing their conformity to his heroic expectations; and as each son rises to the occasion with the language of self-assertion, Tamburlaine values his worth accordingly:

> If thou wilt love the wars and follow me,
> Thou shalt be made a king and reign with me,
> Keeping in iron cages emperors.
> If thou exceed thy elder brothers' worth,
> And shine in complete virtue more than they,
> Thou shalt be king before them.
>
> (*Pt. 2:* 1.4.47–52)

We hear in this an anticipation of Lear's challenge to Cordelia, "what can you say to draw / A third more opulent than your sisters?" (ll. 85–86). Tamburlaine, in the course of the play, teaches his sons to be recreations of himself. He even would have them slash their own arms to prove their legitimacy, so that in death he may be assured that his image still lives:

> My flesh, divided in your precious shapes,
> Shall still retain my spirit, though I die,
> And live in all your seeds immortally.
>
> (5.3.172–74)

His solipsism will be satisfied in the expected issue.

Like Tamburlaine's sons, Goneril and Regan understand the nature of their father's challenge and willingly comply with it. They adopt a hyperbole to suit the occasion and thereby sustain Lear's claim of absolute kingship:

> Sir, I love you more than word can wield the matter;
> Dearer than eyesight, space, and liberty,
> Beyond what can be valued, rich or rare,
> No less than life, with grace, health, beauty, honor. . . .
>
> (1.1.55–58)

Words such as these Lear expects: heroic attempts to express an inexpressible commitment. In such a way did Cressida's protestations of faith permit Troilus to maintain his role as truth; in such a way did the parasites' assurances of friendship permit Timon to play the benefactor still; in such a way did Iago's pledge of honest service permit Othello to maintain his integrity as a just revenger. In each case, the hero put his trust in mutable agents, on wills independent of his own, to measure the absoluteness of his own identity. Only Coriolanus balks at such a means of self-knowing; then he, too, succumbs.

Recognizing the error implicit in such a means of evaluation—that words in fact are *not* tantamount to deeds, that it is too easy to fall prey to flattery—Cordelia chastises her sisters for speaking untruths, hollow phrases signifying no substantial commitment. In the process, she impugns the authenticity of the heroic idiom itself. She will not mirror in verbal felicities the image her father wishes to see reflected in them. Instead, she insists that he regard her as an individual with a will of her own. Using words as absolutely as he—not, like her sisters, as rhetorical artifices—she attests to his kingship according to her bond, which, taken in the most favorable sense (as Lear and many critics of Cordelia fail to take it), suggests a love far nobler than her sisters' because freely given. Her words echo the vows of the marriage ceremony: "You have begot me, bred me, lov'd me. I / Return those duties back as are right fit, / Obey you, love you, and most honor you" (ll. 96–98). More honest in her love for Lear than her sisters are, she nevertheless fails to comply with his vain insistence that she testify to his kingly prerogative.

In her failure she resembles Calyphas, the eldest of Tamburlaine's sons who, in his refusal to bear the stamp of his father's heroic mettle, threatens Tamburlaine's public fame. Rather than come to terms with that threat, Tamburlaine, monolithic hero that he is, spurns Calyphas as a bastard and sacrifices him in a ritual rejection of that side of his own nature that he cannot admit exists:

> Bastardly boy, sprung from some coward's loins,
> And not the issue of great Tamburlaine!
>
> (1.4.69–70)

> The obloquy and scorn of my renown!
> How may my heart, thus firèd with mine eyes,
> Wounded with shame and killed with discontent,
> Shroud any thought may hold my striving hands
> From martial justice on thy wretched soul?
>
> (4.2.17–21)

In Cordelia's self-assertion Lear finds, like Tamburlaine, an explicit threat to his traditional assumptions; and so, in remarkably similar language, he repudiates her. But as he disavows his blood bond with all the rage and indignation that one associates with stage conquerors—the very excess of his disavowal serving as a defense against those who would threaten his authority—Lear takes on a role even older in the history of drama, that of tyrant. "Let it be so!" (l. 108) he declares in a spirit of pagan godhead. "His oath," writes Reuben Brower, "is the *fiat nox* of a king of darkness, an inverted echo of the Homeric Zeus. The style . . . also owes something to the heroic oath of Ovid's Jason: 'By triple Hecates holie rites, and by what other power / So ever else had residence within that secret bower.' "³ Models like these informed the rant and threats of dire punishment for which stage tyrants were notorious:

> Let it be so; thy truth, then, be thy dow'r!
> For, by the sacred radiance of the sun,
> The mysteries of Hecate and the night,
> By all the operation of the orbs
> From whom we do exist and cease to be,
> Here I disclaim all my paternal care,
> Propinquity and property of blood,
> And as a stranger to my heart and me
> Hold thee, from this, for ever.
>
> (1.1.108–15)

Lear's words carry the weight of an unalterable vow. They have the incantatory quality of Timon's curse against the Athenians who have denied him; they contain the invocation to dark powers by whom Othello swears to revenge himself on Desdemona for not loving him "all." Their rather ornate classicism is pressed further in his final curse: "The barbarous Scythian, / Or he that makes his generation messes / To gorge his appetite, shall to my bosom / Be as well neighbor'd, pitied, and reliev'd, / As thou my sometime daughter" (ll. 116–20). The closest Shakespearean analogy comes from his early masterpiece of Ovidian-Senecan grotesquery, *Titus Andronicus,* in which Titus—no Scythian, though barbarous—makes messes of the empress's generation in order to gorge *her* appetite. Lear would sooner embrace a cannibal than his daughter. So great, in his eyes, is the enormity of her crime.

The defensiveness of Lear's posture becomes even more apparent in his response to Kent's intervention:

> Here me, recreant, on thine allegiance, hear me!
> That thou hast sought to make us break our vows,
> Which we durst never yet, and with strain'd pride
> To come betwixt our sentence and our power,
> Which nor our nature nor our place can bear,
> Our potency made good, take thy reward.
>
> (1.1.168–73)

With this self-conscious and apparently self-confident refusal to brook any dissent, Lear would fix his kingship in the hierarchy so dear to Elizabethan myth-makers. He does not bother to address the merits of Kent's argument: merely the thing he is shall make his sentence just. But as in *Othello,* the language of heroic assertion becomes most strident when it is under attack and its speaker, vulnerable. Lear betrays such vulnerability in his confession that he has never "durst" break a vow and his parenthetical admission, "Which nor our nature nor our place can bear": these words reveal the limitations of Lear's self-confidence and suggest that heroic assertion may function for him here as a defense mechanism. For him to deny what his will has elected—banishment of Cordelia—in compliance with the reasons urged by Kent would be tantamount to admitting failure: Lear is not, and has never been, Lear. Rather than risk such an admission, he banishes Kent as well.

Like Timon, Lear soon discovers that he has misplaced his trust. Those loved ones in whom he has invested his own values, and from whom he has received assurances of who he is, defy him when he has no more to give. Lear learns too late that Goneril and Regan are as capable of acting independently of his will as Cordelia is, and worse than Cordelia, because she would still proffer him a daughter's love. They offer him only ingratitude. From the daughter who loved him "As much as child e'er lov'd, or father found," Goneril grows into a monarch who begs obedience from her father, "that else will take the thing she begs" (1.4.244). It is painful for Lear to endure such slights from his daughters, for they demonstrate that the power by which he has always measured the absoluteness of his kingship may have been illusory. They threaten to strip him of self-definition, and that threat prompts him to question the nature of the imperial identity to which those same daughters once so flatteringly attested:

> Does any here know me? This is not Lear.
> Does Lear walk thus? Speak thus? Where are his eyes?
> Either his notion weakens, his discernings
> Are lethargied—Ha! Waking? 'Tis not so.
> Who is it that can tell me who I am?
>
> (1.4.222–26)

"This admiration," as Goneril suggests, may be a prank (ll. 233–34) to shame his daughters into subjection; but it leads to a profound collapse of Lear's character. Like Othello's, Lear's collapses so readily because he allows himself to measure it by finite, mutable means. By reserving one hundred knights as symbols of the kingly power he supposedly is willing to forfeit, Lear repeats his mistake of the first scene, since numbers, like words, are never fixed values. Lear's insistence on calculable measures of his identity is ultimately self-defeating. They are subject to change; his identity as king, he believes, is not. Goneril and Regan, who bartered for his kingdom with calculated flattery, now haggle over his kingly identity by whittling away his knights to nothing.[4] They speak Lear's own language:

> LEAR: I can stay with Regan,
> I and my hundred knights.
> REGAN: Not altogether so.
> . . . .
>   What, fifty followers?

> Is it not well? What should you need of more?
> Yea, or so many, sith that both charge and danger
> Speak 'gainst so great a number?
>
> . . . .
>
>   If you will come to me—
> For now I spy a danger—I entreat you
> To bring but five and twenty. To no more
> Will I give place or notice.
>
> LEAR: I gave you all—
> REGAN: And in good time you gave it.
>
> . . . .
>
> LEAR: *[to Goneril]* I'll go with thee.
> Thy fifty yet doth double five-and-twenty,
> And thou art twice her love.
> GONERIL: Hear me, my lord:
> What need you five and twenty, ten, or five,
> To follow in a house where twice so many
> Have a command to tend you?
>
>   (2.4.229–63, passim)

Lear is guiltiest of the three of reductivism, maintaining that the daughter who will allow him fifty followers instead of twenty-five is twice the love of the other. He alone provides them with the means by which to reduce his being to nothing and reserve all power to themselves. Regan takes away his final prop: "What need one?" Lear's loss of his knights is analogous to Timon's loss of his wealth: without finite symbols to tell them who they are, they are reduced to "nothing." Like Othello, they lose their occupation. Little wonder, then, that Coriolanus was reluctant to display his wounds to the wondering multitude as proof of his heroism, loath to hear his nothings monstered before the senate. In the dialogue of values Shakespeare creates among his later tragic heroes, Coriolanus's belief that true heroism cannot and ought not to be reduced to tangible shows for the public gains credibility when one sees, as in Lear, the dire consequences a hero can suffer when he too credulously equates his heroism with those shows. The trouble with the traditional stage hero is that he cannot survive the strains of a less-than-absolute world; likewise, the idiom in which he is encased cannot survive the pressures of a more complex mode of mimesis. Vaunting conquerors and ranting tyrants may have been credible in plays of their day; but in Jacobean drama, they must either transcend their idiom—grow to something more lifelike—or remain objects of ridicule.

In his tragedies of this period, Shakespeare studies the hero's potential for such growth. Troilus, Othello, Timon, Lear—each of them has a choice: either to confront the inadequacy of his own means of self-evaluation or to banish the persons on whom he has counted to reflect his heroic value but who have failed him. Each, in his own way, opts for the latter. Troilus displaces his hostilities onto Diomedes; Timon withdraws to a wilderness from which he curses Athens; Othello vows revenge against Desdemona; and Lear disavows his paternity of Goneril and Regan. He employs the same language he has used to repudiate Cordelia, an indication of how tenaciously he holds to his imperious self-image, how little he has grown in introspection. "Degenerate bastard!" he curses Goneril; "I'll not trouble thee. / Yet have I left a daughter" (1.4.250–51); and he threatens that if Regan is not glad to see him, "I would divorce me from thy mother's tomb, / Sepulchring an adultress" (2.4.129–30). The curses echo Tamburlaine; and in so doing, they reinforce how Lear will regard his offspring as extensions of himself only so long as they dutifully reflect his self-image. As each daughter challenges that image, he disinherits her. He refuses to acknowledge that Cordelia's self-righteousness and Goneril's and Regan's mean egotism are values that might have sprung from him. Thus, like Timon, he progressively isolates himself from all those who once had affirmed his identity, goes into self-imposed exile divested of all those superfluities that he once thought told him who he was. "Nothing I'll bear from thee / But nakedness, thou detestable town!" exclaims Timon as he tears off his clothes (4.1.32–33); and Lear rivals him when he doffs his lendings in the storm. Nakedness for both of them represents the will to separate the self from society, the true being from the inconstant measures of that being; each wants "to strip away the horror of corruption that is civilization and fight back to the bare, essential, natural condition of man."[5] Only from nakedness will it be possible for Lear to integrate his heroic identity with a new self-awareness, to adapt the traditional ethos to the complexities of life that render that ethos simple-minded, if not downright barbarous: to wake up first to the nature of his own limitations as a man and, following that, to recognize, however begrudgingly, the extent to which his daughters are reflections of himself in ways yet unknown.

The disintegration of Lear's heroic identity is characterized by the same wavering between self-doubt and self-assertion we noticed in Othello, when his belief in Desdemona's constancy was contradicted by the ocular proof of her infidelity.[6] Lear's assertion to Goneril, "Thou shalt find / That I'll resume the shape which thou dost think / I have cast off for ever" (1.4.305–7), must be weighed against his admission to her a few lines earlier, "I am asham'd / That thou hast power to shake my manhood thus" (ll. 293–94). This doubt of his own potency is juxtaposed with a confident declaration of wrath in a later attack on both daughters: in it, the poignant breakdown of a noble, now outmoded, character type exists side by side with a persistent affirmation that the type still lives in threats that would do credit to Atreus himself. Lear begins:

> You see me here, you gods, a poor old man,
> As full of grief as age, wretched in both.

> If it be you that stirs these daughters' hearts
> Against their father, fool me not so much
> To bear it tamely; touch me with noble anger,
> And let not women's weapons, water-drops,
> Stain my man's cheeks!
>
> (2.4.272–78)

Like any good hero, Lear calls on the gods who he always thought were at his beck and call. Though a poor old man, as he now recognizes himself to be, and without the prerogatives of kingship, he would yet be touched with "noble anger" to defend his rights like an Achilles. Impotence, he admits, is a given; but like many an old man, he would not "bear it tamely." Instead, he vents his anger in a threat so hyperbolic that it sounds to Reuben Brower like a "Senecan-Marlovian parody of the hero's vein"[7]—but a parody that only draws more attention to the poignancy of Lear's heroic breakdown:

> No, you unnatural hags,
> I will have such revenges on you both,
> That all the world shall—I will do such things—
> What they are, yet I know not, but they shall be
> The terrors of the earth.
>
> (2.4.278–82)

As a whole, the speech is structured on a tension between Lear's ideal self-image, which insists that he still has absolute sway, and his realistic appraisal that he has no sway at all. Yet he seems not to be aware of the tension. He does not echo Troilus in recognizing that "This is, and is not, Lear." Rather, he manifests his internal division like Othello in wavering between two mutually exclusive beliefs without allowing them explicitly to confront one another. And that way madness lies.

Like a hero in Seneca's tragedies, Lear combats with stoic fortitude the impulse to go mad; he calls on the gods repeatedly to give him patience in adversity. But madness wins out. It permits him to reconcile his imperious self-image with his impotence without having to acknowledge a "bi-fold authority" that, were it acknowledged, would "conduce a fight / Of this strange nature, that a thing inseparate / Divides more wider than the sky and earth" (*Troilus:* 5.2.151–53). When sky and earth part for Lear, he can storm with them and still declare that the elements at war within his mind form a thing inseparate. Madness protects him from disintegrating to the point of idiomatic incoherence that characterized Othello's disintegration. Potency combats impotence; he recognizes the futility of fighting against forces greater than he, yet he still addresses those forces in the imperative mood of his former glory. Such combat yields a rant full of paradoxes to which Lear himself remains oblivious. He commands the elements to physic his pain—"Rumble thy bellyful! Spit, fire! Spout, rain!" (3.2.14)—but would call on those same elements as "servile ministers" (l. 21) to inflict torment on daughters he once thought would, like the thunder, peace at his bidding. He is at the mercy of nature, yet he controls it: he perceives no contradiction. Such mad rant links him to a long line of revengers who find their prototype in Hercules Furens, wonderful and primitive heroes with a logic all their own and whose unrestrained fury, like that of Hieronimo, proved so popular that they held the stage well into the seventeenth century. In Lear's mad rant, Shakespeare appeals to this tradition.

In calling on nature to be his champion in revenge, Lear sounds like the unrequited Timon. Both men share a belief that the hierarchic order of nature has been disrupted; ingratitude in the private sphere is, for them, symptomatic of chaos in the public sphere.[8] Thus they both attack the injustice and hypocrisy of social institutions at all levels. The specificity of Lear's attacks goes well beyond the more generalized railing of traditional revengers and makes them as satiric as Timon's:

> Let the great gods,
> That keep this dreadful pudder o'er our heads,
> Find out their enemies now. Tremble, thou wretch,
> That hast within thee undivulged crimes,
> Unwhipp'd of justice! Hide thee, thou bloody hand,
> Thou perjur'd, and thou simular of virtue
> That art incestuous! Caitiff, to pieces shake,
> That under covert and convenient seeming
> Has practic'd on man's life! Close pent-up guilts,
> Rive your concealing continents, and cry
> These dreadful summoners grace! I am a man
> More sinn'd against than sinning.
>
> (3.2.49–60)

Obsessed in his search for universal retribution, Lear imperiously invokes the gods, those dreadful summoners, to take man to trial. The crimes he would have man tried for are the same ones Timon accuses man of and that he asks Alcibiades to scourge in his great curses. But beneath Lear's hyperbole lies the tacit assumption that the gods will not, because they have thus far failed to, deal justice. Lear raises the terrible question once asked of heaven by Hieronimo:[9]

> How should we term your dealings to be just
> If you unjustly deal with those that in your justice trust?
> (*The Spanish Tragedie:* 3.2.10–11)

The answer, of course, is silence. Lear's revenge, like Timon's, must be enacted if at all by the power of the words alone: he will attain the doubtful satisfaction of a primal satirist who would set the world to rights only by cursing.

A difference in attitude, however, sets Lear and Timon a world apart. Timon, in rejecting society so completely, finds that he must reject even that part of himself which makes him "one of the conspiracy into which society so regularly resolves itself."[10] His revulsion against mankind is so absolute that inevitably it turns inward and becomes self-revulsion:

> Therefore, be abhorr'd
> All feasts, societies, and throngs of men!
> His semblable, yea, himself, Timon disdains.
>
> (4.3.20–22)

He nearly nullifies the impact of his moral indignation by speaking to such excess. His is a progress of exclusion that renders him nearly inhuman.

Lear, on the contrary, begins a slow process of inclusion. Simultaneous with his curses *against* society, evidence shows that he is looking to himself for the source of reaccommodation *to* society. That reaccommodation requires first that he recognize the nature of his error: he has been at least partly responsible for the chaos he has blamed on others. There is an implicit admission of guilt even in the curse quoted above; for although Lear sees himself as a victim of others' sins, he nevertheless includes himself among the sinners. He more explicitly admits his guilt when he observes how the Fool, a "houseless poverty" representative of common man, bides "the pelting of this pitiless storm" unprotected:

> O, I have ta'en
> Too little care of this! Take physic, pomp;
> Expose thyself to feel what wretches feel,
> That thou mayst shake the superflux to them,
> And show the heavens more just.
>
> (3.4.32–36)

Here is no heroic vaunt or curse or lament. Despite the persistence of the imperial imperative, Lear's idiom of rage moves into the humbler tones of homily. From the isolation that has marked him as an enemy to man, he begins to develop a feeling for community. He admits a wrong—he has taken too little care of this—that forms the basis for a more humanistic conception of kingship. The king, as microcosm of his society, must reflect all its constituent parts and reject none. He must be the pattern of all virtue but accept responsibility for vice. He must instruct the rich and also defend the poor. As a starting point for his heroic struggle to achieve such kingship, Lear must expose himself to what wretches feel and become the thing itself, unaccommodated man. By embracing Poor Tom, he takes a first step toward reintegrating those parts of himself that wind, rain, and hubris have rent asunder. G. K. Hunter summarizes the difference between Lear and Timon as follows: "Lear in exile absorbs humanity, and assimilates it to his own condition, rather than . . . rejecting it"; whereas Timon "fixes his gaze not on his own condition, seen as a part of universal evil, but on the evil society of Athens, seen as radically distinct from the self who is leaving it."[11] I disagree only in the last: Timon ultimately cannot divorce himself totally from mankind, and so rejects himself along with it.

This difference is manifest in the substance of their satiric imprecations against society. Although, as we have seen, their style and imagery is often comparable, their aims are patently not the same.[12] Lear's railing, even at its bitterest, moves with a humanistic spirit, never sinks to the misanthropy of Timon's. Consider comparable passages. Timon, when he finds gold in the wilderness, sees in it the alchemical power to transmute loyalties and violate laws. "This yellow slave," he says, "Will knit and break religions, bless th' accurs'd, / Make the hoar leprosy ador'd, place thieves / And give them title, knee, and approbation / With senators on the bench." Gold is the "common whore of mankind," and so Timon would use her: "I will make thee / Do thy right nature" (4.3.34–45, passim). Base commodity, thinks Timon, determines social value. As one who opposes such value, he would use gold to corrupt society further and bring it to destruction. He offers gold to Alcibiades, whores, and banditti—all to serve as instruments of his revenge. Timon's misanthropy can allow no possibility that mankind might someday be redeemed.

Lear likewise recognizes the baseness of social value and the power of gold to divert justice from its rightful course. On the surface, his speech sounds as pessimistic as Timon's—more vindictive, perhaps, because in it, Lear maintains his pose as absolute ruler and would use his authority to corrupt society further:

> Through tatter'd clothes small vices do appear;
> Robes and furr'd gowns hide all. Plate sin with gold,
> And the strong lance of justice hurtless breaks;
> Arm it in rags, a pigmy's straw does pierce it.
> None does offend, none, I say, none! I'll able 'em.
> Take that of me, my friend, who have the power
> To seal th' accuser's lips.
>
> (4.6.164–170)

Whereas Timon denies participation in such general baseness and would be its scourge, Lear would be king of it: paradoxically, he takes upon his shoulders the burden of universal sin. His catalogue of vices, to be sure, sounds like Timon's. But instead of using gold as a weapon to subdue society, as Timon wishes, Lear would "able 'em" with gold in a magnanimous Pauline inversion: none does offend, because all are guilty. Lear's satire includes himself as its object; it lacks the misanthropic force of Timon's. His mad irony softens it, molds it to an expression not of unyielding rage, but chastened self-knowledge. He who has the power to seal the accuser's lips stands self-accused. Lear subverts the traditional call for retributive justice with almost Christian charity.

Lear's growth to self-knowledge, an arduous process for one who began with no more insight than tyrants are allowed, must eventually take account of those daughters who provoked his curses against mankind in the first place. To trace the course of his inclusion of them, I must examine his revulsion against sex, which critics have likened to Timon's as simply part and parcel of the satirist's conventional idiom. For Timon, it may be true that sexual revulsion is simply conventional: nothing in the context warrants his repeated references to whoredom and venereal disease. When he urges Alcibiades's whores to "Plague all, / That your activity may defeat and quell / The source of all erection" (ll. 164–66), he speaks metaphorically: the image is striking in itself but oddly detached, as is Timon himself, from specific dramatic situation. The thrust of Lear's sexual imagery, on the other hand, is specific and motivated by deep-seated accountability. He curses Goneril,

> Hear, Nature, hear; dear goddess, hear!
> Suspend thy purpose, if thou didst intend
> To make this creature fruitful!
> Into her womb convey sterility;
> Dry up in her the organs of increase,
> And from her derogate body never spring
> A babe to honor her! If she must teem,
> Create her child of spleen, that it may live
> And be a thwart disnatur'd torment to her!
>
> (1.4.272–80)

The fact that Lear is cursing his daughter whom he once regarded as an emanation of himself—a babe "to honor" him—provokes him to a far more passionate involvement with his object than Timon ever achieves. The violence of his sexual revulsion has an underlying logic; for in wishing upon her either sterility or a child of spleen, he is betraying a deep revulsion against that part of himself that begot a splenetic daughter. He would have Goneril suffer from a thankless child in the way that he has; thus he unconsciously identifies himself with her as a parent who deserves, because he is the source of, such children.

Every time Lear casts off a daughter as a stranger to his soul, he uses imagery of the blood bond: it ironically suggests his moral complicity in their natures. He is not conscious of such complicity when he banishes Cordelia: "Here I disclaim all my paternal care, / Propinquity and property of blood." It is on the threshold of his consciousness, however, when he banishes himself from Goneril:

> We'll no more meet, no more see one another.
> But yet thou art my flesh, my blood, my daughter;
> Or rather a disease that's in my flesh,
> Which I must needs call mine. Thou art a boil.
> A plague-sore, or embossed carbuncle
> In my corrupted blood.
>
> (2.4.219–24)

Lear intends in this speech to reject his daughter outright as a thing diseased. But there is a strong suggestion that Lear's corrupted blood is receptive to the disease; indeed, that his daughters are a disease he has begotten upon himself.[13] Lear does not own his responsibility for them; but in simply acknowledging that they are one with his own flesh (and thereby betraying a thought that obviously troubles him), he becomes an accomplice in the sins for which he will take them madly to trial.

In madness, Lear consciously—if madness indeed has the clarity of a transcendent consciousness—acknowledges his complicity. The storm's abuse of his flesh, he admits with a kind of stoic self-judgment, is just penance for his having gotten "pelican daughters":

> Death, traitor! Nothing could have subdu'd nature
> To such a lowness but his unkind daughters.

He refers, of course, to Poor Tom; but in Poor Tom he sees an image of suffering mankind onto which (true to form) he projects his own experience.

> Is it the fashion, that discarded fathers
> Should have thus little mercy on their flesh?
> Judicious punishment! 'Twas this flesh begot
> Those pelican daughters.
>
> (3.4.69–74)

Young pelicans feed on the blood of their parents.[14] Lear's metaphor suggests a parasitism for which he takes full responsibility.

Lear, then, transcends Timon in self-knowledge. Timon is poised on the brink of comprehending his own part in human folly, but his heroic character proves too intractable to allow him that comprehension. In divorcing himself from society, he must divorce himself from himself; and the result of that is self-annihilation, not reaccommodation. Lear, however, in the indirection of his madness, finds direction out. Satiric invective for him is not an end, as it is for Timon, but only a means—a rhetoric he uses with increasingly mad irony—to a comprehension of the kingly part he has played so badly, and will play again but better, in a world that is not at his beck and call. In his curses, Lear rejects the image of a heroic kingship that his hypocritical daughters helped to foster in him; but he substitutes for it a humanist kingship that embraces mankind as ardently as Timon shuns it.

The differences between Timon and Lear are dramatically reinforced by their responses to those characters who would presume to educate them to a knowledge of their errors. There are two such characters in each play, a faithful steward and a cynical jester, voices of common sense to counter the voices of heroic hyperbole. The parallels between them—between Flavius and Kent, Apemantus and the Fool—are strong enough to indicate that Shakespeare borrowed from *Timon* in plotting *Lear.*

The Fool shares with Apemantus a cynical, if less systematic, vision of society in which merit never reaps rewards and corruption thrives. His prophecy pits the actual against the ideal. It satirically lists impossible social conditions:

> When every case in law is right;
> No squire in debt, nor no poor knight;
> When slanders do not live in tongues;
> Nor cutpurses come not to throngs;
> When usurers tell their gold i' th' field,
> And bawds and whores do churches build. . . .
>
> (3.2.87–92)

The logical conclusion would be that when all the social injustices implied here have been expunged, the state will be a utopia.[15] But the Fool reverses logic by claiming that such ideal conditions will bring Albion "to great confusion" (l. 86). His message is that society thrives on injustice and would not know how to cope with moral order.

Similarly, he would teach Lear to recognize the world for what it is: a place hostile to old men. Just as Apemantus observes that the "friends" upon whom Timon has built his utopian vision are mere flatterers, so the Fool observes that Lear's utopian hope for an old age spent with all the prerogatives of kingship but none of the burdens is bound to be dashed by hypocritical daughters. Only after Lear has committed himself unalterably to his folly, however, does Shakespeare introduce the Fool, apparently to serve as a tutor to instruct Lear in the nature of that folly. The Fool's pedagogic method, which runs to riddles, homely proverbs, and snatches of old songs, reduces "Lear's behaviour to the simplest, most uncomplicated images of actuality, so that the state of affairs becomes perfectly obvious":[16] Lear has cut his egg in the middle and given away both crowns, leaving his own bald; he is like the hedge-sparrow, who fed the cuckoo so long that it had its head bitten off by its young. The Fool anticipates the image Lear uses when he sees himself as the only begetter of those pelican daughters. In forcing Lear to ponder the meaning of his riddles, the Fool encourages him to come to a realistic understanding of human nature— such an understanding as Apemantus tried to promote in Timon.

But the Fool differs from Apemantus in that he is not an impartial observer. He is, in fact, deeply committed to the welfare of his benefactor. Far less dispassionate than Apemantus, the Fool imparts his lessons to Lear in order to protect him from pain in a hostile universe. He is a "sweet" fool who pines for Cordelia, suffers through Lear's blindness, and is, in a sense, a "natural"—poignant, caring, innocent: Lear's "boy." He obeys his affections rather than his reason to the point of following Lear onto the heath.

In doing so, he abjures the practical advice he has given Kent. The man deserves a coxcomb, he says, for taking the part of one who is out of favor. The line has an Apemantean ring:

> Let go thy hold when a great wheel runs down a hill, lest it break thy neck with following; but the great one that goes upward, let him draw thee after. When a wise man gives thee better counsel, give me mine again. I would have none but knaves follow it, since a fool gives it. (2.4.70–75)

The Fool is playing with an ironic inversion of values that baffled Dr. Johnson.[17] His advice would be regarded as wisdom only by a knave. A fool's wisdom is of another sort. The Fool would not have Kent follow his advice because Kent is a fool who, like him, might better follow the dictates of his heart than of his mind.

By taking Lear's part, the Fool subscribes to a higher morality that lesser men might call folly. His decision to follow Lear onto the heath is in its own right a heroic act, an act of love, an affirmation of intuitive value. Yet his express purpose is to recall Lear to his senses, not to be raised himself to Lear's heroic mode of apprehending the world. He would compromise Lear's values to save Lear's skin:[18]

> O nuncle, court holy-water in a dry house is better than this rainwater out o' door. Good nuncle, in, ask thy daughters' blessing. Here's a night pities neither wise men nor fools. (3.2.10–13)

In his dedication to Lear, the Fool transcends the values of the court; yet, as a creature whose role is defined by the court, he has no internal resources and is not fully capable of understanding Lear's commitment to endure the worst. In this respect he again, in a way, resembles Apemantus, who advises Timon to return to Athens and play the flatterer himself, accommodate himself to social values, be a beast with the other beasts:

> Be thou a flatterer now, and seek to thrive
> By that which has undone thee. Hinge thy knee,
> And let his very breath whom thou'lt observe
> Blow off thy cap; praise his most vicious strain,
> And call it excellent.
>
> (4.3.212–16)

Yet the apparent similarity of the Fool's advice to Lear reveals how essentially different he is from Apemantus; for he would have Lear return to the castle only in order to stay dry—his motive, charitable; whereas Apemantus would have Timon return to Athens only out of professional spite, to prove that Timon is no nobler than the most abject flatterer.

Apemantus, however, anticipates what Lear does, in sarcastic show, when Regan begins to abate his train of knights: kneel and ask his daughter's blessing (2.4.152ff). This unsightly trick points up how alien the Fool's advice is, however well-meant, to Lear's own uncompromising nature. The Fool and Apemantus, then, are limited in their role as educators. They cannot abjure the world, as their great-souled pupils can. Apemantus by profession, and the Fool by innocence, fail to realize that heroic commitment has a logic of its own that no worldly wisdom can hope to understand. Thus their expedient advice does not so much diminish the hero for being a fool as ennoble him for resolving not to take the easy way out.

The Fool and Apemantus are crucial yardsticks by which one measures the magnitude of Lear's and Timon's heroic responses to society. Timon refuses to acknowledge Apemantus's teaching altogether. He admits no error and resists all attempts to enlighten him. Instead of including Apemantus in a general amnesty with society, Timon flytes with him and sends him screaming back to Athens: "Away, thou issue of a mangy dog! / Choler does kill me that thou art alive; / I swoon to see thee" (ll. 371–73). By refusing to come to terms with Apemantus, Timon allows him to remain an autonomous critical voice—a voice to which we listen, to Timon's detriment. Shakespeare ends with a cynical perspective on Timon that encourages us to regard him, as Apemantus does, as too willful in the extremity of his hate to be fully tragic.

In *Lear*, Shakespeare does not allow us the option of *eironic* detachment to the end; for Lear himself fully comprehends the Fool's teaching, benefits from it, then transcends it in the emblematic scene in which he magnanimously protects the Fool from the storm that he, with his less heroic spirit, cannot endure. The Fool, having been thus absorbed by a greater and more inclusive consciousness, disappears after the third act. In becoming self-critical, Lear plays both king and fool: he incorporates the perspective of the one independent critic through whom we might have continued to detach ourselves from him. The inclusion of that voice within his own heroic being causes us to admire him the more.

The second of Lear's tutors, Kent, is patterned on Timon's steward, Flavius: a man of plain and simple integrity who would fain persuade his master to see the error of his ways. The deliberate rudeness of Kent's speech emphasizes the import of his censure:

> Be Kent unmannerly,
> When Lear is mad. What wouldst thou do, old man?
> Think'st thou that duty shall have dread to speak
> When power to flattery bows?
> To plainness honor's bound,
> When majesty falls to folly.

> (1.1.145–50)

Flavius is governed by a like sense of honor when, with plain speaking, he attempts to counsel Timon. "At many times I brought in my accounts, / Laid them before you," he reminds Timon:

Yea, 'gainst th' authority of manners, pray'd you
To hold your hand more close. I did endure
Not seldom, nor no slight checks, when I have
Prompted you in the ebb of your estate
And your great flow of debts.

(2.2.137–38; 142–46)

What Flavius reports to have suffered we in fact *see* Kent suffer from his master's rage—no slight checks indeed: banishment. In this, Kent is more like Flavius than Perillus, the analogous good counselor in the *King Leir* source play who is never rebuked for his advice. Kent and Flavius are alike, too, in their absolute commitment to service. Even having endured checks that could rightly absolve them of all bonds of loyalty, they both return humbly to their masters and offer up their lives to their service. Flavius does so in his own person: "I will present / My honest grief unto him, and, as my lord, / Still serve him with my life" (4.3.474–76). Kent makes his bid in an assumed guise that Lear does not recognize. Their exchange is well know. "What wouldst thou?" "Service." "Who wouldst thou serve?" "You." "Dost thou know me, fellow?" "No, sir; but you have that in your countenance which I would fain call master." "What's that?" "Authority." (1.4.22–30)

Kent, however, has even more in common with Flavius's original, the steward Laches in the *Timon* comedy, than with Flavius himself.[19] Like him, and unlike Flavius, Kent returns in humble disguise to serve his master: Laches as an indigent soldier, Kent as "a very honest-hearted fellow, and poor as the King" (ll. 19–20). Both of them, unlike Flavius, mock the fawning parasites who embody the values of the "civilized" world. Just as Laches hoodwinks the foppish Hermogenes, so Kent soundly beats the obsequious Oswald. And whereas Flavius, who would willingly abide with Timon, is told to return to Athens, Kent, like Laches, is allowed to shepherd his master through spiritual upheaval and admonishes him to have patience in the face of adversity. "Master, why muse you thus?" asks Laches. "what thinke you on? / Why are your eyes soe fixed on the earth? / Pull vp your spirits: all aduersity / By patience is made more tolerable" (3.5.1566–69). Kent delivers his stoic commonplaces with remarkably similar phrasing:

How do you, sir? Stand you not so amaz'd.
· ·
O pity! Sir, where is the patience now
That you so oft have boasted to retain?

(3.6.33; 57–58)

I mention these similarities with the old comedy only to show that the legend of Timon and his heroic excesses was inextricably bound, in Shakespeare's imagination, to the legend of Lear. A source for one play could serve as a source for the other; for in both, he was testing the limits and potentials of the same kind of heroism.

Kent, from the first, champions Cordelia as a defender of virtue against Lear's "hideous rashness" (1.1.152); and when he follows Lear in banishment, he dramatizes the same duty towards him as that Cordelia has spoken of—love freely given. He thus becomes Cordelia's symbolic representative in her absence; his presence by Lear's side insures that Cordelia's values are still a present force. On a more naturalistic level, Kent maintains a correspondence with Cordelia through an unnamed gentleman that prepares us for her reappearance and reconciliation with Lear. Through Kent's good offices, Lear never fully loses touch with her. His acknowledgment of her is the logical conclusion to the process of reaccommodation through which Kent has shepherded him.

Kent, then, plays a more vital role than Flavius. He is directly responsible for bringing Lear to a final reconciliation with the society he has banished forever. Flavius fails to do the same for Timon. As a mere steward, he has not enough dramatic stature to signify the full weight of human dignity and therefore is insufficient to bring Timon to a regenerated view of humanity. Although Timon does not exclude Flavius with as much invective as he excludes other Athenians, he excludes him nonetheless and thereby turns his back on a tragic awareness of his own mistaken judgment of mankind:

> Thou singly honest man,
> Here, take. The gods out of my misery
> Has sent thee treasure. Go, live rich and happy,
> But thus condition'd: thou shalt build from men;
> Hate all, curse all, show charity to none,
> . . . .
> Stay not; fly, whilst thou art blest and free.
> Ne'er see thou man, and let me ne'er see thee.
>   (4.3.528–32; 540–41)

In Flavius, Timon recognizes a blessing of honesty, but he cannot allow that recognition to penetrate his vision. Were he to include one redeemed man in his vision of unredeemed humanity, he would shatter his integrity as a misanthrope—in theatrical terms, forfeit the core of his character. Flavius must remain, for him, the exception to prove the rule. Kent, on the other hand, functions far more effectively as the agent of Lear's spiritual reformation.

Awaking from madness to recognize both Cordelia and Kent, Lear leaves behind, as in a bad dream, his dependence on worldly measures and the spirit of mean rationalism that marred his earlier kingship. From the Tamburlaine-like speeches of banishment that characterized his tyranny, he emerges with humility and the will to fuse together those elements he rent asunder:

> Methinks I should know you, and know this man,
> Yet I am doubtful; for I am mainly ignorant
> What place this is, and all the skills I have
> Remembers not these garments, nor I know not
> Where I did lodge last night. Do not laugh at me;
> For, as I am a man, I think this lady
> To be my child Cordelia.
>
> (4.7.66–72)

The grand cadences of Lear's earlier Marlovian idiom and the satiric invective of his rant on the heath are heard no more. They have given way to a new idiom, simpler and more dignified: its sentiments, more homiletic; its heroism, not of this world. S. L. Goldberg accounts for Lear's emergence from madness as follows: "From the bewildered, fragmented awareness of a world that seems correspondingly fragmented, the speech gradually begins to take a direction in its wandering until it eventually finds its coherence—its heart, as it were—in the final, cohesive acknowledgment."[20]

Cordelia's gentle reassurance that she is indeed his daughter and that she has "no cause" not to love him as freely as before opens Lear's eyes to a regenerated vision of humanity that is irrationally great—a vision of reciprocal and charitable love unlike anything Lear has ever known. In his negative reply to Cordelia's question, "Shall we not see these daughters and these sisters?" (5.3.7), he transcends the cries for justice and revenge that so constricted his vision on the heath, and Timon's vision to the end. For curses, he would substitute a vision of paradise:

> When thou dost ask me blessing, I'll kneel down,
> And ask of thee forgiveness. So we'll live,
> And pray, and sing, and tell old tales, and laugh
> At gilded butterflies, and hear poor rogues
> Talk of court news; and we'll talk with them too—
> Who loses and who wins; who's in, who's out—
> And take upon 's the mystery of things,
> As if we were God's spies; and we'll wear out,
> In a wall'd prison, packs and sects of great ones,
> That ebb and flow by th' moon.
>
> (5.3.10–19)

There is more constancy of purpose and heroic self-assurance in this speech than in any speech spoken by the more idiomatically "heroic" Lear of earlier acts. He echoes Cordelia's stoic resolution to "out-frown false fortune's frown" (l. 6) and vows to forget past injustices. He casts off as strangers all the trappings of temporal power that define "packs and sects of great ones" such as Goneril, Regan, and Edmund and that once defined his own kingship. For them, he substitutes an exalted *contemptus mundi* that dwarfs Timon's unenlightened contempt. Lear becomes a hero of another sort: his conversion alludes to the conversions of Rex Vivus, Rex Mundus, and Humanum Genus in the old Moralities, whose careers took them from tyranny, through humiliation, to reformation. Even what sounds like Lear's old voice of heroic defiance issues instead an affirmation of his new faith. "He that parts us," he tells Cordelia, "shall bring a brand from heaven, / And fire us hence like foxes" (ll. 22–23). His faith is too strong to allow him to credit the power of his enemies. The vengeance he once had sworn against them he now delegates to time: "The good-years shall devour them, flesh and fell, / Ere they shall make us weep!" (ll. 24–25). Biblical imagery, not pagan, now strengthens his will to endure the worst.

Shakespeare does not let Lear linger long in such spiritual affirmations.[21] Cordelia is killed. The act may be a cruel joke played by a merciless God, or perhaps it testifies to a universe where there is no God at all. Lear unleashes his pain in one long howl. Against the "men of stones" (l. 261) he reasserts—as if in defiance of his own helplessness—an idiom of heroic greatness: "Had I your tongues and eyes, I'd use them so / That heaven's vault should crack" (ll. 262–63). But he uses such language only conditionally now—"*Had* I your tongues"—for all he has the courage to do is face the fact: "I know when one is dead, and when one lives; / She's dead as earth" (ll. 264–65). To dramatize such courage, the excesses of heroic speech are superfluous.

Yet Lear struggles still to oppose the fact; and that struggle, too, takes courage. In prison, he instinctively forsakes patience for an act of heroic revenge: "I kill'd the slave that was a-hanging thee" (l. 278). The act prompts him to boast of an earlier self that never would have stood for such insurrection: "I have seen the day, with my good biting falchion / I would have made them skip" (ll. 280–81); and next to such heroic recollection, his subsequent admission, "I am old now," signifies not a return to patience, but remorse for something lost. Even at the end, Lear's old heroic ethos struggles against his patience just as it did in madness. He *wills* Cordelia to live again. In his imagination, the feather stirs. And at last, he confronts the gods with an unanswerable question: "Why should a dog, a horse, a rat, have life, / And thou no breath at all?" (ll. 311–12). There is no humility in the question. By asking it, Lear asserts himself against a universe that has made a mockery of all he knew. He demonstrates how a heroism of self-abnegation can endure but fitfully in a world that is constant only in testing that heroism with horrors.

Our tragic admiration of Lear springs directly from his indomitable spirit, from the failure of the homiletic idiom totally to suppress the "old" Lear. He is willing to look at the world unflinchingly. He persists in questioning causes and is unwilling to settle for pat answers. As Susan Snyder has lucidly shown, Shakespeare invests *Lear* with radically opposed but equally conventional schemes by which characters explain life to themselves: either as divine comedy, wherein all suffering leads to a final heavenly reward, or as absurdist comedy, wherein all acts are meaningless, all suffering without cause. Lear finally stands majestically above these alternatives because he refuses to concede that man is merely a pawn "in a preestablished scheme, following the way laid out for him by a higher intelligence, or . . . an aimless atom in a universe of aimless atoms."²² Certain only that neither scheme can justify the agony of his life, Lear falls in upon himself and trusts only what he knows—his capacity to feel, to question, to cry out. By doing so, he succeeds in maintaining a heroic stance against a world that would deny him all.

Lear's greatness is achieved in part by Shakespeare's juxtaposition and fusion of antithetical heroic traditions. Lear's choice of his evil daughters over his good may find its proper analogue in the willful choice of folly enacted by Rex Vivus in *The Pride of Life* or even by Gorboduc; certainly the emphasis on erroneous moral judgment is the same. But Lear does not speak the language of a Morality. He speaks with a heroic assertiveness that makes the analogy with Tamburlaine's rejection of his defiant son at least as apt. Nor, in madness, does he undergo the process of humiliation in the same way Morality tyrants undergo it. Though Shakespeare may have borrowed the pattern of Lear's spiritual education from native drama, Lear deviates from that pattern by voicing his rage and despair in the language of epic heroism, by railing against society in the voice of a Jacobean satirist, and by never settling absolutely into a Christian patience with life. The profundity of his education may make Lear, as Ruth Nevo says, "the vessel of all ironic knowledge";²³ but such knowledge does not lend him the *eiron*'s detachment from heroic values and their expression. In his most ironic admissions of accountability for the world's sins, Lear holds fast to the imperative mood. He is never a Hamlet. Even at the end, when he seems most chastened, his self-assertion will not down.

The traditional heroic ethos that informs his behavior in the early acts connotes certain values, both positive and negative, that Shakespeare would have us understand as pagan: willfulness and inflexibility, desire for wrath and revenge, magnanimity and greatness of soul. The idiom in which these values are expressed is, as I have tried to show, conventional: Lear himself comes to recognize it as far too defensive and egotistical an idiom for one who would be a truly moral man, and its worldliness contrasts sharply with the idiom of Lear's renunciation of the world. Yet Lear's refusal to let the old idiom die in the crucible of his world is what we most admire about him. He is no saint. Though he accepts responsibility for the world's ills, he does so as a king. As a king, he knows and fears his enemies; he defies them to the end. He would, though in apparent contempt of the world, cling tenaciously to his life with Cordelia; and when he sees that he cannot even be king of that, he looks darkness in the eye and demands to know "Why?" The persistence of Lear's heroic selfhood creates a tension with his growth to patience and conversion to humility. To deny its force is to miss a part of what makes the play so profound a study of human potential.

8

Bellona's Bridegroom or Dwarfish Thief?

*F*ew would dispute that *Macbeth* is heroic tragedy. We customarily speak of Macbeth, in the company of Lear and Othello, as one of Shakespeare's "great" tragic heroes. What qualifies him for heroism, however, is very much in question. It is difficult to separate our conception of Macbeth's heroism from morality, and particularly so because modern criticism has made such progress in discovering a Morality basis for much Elizabethan drama. Striving to correct the nineteenth-century conception of Macbeth as a tormented romantic, a visionary precursor of Milton's Satan, recent critics have tended to subordinate his greatness and individuality as a hero, just as they have Lear's, to the play's moral and aesthetic patterns: they do not willingly concede that he, as hero, embodies values that may be admired apart from or even despite these patterns.[1] Typically, Macbeth is seen to degenerate from a noble warrior to a vicious tyrant—from Bellona's bridegroom to dwarfish thief. His heroism is measured largely in terms of moral criteria. These criteria suggest that we should admire him most for putting duty to the king before personal ambition, for feeling revulsion at the thought of crime, and for apprehending his guilt with horror, and that we should cease to admire him when he hardens in his resolve to sin. A more reductive judgment on him would encourage us to withhold our admiration even from the outset. Macbeth—so the argument goes—is a man of more brawn than brain, more action than thought, whose heroic diction cannot be substantiated by any demonstrable greatness of character. In the words of Richard Moulton, harbinger of much modern criticism of the play, Macbeth's lofty tone may be attributed to "no more than virtuous education and surroundings"; his moral sensibility, to those stock notions he has "retained just because he has no disposition to examine them."[2] If one carries this view to an extreme, Macbeth becomes—paradoxical phrase—a pedestrian hero, a pragmatist who speaks heroic verse without conviction and who thereby reduces it to high astounding hollowness, a villain no better morally than Richard III. In him, idiom is divorced from

169

ethos; Macbeth speaks like a hero but is none. He is incapable of investing heroic speech with enough thought and feeling to make it genuinely expressive of inherent nobility.

Not many would fully subscribe to this view of Macbeth.[3] Yet its exaggeration is symptomatic of how far Macbeth's status as a hero has fallen in our century. The modern bias for antiheroes has encouraged us to put Macbeth in a gray flannel suit, deck him out as an exemplum of our own amorality, and deny to him the self-determination, the will to endure, and the superhuman capacity to suffer that set heroes apart from Everyman. Major studies of the heroic traditions, both Graeco-Roman and Renaissance, that inform Shakespearean tragedy have by and large ignored *Macbeth*.[4] Even those few that *have* acknowledged a certain heroism in Macbeth have failed to agree on what aspect of his character moves us to admiration: his military prowess? his struggle to overcome temptation? his imaginative apprehension of guilt? his stoic acceptance of fate? all of the above?

One reason—perhaps the chief reason—for contemporary uncertainty about the nature of Macbeth's heroism, it seems to me, is our incomplete understanding of Shakespeare's use of the heroic traditions available to him. Shakespeare dramatizes Macbeth's tragedy through subtle shifts in the register of his diction, through the opposition and exchange of traditional idioms, each expressive of certain heroic values and assumptions that conflict with, but do not disqualify, one another. It is necessary to recognize these alternate conceptions of heroism in order to credit Macbeth as a fully heroic figure whose moral quandary is portrayed *through* the conflict of idioms and whom we do not cease to admire when he embraces a career of evil. Although the play concerns the dehumanizing effects of evil, an alertness to the register of Macbeth's diction teaches us not to make a monster of him in the simple-minded manner of a Morality. His tragedy hinges on morality, of course, but it need not be regarded exclusively within the frame of Christian reference.

In the second scene of the play, Shakespeare uses narration to body forth a traditionally heroic Macbeth. Much as the Messenger in *1 Henry VI* details Talbot's achievements in an elevated heroic style, so the bleeding Captain, come fresh from war, reports Macbeth's bravery in the round cadences and epic similes of earlier English practitioners of heroic drama—Kyd, whose ghost of Andrea narrates the epic events that will determine the action of *The Spanish Tragedie,* and Marlowe, whose Aeneas narrates the fall of Troy to his attendant *Dido, Queene of Carthage.* The "merciless Macdonwald," we are told, seems to have whorish fortune smiling on his rebel's cause, but proves too weak:

> For brave Macbeth—well he deserves that name—
> Disdaining Fortune, with his brandish'd steel,
> Which smok'd with bloody execution,

> Like valor's minion carved out his passage
> Till he fac'd the slave;
> Which nev'r shook hands, nor bade farewell to him,
> Till he unseam'd him from the nave to th' chops. . . .
>
> (1.2.18–24)

His victory is no sooner enjoyed, however, than threatened by a new assault by the "Norweyan lord," which the Captain heralds with an epic simile:

> As whence the sun 'gins his reflection
> Shipwracking storms and direful thunders break,
> So from that spring whence comfort seem'd to come
> Discomfort swells.
>
> (1.2.27–30)

This simile is soon overborne by another even more heroic, which asserts that this new assault dismayed Macbeth and Banquo "as sparrows eagles, or the hare the lion. . . . they were / As cannons overcharg'd with double cracks, / So they doubly redoubled strokes upon the foe" (ll. 37–40). Though pared of the excesses of its predecessors, this narration has palpable signs of the English Seneca: graphic blood-letting, jaded adjectives such as "dismal" and "direful," words of abuse such as "slave," and grand personifications of fortune and war. The description of Macbeth's unseaming Macdonwald from the nave to the chops may owe a direct debt to Studley's translation of the *Hippolytus*, wherein the Nuntius relates how "a Stake with Trunchion burnt" rips open Hippolytus's "Paunch": "From rived Grine to th' Navell stead within his wombe it raught." And if Shakespeare was not echoing Seneca's line directly, he may have been echoing its imitation in Marlowe's narration of how Pyrrhus slaughtered Priam: "Then from the nauell to the throat at once, / He ript old *Priam*."[5] If Shakespeare thus patronizes an anachronistic style, he nevertheless does not parody it as he does in *Hamlet*, where the Player's narration of Aeneas's tale to Dido borders on Marlovian burlesque, its sentiments direly undercut by a context skeptical of antique heroism. This early in *Macbeth*, Shakespeare registers no such skepticism.

The Captain's testimony leads us to expect a kind of epic, almost Homeric hero—bloody, bold, and resolute. If Macbeth's brave deeds are done in service to the king—something that would ally him more closely with Virgilian than Homeric warriors—they are nevertheless not entirely benign and selfless. Behind his soldierly virtue lie both an assertive hauteur and an ambivalent cruelty that characterize a host of Elizabethan conqueror heroes, from Tamburlaine to Caesar, all of whom, like Macbeth, disdain fortune and carve out passages for themselves.[6] The Captain's renewed emphasis on such hauteur and cruelty near the end of his narration—"Except they meant to bathe in reeking wounds, / Or memorize another Golgotha, / I cannot tell" (ll. 41–43)—earns Macbeth the epithet

"Bellona's bridegroom" (l. 57), a man of steel who makes love to war as ardently as Coriolanus will: the epithet caps the antique heroic style in which Macbeth is here described.

What we are led to expect is not necessarily what we get. Macbeth's first line recalls not the style of the Nuntius, but the more equivocal style of the Weird Sisters: "So foul and fair a day I have not seen" (1.3.38). A hero such as the one on whom the Captain models his report would never speak a line like this: he must be unambiguous in what he does, absolute in what he says. Any doubt or equivocation, expressive as they are of uncertain values or direction, would cause him to be no epic hero, but Hamlet. The Weird Sisters are the source of linguistic uncertainty in the play: "When the battle's lost and won," "Fair is foul, and foul is fair," "Lesser than Macbeth, and greater," "Not so happy, yet much happier." And if their language is not always paradoxical, it nevertheless employs the *figures* of paradox, antithesis and conundrum to create a rhetorical counterpoint to the straightforward assertiveness of the heroic style.[7]

That counterpoint underlines Macbeth's tragic uncertainty. That he, the Bellona's bridegroom we have been led to expect, utters an equivocal clause indicates immediately his capacity to entertain ambiguities, to weigh what seems against what is. It bears witness that his selfhood is disjoined from the heroic image he projects:

> This supernatural soliciting
> Cannot be ill, cannot be good. If ill,
> Why hath it given me earnest of success,
> Commencing in a truth? I am Thane of Cawdor.
> If good, why do I yield to that suggestion
> Whose horrid image doth unfix my hair
> And make my seated heart knock at my ribs,
> Against the use of nature?
>
> (1.3.130–37)

The rhetorical balance of opposites dramatizes Macbeth's moral uncertainty and reflects his ability to sustain antithetical values—heroic duty to his king, and the ambition that would overwhelm that duty. He cannot easily resolve these antitheses. His thought so shakes his single state of man—the integrity any traditional hero must maintain—"that function / Is smother'd in surmise, and nothing is / But what is not" (ll. 140–42). He enters the realm of relative valuation, as no antique hero would. Constancy, for him, is turned topsy-turvy; "horrible imaginings" prevail; his identification of himself as a hero at one with his world is called into question.

The next scene dramatizes this tension of opposites more fully. Formally, the ceremony at Duncan's court is emblematic of a perfect order. When

Macbeth comes from war, heaped with honors, to vow allegiance to Duncan, he declares himself a defender of that order:

> The service and the loyalty I owe,
> In doing it, pays itself. Your Highness' part
> Is to receive our duties; and our duties
> Are to your throne and state children and servants,
> Which do but what they should, by doing everything
> Safe toward your love and honor.
>
> (1.4.22–27)

Service, loyalty, duty, love, and honor: these are the public virtues by which Romans tamed the hubris of the Homeric hero and made him a hero of state, virtues reinforced by the medieval faith in degree that still obtained in the Renaissance. Titus, who knelt before Saturninus to offer up the spoils of war, manifested such virtues; and so did Talbot, that paragon of courtesy, as he dropped his sword before the feet of Henry VI,

> And with submissive loyalty of heart
> Ascribes the glory of his conquest got
> First to my God and next unto your Grace.
>
> (*1 Henry VI:* 3.4.10–12)

Macbeth pays lip service to such virtues; and the stage picture, as it alludes to Shakespeare's earlier plays, affirms them.

Macbeth's formal adherence to them, however, belies the more complex tension between his ethical and his more willful conceptions of heroism. As the previous scene indicated, Macbeth is capable of masking private desire with shows of public duty. Though he still believes (in an ethical frame of mind) that his chiefest duty is to his king, his progression towards an amoral heroism of self-interest is marked by an aside spoken in the equivocal phrases of his first soliloquy:

> Stars, hide your fires;
> Let not light see my black and deep desires.
> The eye wink at the hand; yet let that be
> Which the eye fears, when it is done, to see.
>
> (1.4.50–53)

The odd dissociation of the self from the hand that acts and the eye that sees—a dissociation that will recur, especially in the dagger soliloquy— indicates how deeply Macbeth would like to divest himself of moral responsibility for the consequences of acting on his will. The tension between his will and his conscience casts an ironic shadow on this otherwise traditional, ceremonial scene.

Lady Macbeth, when she appears in the scene immediately following, defines her husband's nature in the same balanced antitheses he has used:

> Thou wouldst be great,
> Art not without ambition, but without
> The illness should attend it. What thou wouldst highly,
> That wouldst thou holily; wouldst not play false,
> And yet wouldst wrongly win.
>
> (1.5.18–22)

Her imitation of his rhetorical style is reductive, however. She echoes him only to mock the equivocal nature such antitheses represent. In his mouth, they reflect a heroic struggle; in hers, they brand him as weak and indecisive. The ethical man—whom she disparages as "holy"—who has no illness in his nature cannot be great; her husband would be both ethical *and* great. The antithesis forms a stylistic bridge to the idiom of self-assertion she will offer him as an alternative, a diction to beat down his doubt and force him to a resolution:

> Hie thee hither,
> That I may pour my spirits in thine ear,
> And chastise with the valor of my tongue
> All that impedes thee from the golden round. . . .
>
> (1.5.25–28)

She recasts the heroic style of the bleeding Captain in a mold of amoral self-possession; she scorns the ethics of public duty that ensnare the will and invokes in their place a passionate commitment to the self alone, like that shared by the earlier Richard Duke of York, Aaron the Moor, and Richard III. I find evidence, in fact, that Shakespeare had York's famous soliloquy from *2 Henry VI* in mind while he was composing Lady Macbeth's speech—the one that ends with a Tamburlainian resolution not to rest content until he wears "the golden circuit on [his] head" (3.1.352). The resonances are strong:[8]

> Now, York, or never, steel thy fearful thoughts,
> And change misdoubt to resolution.
> Be that thou hop'st to be, or what thou art
> Resign to death; it is not worth th' enjoying.
> Let pale-fac'd fear keep with the mean-born man,
> And find no harbor in a royal heart.
>
> (3.1.331–36)

We hear in this an anticipation of "Glamis thou art, and Cawdor, and shalt be / What thou art promis'd" (ll. 15–16), and just as strongly, an anticipation of her later taunts that Macbeth's hope looks green and pale, that his manhood is suspect, that he fears to be in act and valor what he is in desire—taunts Macbeth takes to heart when he attempts to change *his* misdoubt for resolution. Shakespeare apparently conceived Lady Macbeth's character in part through the idiom of old conqueror drama. He invested her diction with the hyperbole of private ambition for the sweet fruition of an earthly crown, with a heroic drive untamed by the ethics of state—a diction reminiscent of those aspiring conquerors who fired the imaginations of audiences years earlier. But unlike them, Lady Macbeth cannot achieve her heroic ambitions on her own. First, she must implant her will in her husband. She must win him over to her idiom.

Her second soliloquy advances her promise to chastise his equivocal nature with the valor of her tongue. The presence of a woman soliloquizing about cruelty suggests in itself a Senecan influence, and Inga-Stina Ewbank has discovered allusions to the *Medea*—to Studley's embellished translation more than to the original—that strengthen the case for specific influence.[9] Medea invokes Hecate to help her take revenge on Jason by murdering first his royal family, then her own children. She attempts to unsex herself by banishing fear and pity as strangers to her soul so that she may do a "Most divelish, desperate, dreadfull deede": "If ought of auncient corage doe dwell within my brest," she says, "Exile all foolysh Female feare, and pity from thy mynde."[10] Lady Macbeth adopts Medea's incantation to the spirits (though she never explicitly calls on Hecate, who appears later in the play) and her desire to be unsexed so that she may do a deed that, like Medea's, will violate the natural order of the universe—"force heaven, earth, and hell to quake and tremble sore," in Studley's terms:

> Come, you spirits
> That tend on mortal thoughts, unsex me here,
> And fill me from the crown to the toe top-full
> Of direst cruelty! Make thick my blood;
> Stop up th' access and passage to remorse,
> That no compunctious visitings of nature
> Shake my fell purpose, nor keep peace between
> Th' effect and it! Come to my woman's breasts,
> And take my milk for gall, you murd'ring ministers. . . .
> (1.5.40–48)

Lady Macbeth's mind, like Medea's, is suffused with the courage to be cruel, and her thoughts progress likewise from witchcraft, to royal murder, and finally to the slaying of her own children. Medea's imagination of unnatural deeds leads to a climactic image of hands bathed in blood, and it is an image that will be central to the Macbeths' apprehension of *their* unnatural deed as well:

> How wilt thou from thy spouse depart? as him thou followed hast
> In bloud to bath thy handes and traytrous lyves to wast.

From Medea, then, Lady Macbeth derives a language of heroic obsession divorced from moral law. Its Senecanism tempts Macbeth with an attractive alternative to his enervated heroism of state. Macbeth can seize on such emotive language with far more energy than on the ceremonial language of chivalric duty he mouthed in Duncan's court. The temptation is, as much as anything else, rhetorical.

These two heroic idioms, the ethical and the willful, clash head on at the end of act 1. Macbeth remonstrates with his ambition by uttering a series of ethical commonplaces consonant with others' heroic portrayal of him. He recites a sequence of conditions that represent his desire to gain the crown without risk: *If* the deed were done, *If* the assassination could trammel up the consequence, *If* this blow might be the be-all and the end-all. But his recitation only serves to strengthen the moral objections that render these conditions untenable. Judgment teaches him that evil always pays a price, that deeds have consequences. Ideals of chivalry remind him that he owes hospitality to his king and kinsman. Duncan's own virtues choke his ambition in the utterance by kindling in him an image of pity as a newborn babe, and pity deters him from violating the sacred bonds of honor by which he, like Talbot, identifies himself as a hero. Thus armed with reason, Macbeth asserts his nobility against an encroaching will, "straining almost to incoherence for words that can help him believe in his own decency."[11]

Lady Macbeth challenges that decency by accusing him of a cowardly failure of desire—of "Letting 'I dare not' wait upon 'I would,' / Like the poor cat i' th' adage" (1.7.45–46). Daring, of course, is an essential ingredient in any hero; so when she accuses him of being "afeard / To be the same in thine own act and valor / As thou art in desire" (ll. 40–42), she in effect is attacking his manhood. For a true man, she argues, desire should be the only impetus to action: her model for such manhood would be a pagan such as Tamburlaine. Then she compounds her attack by twisting what, in a more amorous context, would be a lady's appeal to her knight into a dare of her own: "Such I account thy love" (l. 40).

In self-defense, Macbeth resorts to the Renaissance ideal of ethical heroism he has espoused in his soliloquy. "I dare do all that may become a man," he protests. "Who dares do more is none" (ll. 47–48).[12] Judgment distinguishes hero from brute; and for such heroism, amoral conquerors do not qualify. But Lady Macbeth will not stand for such qualification. She turns the discussion back to *her* conception of a man as one who translates raw will into action. "When you durst do it, then you were a man," she reminds him, alluding to his earlier dare to kill Duncan; and she further suggests that by gaining the crown, he would become even more manly, in her estimation: "to be more than what you were, you would / Be so much more the man" (ll. 50–52).

Then she shifts tack by reminding him of the vow he has taken. When a traditional hero swears to do something, the deed should be as good as done; this much is central to the ancient heroic ethos. But Macbeth, she asserts, has reneged on his word, and it is up to her imaginatively to demonstrate for him how absolute a commitment an oath requires:

> I have given suck, and know
> How tender 'tis to love the babe that milks me;
> I would, while it was smiling in my face,
> Have pluck'd my nipple from his boneless gums
> And dash'd the brains out, had I so sworn as you
> Have done to this.
>
> (1.7.55–60)

With this, her allusions to *Medea* come full circle. Her cruelty destroys her husband's babe of pity. Like her, Medea in act 4 bares her breasts and sacrifices her own blood to Hecate in order to steel herself "to do the most unnatural of all deeds, kill her own children—though pity, in the shape of her babes, stands literally before her."[13] Medea's mention of her "tender Children," her "naked breast and dugges layde out," and her "hardned heart" all figure in Lady Macbeth's imagery, wherein she persuades her husband how unnatural it would be for him to violate his oath. She uses Senecan diction to argue for the *ethics* of heroism—the very ethics she has previously disparaged in him.

Drawing from the rhetoric of traditional heroism that Macbeth has insistently applied to himself, Lady Macbeth sets out two topoi, the dare and the vow, as snares with which to catch him in a contradiction. Although he has enlisted all the duties of the conventional Renaissance hero in defense of his inaction, he has neglected the hero's greater duty to do what he has sworn to do. She thus traps him on a point of honor where all her arguments *against* honor have failed; and to do so, she depends more on the force of diction than on the force of logic.

In accepting Lady Macbeth's concept of manhood long enough to do the deed, Macbeth persuades himself to view man as a predatory animal unfettered by ethics. Once the deed has committed him to this view, he tries to validate it by sheer force of will, as though insistence of will could *by* itself establish validity and *in* itself be a kind of heroism. His dilemma arises from his inability fully to suppress his fundamental belief in justice, consequence, and the interrelatedness of actions. We may measure his dilemma by the linguistic tension—now within him rather than between him and

her—between the equivocation that signifies moral uncertainty and the
hyperbole that would resolve such uncertainty.

This tension informs the dagger soliloquy. The refusal of the imaginary
dagger to leave his line of vision attests to the strength of his will to murder
Duncan; its appearance with gouts of blood manifests the cruelty of which
he is capable. But the fact that it eludes his grasp indicates the persistence
of his moral revulsion at the deed: he would let his eye wink at his hand and
not see the murder that put the gouts of blood there. He would subject the
air-drawn dagger to a rational analysis that would preclude its use, and the
image is thus held in check by the rhetorical antitheses that characterized
his earlier impotence:

> I have thee not, and yet I see thee still.
> Art thou not, fatal vision, sensible
> To feeling as to sight? Or art thou but
> A dagger of the mind, a false creation,
> Proceeding from the heat-oppressed brain?
> . . . .
> Mine eyes are made the fools o' th' other senses,
> Or else worth all the rest.
>
> (2.1.36–40; 45–46)

The weighing of options here, the will that would verify the dagger versus
the reason that would not, finally leads Macbeth to cease his course of
inquiry or risk impotence once again. He substitutes for it a decidedly more
Senecan diction reminiscent of Lady Macbeth's. Much as Hamlet tries to
muster his courage by reciting the Pyrrhus speech and by stirring himself
to the rant of antique revengers—"'Tis now the very witching time of
night, / When churchyards yawn and hell itself breathes out / Contagion to
this world"—so Macbeth attempts to fortify his flagging resolution by invoking images from the stock idiom of unnatural cruelty—nighttime and
witchcraft, wolves and ghosts:

> Now o'er the one half-world
> Nature seems dead, and wicked dreams abuse
> The curtain'd sleep; witchcraft celebrates
> Pale Hecate's off'rings, and wither'd murder,
> Alarum'd by his sentinel, the wolf,
> Whose howl's his watch, thus with his stealthy pace,
> With Tarquin's ravishing strides, towards his design
> Moves like a ghost.
>
> (2.1.50–57)

His attempt is only partly successful; for a disjunction between the self and
the deed, an objectification of the self as Murder and Tarquin, implies a
moral uncertainty even in the context of heroic self-assertion. His fear that
the stones' prating of his whereabouts may "take the present horror from

the time" further attests to his uncertainty, because the word "horror" is tellingly judgmental. Medea would have recoiled at such moralizing. Macbeth's ultimate concern with Duncan's spiritual fate—"it is a knell / That summons thee to heaven or to hell" (ll. 64–65)—confirms his fear of consequence and his detachment from the amoral role he has assigned himself. The contention between two idioms in this soliloquy, therefore, helps to portray the struggle within Macbeth between two contrary systems of value.

The hyperbole of the dagger speech harks back not only to Seneca, but also to the ornate Ovidian images of Shakespeare's early work such as *Titus Andronicus* and *The Rape of Lucrece.* In the soliloquy following the murder of Duncan, Shakespeare shows more clearly the dramatic use he could make of an exclusively Senecan diction. Macbeth apprehends his guilt with images of heroic amplitude. They represent the moral greatness of which his nature is capable:

> What hands are here? Ha! They pluck out mine eyes.
> Will all great Neptune's ocean wash this blood
> Clean from my hand? No, this my hand will rather
> The multitudinous seas incarnadine,
> Making the green one red.
>
> (2.2.57–61)

If we hear an echo of Medea bathing her hands in blood, the tone, expressive of fear and disbelief, is different from hers. More helpful to an understanding of the tone, as critics since Lessing have recognized, is the image of great Neptune's ocean. Macbeth's lines are an amalgamation of two Senecan passages, one from the *Hercules Furens,* the other from the *Hippolytus.*[14] Hercules awakens from madness to discover that he has slaughtered his wife and children, and he responds with horror:

> What Tanais, or what Nilus els, or with his Persyan wave
> What Tygris violent of streame, or what fierce Rhenus flood,
> Or Tagus troublesome that flowes with Ibers treasures good
> May my ryght hand now wash from gylt? although Meotis cold
> The waves of all the Northen sea on me shed out now wolde,
> And al the water therof shoulde now pas by my two handes,
> Yet wil the mischiefe deepe remayne.
>
> (1, 51)

Likewise Hippolytus, horrified to discover the unnatural lust he has awakened in his father's wife, casts aside his sword with which she has threatened to immolate herself and turns on himself with moral revulsion:

> What bathing lukewarme Tanais may I defilde obtaine,
> Whose clensing watry Channell pure may washe mee cleane againe?
> Or what Meotis muddy meare, with rough Barbarian wave

That boardes on Pontus roring Sea? not Neptune graundsire grave
With all his Ocean foulding floud can purge and wash away
This dunghill foule of stane.

(1, 162)

The form and wording of the second passage, with its hyperbolic negation of the rhetorical question ("not Neptune graundsire grave . . . can purge and wash away / This dunghill"), more closely approximates Macbeth's lines; but the contexts of both help to enrich one's understanding of Macbeth's dilemma. For both Hippolytus and Hercules, each an essentially noble hero innocent of but victimized by the criminal passions of another, come to a horrified apprehension of their guilt and respond with fear, remorse, and violent self-loathing. The Senecan resonances heard in Macbeth's speech indicate how Shakespeare had learned to use the power of allusion, not mere imitation, to establish a heroic ethos. Through allusion, he dramatizes moral horror in a man who once found moral safety in a system of rational heroism.[15]

Shakespeare, therefore, taps the two forms of Senecan *virtus* to give heroic definition to Macbeth's dilemma. *Virtus*—the word for Roman manly courage—was the essence of Stoicism, the prime manifestation of the greatness of soul that made the Stoic a hero. But *virtus* could be either active or passive. The hero of passive *virtus*, like Hercules and Hippolytus, endured a martyrlike suffering: his great soul stood unshaken by the buffets of fortune. The hero of active *virtus*, on the other hand, had to display that great soul in enterprises of great pitch and moment. Seneca the dramatist (as opposed to the philosopher) was obsessed with the perversion of this active *virtus* as *scelus*, or crime; and his most actively courageous heroes such as Atreus, Clytemnestra, and Medea committed crimes of a monstrous, sometimes insane kind.[16] By dramatizing *virtus* as *scelus*, Seneca turned Stoic idealism on its ear and allowed passion to triumph over an endurance of adversity: thus the two types of Senecan hero—sufferer and criminal—are morally at odds. Nevertheless, the language of both types is remarkably similar since it conveys a violence of action and suffering that is of equal intensity. Shakespeare draws from both extremes to establish a tragic counterpoint in Macbeth. The cruel bravado Macbeth learns from his wife in an attempt to divest himself of conscience leads him to an equally assertive diction of furious remorse, the consequence of his old moral values filtering through his newly adopted language.

Macbeth's need to affirm his integrity as a hero overcomes his compulsion to judge his own crime. He tries to suppress his remorse by mouthing the language of criminality that his wife has foisted upon him. He *wills* himself to become a villain. He takes tentative steps in this direction by assuming full responsibility for what earlier she would have to have spurred him to do: kill Banquo. Banquo dares do all that may become a man in reason and good conscience; and by so daring, he embodies the ethical heroism that Macbeth himself forsook when he swore to kill Duncan:

> 'Tis much he dares;
> And to that dauntless temper of his mind
> He hath a wisdom that doth guide his valor
> To act in safety. There is none but he
> Whose being I do fear.
>
> (3.1.50–54)

Fear reminds Macbeth of how far he has fallen from the heroic ideal. He would destroy that ideal *virtus* not only by killing Banquo, but also by adopting Lady Macbeth's diction to stifle the pity that might become a woman:

> Come, seeling night,
> Scarf up the tender eye of pitiful day,
> And with thy bloody and invisible hand
> Cancel and tear to pieces that great bond
> Which keeps me pale!
>
> (3.2.49–53)

His incantation echoes her "Come, thick night" (1.5.50) and, further back, Medea's incantation to Hecate, a goddess Macbeth has mentioned a few lines earlier. If this passage still betrays in him a will to dissociate himself from the deed—Night, not Macbeth, must do and then hide the murder—he nevertheless uses the idiom of revenge tragedy more conventionally, less judgmentally than he does in the dagger soliloquy:

> Light thickens, and the crow
> Makes wing to th' rooky wood;
> Good things of day begin to droop and drowse,
> Whiles night's black agents to their preys do rouse.
>
> (3.2.53–56)

These lines are reminiscent of the language antique revengers spoke in plays that Shakespeare parodied in *The Murder of Gonzago*. Lucianus's "Thoughts black, hands apt, drugs fit, and time agreeing, / Confederate season, else no creature seeing," though triter than Macbeth's couplets, nevertheless creates a mood in much the same vein, and his address to the poison anticipates the imagery of Macbeth's dark world:

> Thou mixture rank, of midnight weeds collected,
> With Hecate's ban thrice blasted, thrice infected. . . .
>
> (*Hamlet*, 3.2.253–56)

Macbeth, however, has no Hamlet to stand up and protest, "Leave thy damnable faces, and begin!" Shakespeare does not subject the archaism of the Vice-like revenger's idiom to such ruthless mockery here, for the realism of *Macbeth* is of a different sort, and Shakespeare can employ without apology an outmoded diction to help establish Macbeth's mimetic credibility.

Macbeth's success in hardening himself to moral depravity is punctuated by lines that allude directly to Clytemnestra's brazen sentence from the *Agamemnon,* "per scelera semper sceleribus tutum est iter":[17]

> Thou marvel'st at my words, but hold thee still;
> Things bad begun make strong themselves by ill.
>
> (3.2.57–58)

Clytemnestra's sentence was popular in Elizabethan revenge tragedy. Hieronimo had used it to oppose "the imperative of religious patience" conveyed by his Pauline quotation, *Vindicta mihi:*[18]

> *Per scelus semper tutum est sceleribus iter.*
> Strike, and strike home, where wrong is offred thee;
> For euils vnto ils conductors be,
> And death's the worst of resolution.
>
> (*The Spanish Tragedie:* 3.13.6–9)

Kyd, however, casts the Senecan sentiment into a more sympathetic context: we grieve with Hieronimo for the loss of his son and thus understand the moral righteousness of his will to revenge. Macbeth's version is closer to the original, more an expression of criminal hubris than moral justice. A knowledge of Seneca enriches our understanding of Macbeth's desperate assertion; for like Clytemnestra, he is attempting to make a *virtus* of *scelus.*

The appearance of Banquo's ghost at the banquet devastatingly undercuts that attempt. Like the ceremonial scene in which Duncan and his nobles pledged their mutual duties to one another, Macbeth intends his banquet to serve as an emblem of the heroic order he wishes to reinstate. Banquo's ghost disturbs that order. Macbeth, who "had else been perfect, / Whole as the marble, founded as the rock" (3.4.21–22)—all similes for amoral invulnerability such as the hardest of Senecan heroes achieved—instead is racked with uncertainty. He responds to the ghost with a half-hearted denial of guilt that here, as before, makes us realize how deep-seated that guilt really is: "Thou canst not say I did it. Never shake / Thy gory locks at me" (ll. 50–51). In an effort to recall him to at least a show of integrity, Lady Macbeth taunts him as she has done before with the question, "Are you a man?" (l. 58); but this time he rejoins not with a defense of ethical heroism, but with a hyperbolic daring that brings her up short: "Ay, and a bold one, that dare look on that / Which might appall the devil" (ll. 59–60). When she pursues him with images of female weakness to shame him into courage, his ultimate rejoinder is to rant at the ghost in a diction she should be proud to hear—a parody of his earlier assertion that he dares do all that may become a man:

What man dare, I dare.
Approach thou like the rugged Russian bear,
The arm'd rhinoceros, or th' Hyrcan tiger;
Take any shape but that, and my firm nerves
Shall never tremble.

(3.4.100–104)

His bravado borders on fustian: in an earlier play, Shakespeare might have ridiculed it as braggadocio by putting it in the mouth of a Pistol. But in *Macbeth*, it is expressive of heroic desperation: language designed to combat the fiercest opponent. Its epic origins are apparent in terms such as "th' Hyrcan tiger," a Virgilian epithet that branded Shakespeare's earliest and cruelest heroine, Margaret in *3 Henry VI*, as a heartless beast and that appeared again in the Hamlet's archaic description of the "rugged Pyrrhus."[19] Such language is an apt vehicle for Macbeth to address a ghost who may have been inspired by Creon's description of meeting Laius in hell, in act 3 of Seneca's *Oedipus:*[20]

Til out at length comes Laius with foule and grisly hue:
Uncomly drest in wretched plight with fylth all overgrowne:
All perst with wounds, (I loth to speake) with bloud quight overflown.

(1,212)

Macbeth's rant, however, cannot combat a self-created image. The horrible imaginings that father fear cannot be defeated by a bravado intended to intimidate others. "Take any shape but that": Macbeth's is the language of external combat, and its failure to daunt the ghost indicates his inability to engage himself fully with the Senecan role that would enable him to use such language unselfconsciously.

Does this mean, then, that Macbeth is detached from the heroic style he wields, and that his insincerity makes rhetoric out of poetry? Does he vow to dare and to outdo in the idiom of Cambyses or Tamburlaine only to disguise his doubt and fear? Does he use the idiom *ironically?* It would be tempting to answer yes; for Macbeth's vaunt is similar to that of Hamlet who, when provoked by Laertes' excessive lament for his dead sister, leaps out of hiding to forge a bold heroic identity—"This is I, / Hamlet the Dane"—and to contest with Laertes by using the same outdoing topos that Macbeth uses against the ghost:

'Swounds, show me what thou 't do.
Woo't weep? Woo't fight? Woo't fast? Woo't tear thyself?
Woo't drink up eisel? Eat a crocodile?
I'll do it.

(5.1.274–77)

As I argued earlier, Hamlet here indulges in Ercles' vein, an idiom that even in madness he would not use for self-expression. Even in this act of passionate commitment, half of Hamlet's character remains uncommitted, a wry observer of the other half playing a conventionally heroic role. This is not true of Macbeth. He has been a warrior, a general; and throughout he has adopted a heroic diction far less self-consciously than the more studious Hamlet. Next to Hamlet's, Macbeth's bravado sounds like high seriousness; and if he recognizes that it will not adequately serve his ends ("Take any shape but that" suggests its failure to defeat the ghost), he nevertheless speaks with far more sincerity and less irony than Hamlet. The rhetorical topos is but one element of an allusive and constantly shifting heroic idiom that defines the complexity of Macbeth's character. If that idiom on occasion sounds conventional, it in no way lessens his individuality: rather, it provides a dramatic shorthand for the absoluteness of self-possession and ruthlessness of will that Macbeth struggles, against his conscience, to achieve.

Many critics think he succeeds. His "powers of self-recognition seem to have been squandered on the night of the first murder," according to one, leaving him, in the words of another, "a diminished thing" who discards large areas of consciousness and, monsterlike, loses his capacity for feeling.[21] They take his speech at the end of 3.4 as an index of how far he will shrink in stature, from hero to villain, in the two remaining acts. Macbeth will once again interrogate the Weird Sisters:

> for now I am bent to know,
> By the worst means, the worst. For mine own good,
> All causes shall give way. I am in blood
> Stepp'd in so far that, should I wade no more,
> Returning were as tedious as go o'er.
>
> (3.4.135–39)

Here, it is argued, Macbeth resolves his moral dilemma, overcomes his fear of consequence by devoting himself entirely to crime. That the "worst" becomes his "own good" suggests how far he has perverted conventional moral judgment, and he is the less human for that. It follows that sympathy for his suffering and admiration for his courage must be tempered by disgust for his callousness. And yet, unless we are willing to judge him by the narrow criteria of Christian morality alone and settle for Malcolm's simple verdict that Macbeth is a butcher, we must recognize that his determination to know the worst and act accordingly is qualified by allusions in the verse that humanize him still, that allow us to preserve a certain sympathy and admiration for him that transcend pat moral judgment.

Macbeth's image of wading in blood recalls the earlier image of multitudinous seas that he has incarnadined with his bloody hands, but the Herculean remorse that so oppressed that earlier speech seems to have given way to insensitivity. Shakespeare used the same metaphor in *Richard III* to signify an irreversible commitment to sin:

> Uncertain way of gain! But I am in
> So far in blood that sin will pluck on sin.
> Tear-falling pity dwells not in this eye.
>
> (4.2.63–65)

This is the language of a tyrant who, like Macbeth (so one could argue), divests himself of pity and moral uncertainty. And the Senecan sources for such commitment to crime seem likewise, at first, to be amorally direct. Clytemnestra's sentence, "The safest path to mischiefe is by mischiefe open still"—one Macbeth already echoed in declaring that things bad begun strengthen themselves by ill—can be heard distinctly in Richard's assertion that sin will pluck on sin and again, though transmuted by images of blood, in Macbeth's admission that it would be as tedious to repent as to sin further. And Medea's vow that she will "have no respect of ryghte, / From mynde on mischiefe fixed fast let shame be banisht quyte (2, 94), antici-pates Macbeth's "For mine own good, / All causes shall give way."

The heroic resolution with which both women speak, however, is far from absolute. Medea, in the speech from which I quoted, begins by ad-dressing her faltering soul: she is torn between a lust for revenge and a natural affection for her children. Thus, her vow to banish shame becomes not a manifestation of moral callousness, but a desperate remedy for her anxiety. Clytemnestra, in her speech, begins similarly by chastising her "drowsie dreaming doting soule" for wavering in its commitment. She muses elegiacally that her world is not now what it once was:

> The fittest shift prevented is, the best path overgrowne
> Thou mightest once mayntayned have thy wedlocke chamber chast,
> And eake have ruld with majesty, by fath conjoyned fast:
> Now natures lore neglected is, all ryght doth clean decay,
> Religion and dignity with faith are worne away.
>
> (2, 106)

By subsequently resorting to a hardened declaration of criminal intent— "The safest path to mischiefe is by mischiefe open still," the sentence twice imitated in *Macbeth*—she tries to find a way out of the bewilderment of contrary passions and to summon the courage to kill Agamemnon: like Medea, she speaks out of moral desperation, not insensitivity. The reso-nance of a conviction spoken in doubt, of determination tainted by a sense of loss, admirably suits Macbeth's situation when he vows to bend his will to crime. Such resonance suggests how self-deceptively he is using Senecan diction to affirm an absoluteness he does not feel.

Allusion, therefore, helps to dramatize the uncertainty of Macbeth's heroic stance; but it is *by* such allusion, ironically, that Macbeth would squelch his uncertainty. As Othello seeks ocular proof of Desdemona's infidelity in order to maintain his heroic integrity—"To be once in doubt, / Is once to be resolv'd"—and as Gloucester seeks auricular proof of Edgar's infidelity to eliminate the doubt he is incapable of sustaining—"I would unstate myself to be in a due resolution"—so Macbeth seeks proof of his fate from the Weird Sisters in order to bolster his resolution and dedicate himself to the diminished goal of heroic self-preservation. The irony is that the Sisters are themselves the linguistic center of the equivocation that throughout has characterized Macbeth's *ir*resolution. In going to them for absolute knowledge, he makes the same mistake Othello makes in seeking proof from Iago, or Gloucester from Edmund. His attempt to embrace their prophecies as truths becomes an embrace of the very duplicity he is trying to rid himself of in asking for proof in the first place.

The cataclysmic force with which he conjures the Weird Sisters reveals the insecurity of his resolution:

> I conjure you, by that which you profess,
> Howe'er you come to know it, answer me.
> Though you untie the winds and let them fight
> Against the churches, though the yesty waves
> Confound and swallow navigation up,
> Though bladed corn be lodg'd and trees blown down,
> Though castles topple on their warders' heads,
> Though palaces and pyramids do slope
> Their heads to their foundations, though the treasure
> Of nature's germains tumble all together,
> Even till destruction sicken, answer me
> To what I ask you.
>
> (4.1.50–61)

Behind this wild apostrophe to the storm, this apocalyptic command that nature pervert herself rather than defy him, we hear Timon in the wilderness invoking the elements to destroy mankind, Lear on the heath raving against his unnatural daughters—

> Crack nature's molds, all germains spill at once,
> That makes ingrateful man!

—and, further back, the ravings of Seneca's mad heroes. To a degree, the Weird Sisters' apparitions support Macbeth's heroic resolution: "Be bloody, bold, and resolute," they tell him (l. 79); "Be lion-mettled, proud, and take no care / Who chafes, who frets, or where conspirers are" (ll. 90–91). But these reassurances are matched by apparently contradictory, and therefore less supportive, prophecies about Macduff, "none of woman born," Birnam Wood, and Banquo's heirs. The epic *virtus* the Sisters would inspire in Macbeth they also make impossible for him to achieve.

It is commonly argued that Macbeth takes the prophecies literally as his single reality, his *carte blanche* for villainy, his "bond of fate."[22] He is said to ignore their contradiction and enigma. I think, on the contrary, that he expresses doubt at every turn—sometimes implicitly, as when his response to the first prophecy, "Thou hast harp'd my fear aright" (l. 74), is too easily checked by his response to the second, "what need I fear of thee?" (l. 82); sometimes explicitly, as when he acts annoyed that the prophecies are not unequivocal enough to alleviate his doubt. Thus he asks the first apparition for "But one word more" (l. 74), determines to "make assurance double sure" after the second (l. 83), and admits that his "heart / Throbs to know one thing" after the third (ll. 100–101). The show of Banquo's heirs confirms his doubts, and he departs muttering a curse at the equivocation in the Sisters' proofs: "Infected by the air whereon they ride, / And damn'd all those that trust them!" (ll. 138–39). To take this curse ironically as Macbeth's self-damnation is to miss the point. Macbeth does *not* have perfect trust in them, nor has he lost his powers of introspection. To suggest that he takes the prophecies literally and thereby gains heroic composure by shrinking into unobstructed villainy is to ignore the verbal cues Shakespeare amply provides.

Throughout act 5, Macbeth suffers the same uncertainty he has suffered since he first dedicated himself to crime. Therefore, his insistence on the validity of the prophecies may be more rhetorical than substantial, a desperate attempt to delude himself as well as his followers. Although he presumes to defend himself as if he took the prophecies for unequivocal truths, he knows better. Before his men he vaunts in the language of heroic certitude spoken by such forbears as Tamburlaine, Titus, and Richard III. Yet he trails each vaunt with a somber acknowledgment of the penalty he has paid for trying to adopt the role to suit the language. He boasts in good set terms,

> Till Birnam wood remove to Dunsinane,
> I cannot taint with fear. What's the boy Malcolm?
> Was he not born of woman?
> . . . .
> The mind I sway by and the heart I bear
> Shall never sag with doubt nor shake with fear.
>
> (5.3.2–4; 9–10)

But perhaps he protests too much; for his boast leads straight to an elegiac lament that he has lived long enough; his way of life is fallen into the sere, the yellow leaf; his violation of the ethics of heroism—loyalty, duty, honor— will deprive him of like fruits in his old age. "Honor, love, obedience, troops of friends, / I must not look to have" (ll. 25–26). His recognition glances back to Hercules' lament to Amphitryon and indicates once again the magnitude of Macbeth's apprehension of crime's consequence:[23]

Wherfore I longer should sustayn my life yet in this light,
And linger here no cause there is, all good lost have I quighte,
My mynd, my weapons, my renoume, my wife, my sonnes, my handes. . . .

(1, 49)

Macbeth's defiance of report in swearing to "fight till from my bones my flesh be hack'd" (l. 32) yields likewise to the melancholy query about his wife that reflects his own mental strife more than hers:

> Canst thou not minister to a mind diseas'd,
> Pluck from the memory a rooted sorrow,
> Raze out the written troubles of the brain. . . ?

(5.3.41–43)

In these lines Macbeth echoes again the same Herculean lament: "And fury to[o] no man may heale and lo[o]se from gylty bandes / My mynd defyeld." And his extravagantly heroic dismissal of the enemy—

> Hang out our banners on the outward walls.
> The cry is still "They come!" Our castle's strength
> Will laugh a siege to scorn. Here let them lie
> Till famine and the ague eat them up.

(5.5.1–4)

—is soon vanquished by his despondent account of life that mocks the value of heroic resolution and serves even as a gloss on the role of villain-hero he is trying so hard to play:

> Life's but a walking shadow, a poor player
> That struts and frets his hour upon the stage
> And then is heard no more. It is a tale
> Told by an idiot, full of sound and fury,
> Signifying nothing.

(5.5.24–28)

Undeluded by the heroic posturing with which he deludes others, Macbeth may see himself as that poor player who frets to make meaning out of fustian, a verse full of sound and fury but ultimately incapable of signifying his own heroic complexity, a verbal disguise for the doubt that will not sleep.

The alarums and retreats that end the play invoke the traditionally heroic world of Shakespeare's early histories. They allow us to admire Macbeth more conventionally as the military man as he once again dons his armor, and they invest his hyperbole with a certain heroic credibility against the encroaching prophecies. To the fear he feels when he learns that Birnam Wood is indeed come to Dunsinane—

> I pull in resolution, and begin
> To doubt th' equivocation of the fiend
> That lies like truth.
>
> (5.5.42–44)

—he responds with an assertion of raw will that fuses Richard III's bravado in battle with Lear's call to the elements: "Blow, wind! Come, wrack! / At least we'll die with harness on our back" (ll. 51–52). To the despair that would coax him to suicide, he responds like Clytemnestra with a most unstoic greatness of soul:

> Why should I play the Roman fool, and die
> On mine own sword? Whiles I see lives, the gashes
> Do better upon them.
>
> (5.8.1–3)

In short, he will be General Macbeth still. But how changed from the general who so confidently redoubled strokes upon Macdonwald! He feels anxious at confronting Macduff face to face, and so responds to his anxiety with a command that, to many, seems to taunt Macduff with the murder of his family: "But get thee back! My soul is too much charg'd / With blood of thine already" (ll. 5–6). The ambiguous phrasing of this taunt, however, shows that Macbeth still thinks in terms of his soul and that he harbors in his soul a horrible blood guilt. The taunt is also an admission: it attests to the persistence of his tragic irresolution.

Macbeth confronts doubt one last time and like a soldier tries to batter it down when Macduff reveals that he was of no woman born. Macbeth responds with less surprise than resignation. His vow not to believe "these juggling fiends . . . That palter with us in a double sense" (ll. 19–20) reawakens in him the doubt that cows his "better part of man" (l. 18); and doubt suppresses his heroic will and causes him to refuse to fight. Macduff's consequent threat, however—"Then yield thee, coward, / And live to be the show and gaze o' th' time!" (ll. 23–4)—provokes him to assert his *virtus* boldly in a last stand against the enemy within:

> Yet I will try the last. Before my body
> I throw my warlike shield. Lay on, Macduff,
> And damn'd be him that first cries "Hold, enough!"
>
> (5.8.32–34)

The sound and fury of these lines signify some nobility—even nobility of a conventional sort—despite the detachment with which the morally equivocal context requires us to regard them. That Macbeth dies affirming a heroic role to which he is never fully committed invests his language with a theatrical vitality that challenges his more skeptical assessment of such language as bombast that signifies nothing.

The real vitality of Macbeth's character, therefore, derives from the interplay of idioms that dramatizes his war within himself. The alternation of heroic styles, one against another, and of those styles with the less obviously rhetorical style of equivocation (and the linguistic cross-pollination that often occurs), compels a shifting and complex response to Macbeth. It engages us in trying to resolve an unresolvable tension between sympathy for him in his suffering and recognition that his suffering is deserved, between admiration for his unflinching courage to face up to his deeds and moral censure for the deeds themselves. The play is, of course, *about* the dehumanizing effects of evil. But to see heroic assertion only as the amoral expression of such effects fails to consider not only the variety of heroic traditions on which Shakespeare draws, but also the disparate moral values implicit in those traditions. Shakespeare's manipulation of the heroic idiom imbues Macbeth with an intellectual life that transcends any conventional ethos and defies pat judgments. That idiom, though it sometimes appears to serve ignoble ends, is in fact an allusive and flexible instrument through which Macbeth fiercely attaches himself to values he abhors and just as fiercely suffers the consequences for having done so. It charges his character with enough greatness of soul, in both the crime and the punishment, to form a tragic counterpoint to his rational uncertainty and to redeem him from the dwarfish stature to which too narrowly moral a reading of the play diminishes him.

9

Antony, Cleopatra, and Heroic Retrospection

Can hyperbole alone persuade us that mortals are gods? That question lies at the heart of *Antony and Cleopatra*. Scenes shift the ground from under our judgments, either reinforcing or diminishing the heroic images Antony and Cleopatra try to project: we see them here as Mars and Venus, as Falstaff and Doll there. The play's dramatic tension thus resides not in the plot, not in the question of whether Antony will be true to Octavia or fly again to his Egyptian dish, nor even in the moral dilemma posed by such a choice, but in the interplay between a grandiloquent idiom and a stage behavior that often belies that idiom. In *Antony*, Shakespeare cast a retrospective eye over the various ways he had recreated heroism earlier in his career. In its cumulative allusions to those recreations, the play brings up the crucial problem of *mimesis:* whether the heroic idiom itself and the impact of its allusions are adequate to make us credit a character as heroic, even when the context encourages us to be skeptical—whether Antony and Cleopatra have the power to suspend disbelief, ours as well as their own, sufficiently to make their heroic fictions a credible reality.

The passage that raises the question of heroic reality most explicitly is Cleopatra's portrait of a godlike Antony:

> His legs bestrid the ocean, his rear'd arm
> Crested the world, his voice was propertied
> As all the tuned spheres, and that to friends;
> But when he meant to quail and shake the orb,
> He was as rattling thunder.
>
> (5.2.81–85)

To him she attributes the powers of Jove; his bounty outdoes that of Timon—"There was no winter in 't" (l. 86); as a conqueror, he puts Tamburlaine to shame: "In his livery / Walk'd crowns and crownets; realms and islands were / As plates dropp'd from his pocket" (ll. 89–91). In this heroic

191

description, Cleopatra makes an impassioned plea for belief: "Think you there was, or might be, such a man / As this I dreamt of?" (ll. 92–93). Shakespeare covertly addresses the same question to us: Can we believe that such a play, making use as it does of heroic conventions and stock hyperbole, actually bodies forth heroes? In his use of that hyperbole and those conventions, Shakespeare entreats us to assent: illusion disarms our critical defenses and permits us, to use Janet Adelman's Kierkegaardian phrase, to make a leap of faith even as we doubt.[1] But in Dolabella, the intellect responds: "Gentle madam, no" (l. 93). The play, by its very nature as drama rather than ritual, keeps us from participating fully in the illusion, makes us question legendary fame as rigorously as we did in Henry V, allows us to analyze heroic conventions and hyperbole for what they are: incredible fictions. At stake here is no less than the ancient controversy over the power of art to move and persuade. This play has provided ample ground for those who have wished to renew the fray.

Imagine, for a moment, Antony's death as Antony himself would have it remembered. No longer able to live honorably in the world and inspired by Cleopatra's stoic example, he defies fortune in a final exertion of heroic will. He falls on his sword, allows his soul to regain its grandeur by triumphing on itself—but not before he is carried to a last reunion with the still-living Cleopatra, to whom he begs to be remembered as he was,

> the greatest prince o' th' world,
> The noblest, and do now not basely die,
> Not cowardly put off my helmet to
> My countryman—a Roman by a Roman
> Valiantly vanquish'd.
>
> (4.15.55–59)

Antony echoes the sentiment Ajax speaks as he plunges a sword into his own breast in Ovid's *Metamorphoses: ne quisquam Aiacem possit superare nisi Aiax*. But Antony's quest for integrity is nobler than Ajax's; his stoicism moves beyond Ajax's *dolor*.[2] As he passes, Cleopatra honors him with an encomium such as Marlowe might have bestowed on him—"The crown o' th' earth doth melt" (l. 64)—and his victors, those who remain to triumph in *this* world, speak heroic elegies over him, recognizing their loss.

Antony's death scene conforms to all those conventions of stoic fortitude and heroic assertion that so ennobled the deaths of Cassius, Brutus, and even (though in a Christian context) Othello. Cassius's death will serve to illustrate the form. Having been told that his man Titinius is surrounded by the enemy, Cassius acknowledges that he has fallen from honor and, like a good stoic, runs on his sword:

> O, coward that I am, to live so long,
> To see my best friend ta'en before my face!
>
> (*Julius Caesar*: 5.3.34–35)

An irony comes full circle here, and it anticipates an irony to come in Cleopatra's confessing her ruse too late. For Titinius is in fact not dead at all, but he fails to return in time to save Cassius and so stays to deliver an encomium over him instead. Its imagery is the same that Achilles will use at Hector's death, in a slightly later play, to mark the fall of chivalry:

> Look, Hector, how the sun begins to set,
> How ugly night comes breathing at his heels.
> Even with the vail and dark'ning of the sun,
> To close the day up, Hector's life is done.
> *(Troilus: 5.8.5–8)*

Titinius's cliché is identical, and he expresses it in the sort of rhyme that punctuated not only Hector's death, but the deaths of heroes in the early tragedies as well—Talbot and York—as if to suggest that when Cassius falls, so falls the old order:

> O setting sun,
> As in thy red rays thou dost sink to night,
> So in his red blood Cassius' day is set!
> The sun of Rome is set. Our day is gone;
> Clouds, dews, and dangers come; our deeds are done!
> (5.3.60–64)

Furthermore, Titinius holds up his dead master as a model of stoic resolution, much as Cleopatra takes her cue from Antony; and he vows to take his own life in the same archaic style that characterized the encomium: "By your leave, gods!—This is a Roman's part. / Come, Cassius' sword, and find Titinius' heart" (ll. 89–90). What remains is for Brutus to discover these erroneous deaths and to deliver a heroic elegy over the bodies, like Octavious over Antony and Cleopatra: "Are yet two Romans living such as these? / The last of all the Romans, fare thee well!" (ll. 98–99).

Cassius's death serves to instruct Brutus in the next scene. There, Lucilius reports that Brutus "will be found like Brutus, like himself" (5.4.25), an affirmation of the stoic's will to control his own destiny that echoes the phrase Ovid used to praise Achilles' determination to remain himself alone when all else changed[3]—a phrase Shakespeare adapted to a more vernacular hero in a history play written in perhaps the same year as *Julius Caesar*: "Then should the warlike Harry, like himself, / Assume the port of Mars" (*Henry V:* Prologue, 5–6). More self-consciously than Cassius, Brutus explains his motives for suicide: "It is more worthy to leap in ourselves, / Than tarry till they push us" (5.5.24–25). He rejects the humiliation of having to ride in Caesar's triumph and determines to preserve his honor at all costs: "I shall have glory by this losing day / More than Octavius and Mark Antony / By this vile conquest shall attain unto" (ll. 36–38). The note of "the world well lost," the almost romantic emphasis on glory, belies the stoic's simple trust in honor. Brutus proclaims, as Antony will later, that the death is glorious that escapes the ignominy of heroic failure. Even more like Antony, Brutus speaks his own epitaph in a public bid for noble memory:

> Countrymen,
> My heart doth joy that yet in all my life
> I found no man but he was true to me.
>
> (5.5.33–35)

And this bid grows in artifice as he transforms his life into a moral exemplum recounted to educate his hearers, as though to make his own contribution to the *Mirror* tradition:

> So fare you well at once; for Brutus' tongue
> Hath almost ended his life's history.
>
> (5.5.39–40)

The self-dramatization of this epitaph is something Othello expanded in his final plea, "When you shall these unlucky deeds relate, / Speak of me as I am," and Hamlet in his request that Horatio "Report me and my cause aright."

Antony speaks like a true stoic when he laments that "Since Cleopatra died / I have liv'd in such dishonor that the gods / Detest my baseness" (4.14.55–57). And if, unlike Cassius and Brutus, he dismisses his career with the brief "No more a soldier" (l. 42), he nevertheless exchanges martial heroism for a heroism of the heart that demands an equal commitment. His exchange of public for private value, requiring just as heroic an investment of the self, informs his vision of himself playing Aeneas to Cleopatra's Dido, forsaking civil duty to "couch on flowers" (l. 51). Determined to commit suicide for love, Antony recalls his deeds of martial glory elegiacally, in the manner of Othello's noble *ubi sunt*. "I have seen the day," Othello reminisces, "That, with this little arm and this good sword, / I have made my way through more impediments / Than twenty times your stop." But Antony's civic memories are tucked self-consciously into a subordinate clause:

> I, that with my sword
> Quarter'd the world, and o'er green Neptune's back
> With ships made cities, . . .

Such memories only set off the more strikingly his worship of Cleopatra as a model for heroic action, by whose standards he, like Cassius before him, chastises himself for cowardice:

> . . . condemn myself to lack
> The courage of a woman—less noble mind

Than she which by her death our Caesar tells
"I am conqueror of myself."

(4.14.57–62)

This last stoic affirmation recasts "For Brutus only overcame himself" and anticipates Antony's later interpretation of his own death for Cleopatra: "Not Caesar's valor hath o'erthrown Antony, / But Antony's hath triumph'd on itself" (4.15.15–16). He would have her believe that he has lived up to the standard she set. And why not? All the conventions of heroic death scenes Shakespeare here employs, recalling as they do similar death scenes in *Julius Caesar* and *Othello,* beg us to believe, too, that Antony is what he claims to be: an epic hero dying an honorable death in traditional fashion.

If Antony's suicide adheres to the conventions of heroic death, it nevertheless is bound up in ironies that make it impossible fully to credit those conventions as representing "reality." First, the report of Cleopatra's death is a trick intended to prove to him her stoic constancy. To the audience, it proves the opposite. Unlike the honest error that causes Cassius to think Titinius dead, Cleopatra's error is deliberate—cunning falsification, consistent with other strategies by which one has come to know her inconstancy. The black humor of this particular misguided strategy robs some of the tragic pathos from Antony's death; for even as he revises Virgil in daring to think that he, a doting Aeneas, will join his Dido for an amorous eternity in Elysium, we know that he must love there alone: Cleopatra still lives. The slyness of her trick cheapens his tributes to her stoic resolution; each time he invokes her as a model, we smell a rat. At worst, Cleopatra's ruse reduces Antony to a gull, herself to a trickster. That Antony is unaware of the ruse makes him more pathetic, but his pathos is not exactly that of a Cassius or a Brutus.

Eros, too, qualifies Antony's bid for noble memory. Unlike the servants of Brutus and Cassius, who hold the sword like good subordinates and in no way detract from their masters' resolution, Eros provides a model of resolution that points up Antony's wavering. Rejecting Antony's command that he "Draw that thy honest sword" (4.14.79) and "Do it at once" (l. 82)— a command that indicates Antony would prefer to be *passive* in his suicide, letting the wound come to *him*—Eros takes his own life instead and thus steals the dramatic fire:

Thrice-nobler than myself!
Thou teachest me, O valiant Eros, what
I should, and thou couldst not.

(4.14.95–97)

Antony's recognition is magnanimous. It confirms his reputation as a greatsouled general. But he proceeds to botch his chance to redeem himself by playing the apt student to Eros's teacher. "To do thus," he says, falling on his sword, "I learn'd of thee." But the lesson has not sunk in far enough:

How, not dead? not dead?
The guard, ho! O, dispatch me!

(4.14.102–4)

Rather than dying cleanly in the tradition of his stoic progenitors, he writhes onstage in heroic impotence. To comment on the sour comedy enacted before us, Shakespeare uses the guards much as he used the wailing chorus at Juliet's bedside. There, we recall, the "O woeful day's" are made humorous both by the context—Juliet is not dead—and by their stylistic excess, lamentation borrowed from an outmoded tragic style.[4] So Antony's guards, heedless of his recurrent pleas to them to finish him off, recite their conventional threnodies as though the body writhing before them were already dead. The imagery they use, full of *Revelations*, harks back to the imagery of the choric elegies spoken over Henry V's corpse at the opening of *1 Henry VI*:

SECOND GUARD: The star is fall'n.
FIRST GUARD: And time is at his period.
ALL: Alas, and woe!
ANTONY: Let him that loves me strike me dead.
FIRST GUARD: Not I.
SECOND GUARD: Nor I.
THIRD GUARD: Nor anyone.

(4.14.106–10)

Antony's interruption underscores the irony: premature threnodies are a bit absurd. Decretas's departure with Antony's sword deals another blow to tragic decorum, for the sword will be given to Caesar as a peace-offering before Antony has even used it to make peace with himself. When Antony hears that Cleopatra has tricked him—information to which he responds, again, with magnanimous silence—he knows he must stop the *Romeo*-like lamentation, now abetted by two more guards, in order to proceed with the action:

ANTONY: Bear me, good friends, where Cleopatra bides;
                 'Tis the last service that I shall command you.
FIRST GUARD: Woe, woe are we, sir, you may not live to wear
                 All your true followers out.
ALL: Most heavy day!
ANTONY: Nay, good my fellows, do not please sharp fate
                 To grace it with your sorrows. . . .
                 . . . .
                                          Take me up.

(4.14.131–36; 138)

One imagines him speaking these last lines with a certain peevishness and frustration that tragic closure has eluded him.

His taking up, as many producers would testify, is a cumbersome stage business that Cleopatra lightens with her wit: "Here's sport indeed! How heavy weighs my lord!" (4.15.33). Her sexual innuendo reminds us that their relationship has often lain in the bed of comic romance, and it is in that vein that she suggests an apotheosis that would fetch him up on air: "Had I great Juno's power, / The strong-wing'd Mercury should fetch thee up, / And set thee by Jove's side" (ll. 35–37).[5] In the next breath, however, she acknowledges a humanity that deflates such Ovidian hyperbole and reduces the scene once more to tragic awkwardness: "Yet come a little— / Wishers were ever fools" (ll. 37–38); and if we imagine that the accompanying stage direction, *They heave Antony aloft to Cleopatra*, leads to anything other than folly, we may count ourselves among the wishers.

Such counterpointing of heroic hyperbole and diminished reality also characterizes Antony's final exchanges with Cleopatra. These exchanges ought, by tradition, to affirm at the last an absolute heroic commitment to one another; and formally, they do. But a thread of suspicion woven through them qualifies their heroic affirmation. His chief concern is whether she will trick him again by making peace with Octavius. She has already assured him, in language such as Juliet used when she swore never to marry Paris, that she will never be taken in triumph to Rome, "if knife, drugs, serpents, have / Edge, sting, or operation" (ll. 26–27). And with a dig at Antony's past inconstancy, she vows that "Your wife Octavia, with her modest eyes / And still conclusion, shall acquire no honor / Demuring upon me" (ll. 28–30)—the personal invective is conclusive proof, one would think, that she means business. But Antony tests her resolve further by suggesting that she seek her "honor" of Caesar with her "safety," harping on that Roman term *honor* with which she has just disparaged Octavia, and invoking a principle of compromise antithetical to the stoic resolve she has sworn to live (or die) by. Even Antony's choice of confidants for Cleopatra is suspect. "None about Caesar trust but Proculeius," he admonishes her (l. 49); but Proculeius woos her with false promises to preserve her for Caesar's triumph. Antony's advice to her may be a gross misjudgment, or he may be testing her faith with temptations to survive. In either case, she responds as he would have her respond—like a Roman: "My resolution and my hands I'll trust; / None about Caesar" (ll. 50–51).

Her fortitude tested and (apparently) believed, Antony moves to his greater concern that she remember him not as he is, but as he tells her he has been. He wishes to rely on the transfiguring power of her imagination to feed her thoughts "with those my former fortunes" (l. 54), as if they could make his suicide an even more heroic feat. We regard his former fortunes less credulously, however, because the evidence of his death scene alone, not to mention his earlier defeats in the play, does not fully support the heroic construction he puts on it. From his boast before he is raised to the monument—"Not Caesar's valor hath o'erthrown Antony, / But Antony's hath triumph'd on itself"—to his parting assessment of himself as "a

Roman by a Roman / Valiantly vanquish'd," Antony fictionalizes his death as a complete heroic achievement, unaided and self-executed.[6] In a sense, of course, it is: the allusion to heroic deaths in plays past bear witness to its legitimacy. And yet we know better. Shakespeare creates enough disparity between our conventional expectations and what we see enacted onstage to keep us alert, and ambivalence characterizes our appreciation of Antony's encomium on his whole career. The heroic image he projects is in part belied by the circumstances of his death, but he challenges Cleopatra to keep it alive. The most satirical instance of this method in all of Shakespeare is Achilles' bid for public fame at the end of *Troilus*. If Antony's bid for noble memory is neither so jaded nor so calculated as Achilles', neither is it quite so honest or unselfconsciously conventional as Brutus's and Othello's. Antony's concern is the same as theirs; but that events do not corroborate the fame that grows up around them is as much a part of Shakespeare's presentation of Antony's death as it is, though more devastatingly, of Hector's. The recollection and recasting of Shakespeare's earlier uses of tragic conventions yield a death scene for Antony that at once encourages and discourages belief in the heroic myths that those conventions usually foster.

A choir of elegies rounds out Antony's death and caps Shakespeare's ambivalent appeal to tragic tradition. These elegies are spoken by noble Romans who, like Antony himself at Brutus's death, can afford the magnanimity of praising a dead competitor. As Decretas comes bearing his master's sword, swearing that Antony's hand "writ his honor in the acts it did" (5.1.22), the victorious Caesar, Agrippa, and Maecenas—a grandiose copy of the trio of guards who lamented Antony prematurely—heap tragic honors upon him.[7] "A rarer spirit never / Did steer humanity," declares Agrippa; "but you, gods, will give us / Some faults to make us men" (ll. 31–33), a possible reference to Aristotelian hamartia as it filtered through Renaissance tragic theory. Maecenas, in response, finds more meat in the *Mirror* tradition, which would fix Antony as a moral exemplum for erring greatness: "When such a spacious mirror's set before him," he says of Caesar, "He needs must see himself" (ll. 34–35). It remains for Caesar to utter the most hyperbolic praise, baiting us with convention only to catch a smaller reality. He predictably speaks of Antony's fall as the passing of an old order:

> I must perforce
> Have shown to thee such a declining day,
> Or look on thine; . . .
>
> (5.1.37–39)

The diurnal image places Antony among those earlier representatives of antique virtue, Cassius and Hector. Caesar invokes a stock Elizabethan analogy to cataclysm:

> The breaking of so great a thing should make
> A greater crack. The round world
> Should have shook lions into civil streets,
> And citizens to their dens.

(5.1.14–17)

His use of "should," however, implying an unfulfilled probability, indicates at what a remove Antony's death is from the heroes' deaths in other Shakespearean plays, for which cosmic upheaval and unnatural events are portents or consequences: storms rain blood on the Capitol and a lioness whelps in the street the night before Julius Caesar's murder; there is darkness at noon and horses eat each other following Duncan's. In the world of Antony, such cataclysms and events exist only in the imagination, not in nature. Caesar completes his movement from heroic elegy to Realpolitik when he postpones his fulsome praise of Antony as his "mate in empire, / Friend and companion in the front of war" (ll. 43–44) to deal with matters at hand:

> Hear me, good friends—
> *Enter an Egyptian.*
> But I will tell you at some meeter season.
> The business of this man looks out of him;
> We'll hear him what he says.

(5.1.48–51)

The interruption fulfills our expectation of his sincerity. Caesar has paid his dues to heroic tradition; the form has served him; the Egyptian's arrival is convenient. It also provides an apt conclusion to the extended scene of Antony's death, a formal digression into a world of heroics that cannot hold up against the pressure of the Augustan moment. By recapitulating honorable death scenes through the Shakespeare canon, Antony's death raises formal expectations in us; but the patness of convention, the predictability of forms, and the determination of all involved to construct a heroic drama even against their natures, keep those expectations from being satisfactorily fulfilled.

Antony's death comes not as an isolated instance of heroic drama tinged with comedy, but as the culmination of a whole sequence of scenes in which the heroic idiom is tested against less-than-heroic stage business. The play is full of testaments to the greatness of its legendary protagonists, but Antony and Cleopatra themselves are aware that praise is a relative commodity, to be said and gainsaid at will. The heroic ideals they presumably believe in may be vowed and disavowed, as is expedient for their political interests. And so the play finally focuses on whether Antony and Cleopatra together can overcome their seasoned skepticism enough to embrace the roles that the circumstances of epic warfare require them to play.

Their attempt to make a heroic stand in defense of what they believe in—love for one another—is characterized by a pattern Shakespeare had evolved in earlier plays. A hero laments his loss of selfhood until his partner helps him to restore it by inspiring him to a renewed heroic assertion. Iago's hyperbolic pledge to be Othello's just revenger and Lady Macbeth's challenge to her husband to dare to be a man establish the pattern; but Antony and Cleopatra elaborate upon it and use it three times in succession, so that it becomes a structural *tour de force*.

The pattern works as follows. Antony fails to assert himself as a hero should and blames his failure on Cleopatra's perfidy. After confronting her in rage and despair, he turns inward to enlarge on his elegiac sense of lost heroism. Cleopatra then helps him restore confidence in that forsaken cause so that he may once again go forth to assert his courage against Caesar. From that assertion, he descends to self-doubt, and the pattern begins anew. It embodies the play's central issue: the power of heroic artifice to validate itself in action.

The pattern's first appearance is clear. Antony's navy is forcefully opposing Caesar's at Actium; but when Cleopatra turns tail, Antony follows her, thus violating his "Experience, manhood, honor" (3.10.23). He condemns himself "for rashness . . . For fear and doting" (3.11.14–15)—doting, a word used throughout to denote his desertion of reason for Cleopatra—and laments, "I have lost command" (l. 23): unstoically, he has failed to govern himself. In much the same manner as Othello after he has lost his occupation in doubting Desdemona's fidelity, Antony bemoans the loss of such soldiership as once put the boy Octavius to shame:

> He at Philippi kept
> His sword e'en like a dancer, while I struck
> The lean and wrinkled Cassius; and 'twas I
> That the mad Brutus ended. He alone
> Dealt on lieutenantry, and no practice had
> In the brave squares of war; yet now—No matter.
>
> (3.11.35–40)

This encomiastic recollection of his own valor at Philippi is not confirmed by the events of *Julius Caesar,* in which we never see Antony in battle, and in which the conspirators come to embody nobler heroic values than the politic Caesar and Antony do. Antony presumably finds that an *imagined* heroic past may serve as both an inspiration and a measure of how far he has fallen. His remark to Cleopatra thus applies not simply to his loss of honor at Actium but to the price he has paid for having loved her at all:

> O, whither hast thou led me, Egypt? See
> How I convey my shame out of thine eyes
> By looking back what I have left behind
> 'Stroy'd in dishonor.
>
> (3.11.50–53)

Cleopatra's humble begging of "Pardon, pardon!" (l. 67), however, prompts Antony to make a heroic counter-claim that even one of her tears (he does not regard *them* as crocodile, at least) "rates / All that is won and lost. Give me a kiss. / Even this repays me" (ll. 68–70). A pledge of love, in the best chivalric tradition, assuages his loss of soldiership but does not compensate for it. On the contrary, it spurs him to perform more heroic feats to maintain the image Cleopatra dotes on. His reaffirmation of the stoic fortitude he thought he had lost at Actium—"Fortune knows / We scorn her most when most she offers blows" (ll. 72–73)—leads directly to his challenging Caesar to hand-to-hand combat. He would dispense with legions and test an individual bravery:

> I dare him therefore
> To lay his gay comparisons apart,
> And answer me declin'd, sword against sword,
> Ourselves alone.
>
> (3.13.25–28)

He echoes the heroic assurance with which Hector issues a challenge to the best Greek and, with equal aplomb, Hal issues one to Hotspur in his bid to win fame and honor. He echoes, further back, Talbot's valiant attempt to rescue a lost cause by tempting Joan La Pucelle off the wall and into single combat:

> Damsel, I'll have a bout with you again,
> Or else let Talbot perish with this shame.
> . . . .
> Dare ye come forth and meet us in the field?
>
> (*1 Henry VI:* 3.2.56–57; 61)

Antony anticipates just as surely the epic bravado of Coriolanus, who can boast of his victories for Rome, "Alone I did it." Antony's emphasis on the self alone in matters of honor appears, in the context of empire, at once outmoded and paradoxically noble—much like Talbot's self-reliance in the network of political intrigues that determined the War of the Roses. We recognize his challenge as a naive gesture that Caesar would be a fool to take up, as he hides behind his mass of legions. Joan likewise mocks the naiveté of Talbot's presumption: "Belike your lordship takes us then for fools, / To try if that our own be ours or no" (ll. 62–63). Nevertheless, we are compelled to admire Antony's challenge, much as we admire Talbot's, Hal's and Hector's, as a reversion to the nobler values of epic warfare and to confidence in an individual merit that Caesar cannot match.

The second time the pattern occurs, the threat of Cleopatra's perfidy grows more real for Antony. He has just regained, with her aid, an epic sense of himself. But finding Caesar's servant Thidias kissing her hand, he at once suspects her of compromising her faith—a faith only fragilely restored since Actium—and he responds with rage:

> Moon and stars!
> Whip him. Were 't twenty of the greatest tributaries
> That do acknowledge Caesar, should I find them
> So saucy with the hand of she here—what's her name,
> Since she was Cleopatra? Whip him, fellows,
> Till, like a boy, you see him cringe his face,
> And whine aloud for mercy.
>
> (3.13.96–102)

Like Troilus, who displaces his anger with Cressida onto another, so Antony vents his spleen on Thidias instead of Cleopatra. Such tryannical abuse calls to mind Cleopatra's earlier abuse of the messenger who brings word of Antony's marriage. There she, like Antony here, shores up the tottering realm of her pride with the prop of another's humiliation.[8] Her methods are savage. "The most infectious pestilence upon thee!" (2.5.61), she curses as she strikes the messenger; and as she hales him up and down, she echoes Othello's most violent expressions of self-abuse, in which he calls devils to whip him, blow him about in winds, roast him in sulpher, and wash him in steep-down gulfs of liquid fire.[9] "Thou shalt be whipp'd with wire," she rants, "and stew'd in brine, / Smarting in ling'ring pickle!" (ll. 65–66). And when she assumes a Jovian authority in dealing out punishment, she parodies Antony's most hyperbolic protestation of love, "Let Rome in Tiber melt." "Some innocents scape not the thunderbolt," she warns Charmian; "Melt Egypt into Nile! And kindly creatures / Turn all to serpents!" (ll. 77–79).

Cleopatra's parody of heroic rant in this scene makes Antony's later abuse of Thidias sound excessive by association. It is hard to take his rage seriously when we hear in it an echo of Cleopatra's ludicrous self-indulgence. His tone shifts, however—and with it, our sympathies—when rage gives way to an elegiac expression of lost heroism. "Approach, there!" he summons his servants; and when they do not come, "Now, gods and devils! / Authority melts from me. Of late, when I cried 'Ho!' / Like boys unto a muss, kings would start forth / And cry, 'Your will?'" (ll. 90–93). One expects him to follow this with an admission that he has Tamburlaine's power no longer. Instead, he briefly restores his heroic confidence in an echo of Medea's assertion of heroic staying-power, *Medea super est*—a Senecan line that haunted Shakespeare's imagination ever since the *Henry VI* plays. "I am Antony yet," he boasts (l. 93); and with this assertion, he turns his ire directly on Cleopatra: she is "a morsel" he found "cold upon / Dead Caesar's trencher" (ll. 117–18); she is an intemperate wanton who will live not in heroic, but "vulgar fame" (l. 120). She has made a cuckold of him, and so he biblically cries out, "O, that I were / Upon the hill of Basan, to outroar the horned herd! For I have savage cause" (ll. 127–29). He may allude to the Psalms, but his tone out-Herods Herod.

This desperate resumption of heroic bravado cannot long stave off Antony's more considered judgment that his glory is past. Caesar, he admits, angers him by "harping on what I am, / Not what he knew I was" (ll. 143–44); Antony pays homage again to that image of a Herculean self he knows is unrecoverable. His "good stars," he laments, have "left their orbs, and shot their fires / Into th' abysm of hell" (ll. 146–48). And in one last cosmic metaphor for the fall of a great man—the sort of metaphor Shakespeare had used many times before—Antony proclaims his own tragedy: "Alack, our terrene moon / Is now eclips'd, and it portends alone / The fall of Antony!" (ll. 154–56).

Responding to his self-dramatized *de casibus* fall, Cleopatra adopts an almost Senecan hyperbole to assure him of her faith: her goal is to renew his faith in himself. Her method resembles that of Iago, who adopts an extreme revenge diction to reform Othello's self-image. If I be coldhearted to you, she vows,

> From my cold heart let heaven engender hail,
> And poison it in the source, and the first stone
> Drop in my neck; as it determines, so
> Dissolve my life!

She continues more in the vein of Macbeth's wife, who grotesquely swears she would sooner dash out her baby's brains than break her oath:

> The next Caesarion smite,
> Till by degrees the memory of my womb,
> ·······································
> Lie graveless.
>
> (3.13.160–67, passim)

By resorting to an idiom more heroically daring than his, Cleopatra convinces Antony that his doubt of her was groundless: "I am satisfied," he assures her (l. 168). This satisfaction allows him once again to reassert the glory he thought gone forever. "Where hast thou been, my heart?" he asks, sounding much like a soldier from the old English history plays:

> If from the field I shall return once more
> To kiss these lips, I will appear in blood;
> I and my sword will earn our chronicle.
>
> (3.13.174–76)

He will be Hotspur to Cleopatra's Kate. She interjects, "That's my brave lord!" (l. 178); and her cheerleading spurs him on to new goals: "I will be treble-sinew'd, hearted, breath'd, / And fight maliciously. . . . I'll set my teeth, / And send to darkness all that stop me" (ll. 179–80, 182–83). His vaunting here is just as theatrical as his rage in defeat; and fully conscious of the ludic element in it, Cleopatra crowns the scene with an allusion to the roles they play, to the fictions that would disguise their awareness of impending doom: "since my lord /Is Antony again, I will be Cleopatra" (ll. 187–88).

In a famous interlude that follows, they play these roles to the hilt. Cleopatra arms Antony for battle. By doing so, she calls up the whole literary and iconographic history of Mars and Venus.[10] These deities serve as mythic analogues for Antony and Cleopatra throughout the play. When, early on, Cleopatra exchanges her clothing for his and wears his sword Philippan, for example, she evokes the traditional emasculation of Mars by Venus, love's power over war: she becomes herself a descendant of the *Venus armata*, iconographically akin to Diana. Antony, after his defeat at Actium, rues that "She has robb'd me of my sword," a further evocation of Mars' defection to venery. When Cleopatra helps Antony to arm, then, she counters the mythic tradition by undoing what she has done. Her action suggests emblematically that love may work in the *service* of war, that the proper devotion may cause Antony to resume the martial valor he has cast off. "Is not this buckled well?" she asks (4.4.11); and he responds, "Rarely, rarely. / He that unbuckles this, till we do please / To daff 't for our repose, shall hear a storm" (ll. 11–13).

Although Cleopatra's action, with great histrionic flair, renews their faith in Antony's heroic possibility, we would do well to recall the scenes of arming in Shakespeare's previous plays before renewing our own faith in him. Most recently, Macbeth called Seyton to arm him against Birnam Wood's move to Dunsinane; further back, Hector sought the prize of a Greek's sumptuous armor and made the fatal mistake of taking his own off to put the other on; even further, Richard II tried to pluck up his resolution by calling for a more unsubstantial armor: "Arm, arm, my name!"; furthest of all, Richard III armed defiantly, though racked with bad dreams, to meet Henry Tudor at Bosworth Field. Each time, the hero's bravado rings hollow in a scene that dramatizes the poignancy of lost causes. The elegiac undertone of Antony's arming scene is reinforced by his and Cleopatra's history of abandoning epic ideals for practical expedients. It is possible, of course, to argue that by arming, Antony signifies a glorious return to his heroic past.[11] The morning's victory would seem to bear this out:

> I thank you all,
> For doughty-handed are you, and have fought
> Not as you serv'd the cause, but as 't had been
> Each man's like mine; you have shown all Hectors.
>
> (4.8.4–7)

But Antony's allusion to Hector—a figure by now equated, in Shakespeare's world, with fallen chivalry—and his use of the old-fashioned word *doughty* reveal a mustiness in his heroism that dulls even the brightest sword. If these references are understood correctly, they do not augur well for Antony, for they undercut a fiction that Cleopatra, like him, feeds on but knows is insubstantial:

> He goes forth gallantly. That he and Caesar might
> Determine this great war in a single fight!
> Then, Antony—but now—Well, on.
>
> (4.4.36–38)

Her descent from the expansively expressed chivalric condition to the fragmented syntax of a broken dream says it all.

The third time the pattern occurs, Antony most wrathfully accuses the "Triple-turn'd whore" of betraying the heroic achievement to which she has egged him on (4.12.13). From the battle by sea in which Antony hopes to solidify his victory by land, Cleopatra's ships fly to Caesar. Shakespeare leaves us with the distinct possibility that Cleopatra directed them to do so. Antony has do doubt she defected; and though his arms continue to make war on Rome, "my heart," he says, thinking of her, "Makes only wars on thee" (ll. 14–15). He sees clearly that venery has weakened his valor. And in her perfidy, he prophesies (yet again) his own fall in the traditional diurnal imagery of earlier Roman and chronicle plays: "O sun, thy uprise shall I see no more. / Fortune and Antony part here" (ll. 18–19).

To deal with her, he adopts the posture of a revenge hero. His last heroic deed in this life, like Othello's, will be to punish the woman who has caused him to lose his occupation. "For when I am reveng'd upon my charm, / I have done all" (ll. 16–17). The most monstrous revenge he can imagine is to let her "blemish Caesar's triumph," be hoisted up "to the shouting plebeians," and, most cruelly, to "let / Patient Octavia plough thy visage up / With her prepared nails" (ll. 33–39). With this last image he passes into the world of the Senecan grotesque. And in fact, in a passage customarily taken as Antony's most passionate declaration of wrath, he invokes the spirit of the Hercules Oetaeus:[12]

> The shirt of Nessus is upon me. Teach me,
> Alcides, thou mine ancestor, thy rage.
> Let me lodge Lichas on the horns o' th' moon,
> And with those hands, that grasp'd the heaviest club,
> Subdue my worthiest self. The witch shall die.
>
> (4.12.43–47)

A tension in these lines, true to the tension in Seneca's Hercules, illuminates Antony's ambivalent nature. For just as Hercules, in wrath, wished to avenge himself on Deianira for bringing him the poisoned shirt but resigned himself to suffer with stoic endurance once he heard she was not to blame, so Antony's urge to kill Cleopatra is tempered by a more stoic will to turn his wrath inward and subdue his worthiest self. Impulses of revenge and self-conquest exist side-by-side in him, whereas one succeeded the other in Hercules. Antony may feel a greater rage at his betrayal of himself than at hers of him. Furthermore, his request that Hercules "teach" him indicates how incapable he is of acting on the passion he knows he *ought* to feel. The spirit of his ancestor, as a soldier in an earlier scene observes, has indeed departed from him, and circumspection leads him to lament its loss.[13] Even his mention of "those hands, that grasp'd the heaviest club" elegiacally recalls a forgotten *virtus.*

In an ensuing scene with Eros, Antony muses on his inability to hold a heroic shape. The image of a noble Antony that he, Cleopatra, and Caesar have all professed to believe in, and which has still been invoked after each defection, he now confesses is no more substantial than a cloud, a vaporous succession of heroic poses that melt as soon as they are formed:

> That which is now a horse, even with a thought
> The rack dislimns, and makes it indistinct,
> As water is in water.
> . . . .
> My good knave Eros, now thy captain is
> Even such a body. Here I am Antony,
> Yet cannot hold this visible shape, my knave.
>
> (4.14.9–14)

Antony's despondent assessment of his life as a heroic fiction is hard to contradict. His *belief* in the fiction can be restored only by a testament of faith far more convincing than any that have gone before; for the more extreme his disillusion with the fiction becomes, the more extreme must be the provocation to renew that fiction. Cleopatra's solution lies in a bodily demonstration of her faith in him: "Mardian, go tell him I have slain myself; / Say, that the last I spoke was 'Antony'" (4.13.7–8). The falseness of her report is true to form: she will use any means to spur Antony to be Antony yet. To this witness of her faith, he responds by falling on his sword: in his end, he ties together the heroic conventions of which the whole pattern has been woven.

The scene of Antony's death, then, with all its ironic qualification of the noble values implicit in those conventions, comes as the logical climax of a pattern that shapes the play as a sequence of tests of our faith in heroic dramaturgy. Like so much else in the play, it is a scene of parodic high-seriousness. In it, Shakespeare holds up the traditions of heroic tragedy for critical scrutiny: he affirms their legitimacy even as he exposes their inadequacies. He could not have conceived of the epic drama of Antony and Cleopatra without relying on conventions he had employed throughout his career. There would have been no sense of legendary greatness, no nobility, no way of measuring the *fall* from greatness without them. But he uses them in such a way that they appear artificial, old-fashioned, and finally inadequate to describe a heroic reality; and by doing that, he allows us, if we so choose, not to credit them at all. He makes us aware that only with the aid of imagination can we preserve a belief in traditional heroism—and in the traditional ways of representing it—such as conventions bid for. Our success in suspending disbelief depends on an understanding of Cleopatra's power to convince herself, and us, of the nobility embodied in *her* end.

Janet Adelman argues that the play strives to command our belief not despite but *through* its insistence on doubt. We emerge from the short, unsettling scenes of the first four acts that constantly shift point of view and thus detach us from the lovers' view of themselves, into the expansive resolution of act 5, a scene in which time is at its period and Cleopatra's point of view prevails. "If the dramatic structure now permits us to become engaged with the lovers," Adelman suggests, "it also works to give us the feeling of assent in spite of all logic" (159). In other words, engagement with Cleopatra anesthetizes our critical faculties, and a "new ease" releases us from the "restless tension . . . which action and language had imposed on us earlier" (160). Adelman attributes to Cleopatra, in this act, the power of a Phaedria to lure our unguarded intellectual temperance onto a lake of idleness and to beguile us into a belief that her hyperbolic dream is reality.

Adelman persuasively articulates an opinion many critics share: that act 5 grandly fulfills our expectations of heroic tragedy and restores heroic conventions—even those parodied in Antony's death—to full dramatic currency.[14] Cleopatra controls the scene with a remarkable sense of theatrical illusion. "Give me my robe, put on my crown; I have / Immortal longings in me" (5.2.280–81), she commands, and in seconds we witness her apotheosis. "I am again for Cydnus, / To meet Mark Antony" (ll. 228–29), she declares, and we remember vividly Enobarbus's description of her on her barge, a beauty surpassing Venus. "Methinks I hear / Antony call; I see him rouse himself / To praise my noble act" (ll. 283–84), she imagines, and we at once see her fulfilling the stoic promise for which Antony has already praised her. From attiring herself as a queen of love to dying artfully in the high Roman fashion, Cleopatra renews those myths that satisfy our expectations of heroic tragedy. In the words of Rosalie Colie, who apparently thinks that form ought to determine content, "the play begins to live up to itself."[15] And in the words of Phyllis Rackin, "the truth of the imagination has become reality"; the heroism of Cleopatra is "evoked by all the resources of Shakespeare's theater, by spectacle as well as poetry, and the show will be theatrical reality. The stage itself, no less than the audience, is here freed from the demands of rationally plausible neoclassic verisimilitude."[16]

This is heady stuff, and it would be imprudent for me to deny the generations of critics and theater-goers who have acquiesced in this vision of heroic transcendence. Cleopatra *does* have the power to beguile. But a close examination of act 5 will demonstrate, I think, that Shakespeare provides ample means to keep one's critical faculties from being *totally* beguiled. Just as he does in the first four acts, he sustains in act 5 a wonderful interplay between heroic vision—Cleopatra's immortal longings—and the diminished truth of human fleshly existence. Cleopatra punctuates Antony's death with rage:

> It were for me
> To throw my scepter at the injurious gods,
> To tell them that this world did equal theirs
> Till they had stol'n our jewel.
>
> (4.15.75–78)

The sentiment is defiantly heroic; but, like Antony's request that Hercules teach him a rage he does not feel, it is qualified by a subjunctive that in part detaches her from the passion which her hyperbole presumably expresses: "It were for me. . . . " Shakespeare makes us aware of a rhetorical quality in her speech to which we would be oblivious if we (and she) were fully engaged with her words. But, as she tells her women, she is "No more but e'en a woman" (l. 73), and she uses heroic artifice as an incentive to revive her fainting spirits. As they revive, she assumes the heroic role with increasing confidence. Antony has provided her with a model stoic suicide, and she resolves to follow suit:

> Good sirs, take heart.
> We'll bury him; and then, what's brave, what's noble,
> Let's do 't after the high Roman fashion,
> And make death proud to take us.
>
> (4.15.85–88)

Yet her resolve is questionable even as she swears it. She may say to her women, "Come; we have no friend / But resolution, and the briefest end" (ll. 90–91), but over three-hundred lines later, the "briefest end" has not yet come. She is, of course, afraid to die, and more afraid to kill herself. This leads her, through act 5, to hesitations and equivocations that alternate with her attempts to live up to the heroic Roman ideal she has chosen. Heroic will and mortal fears stand at odds: in no character does Shakespeare dramatize their conflict better than in Cleopatra.

She plays for time by hinting that she may make terms with Caesar. She assures Proculeius that she will comply with Caesar's wishes if he will guarantee the kingdom for her son. Perhaps she is simply trying to secure the best deal for her children before taking her own life; perhaps not. She berates Seleucus for revealing that she has not itemized all her money, plate, and jewels, in what may be a ploy to deceive Caesar into thinking she intends to live, or may be evidence that she *does* plan to live. Shakespeare leaves her motives tantalizingly opaque. She renews her stoic vow, in fact, only when surprised by Roman soldiers. "Where art thou, death?" she asks, drawing a dagger and continuing to play to her audience: "Come hither, come! Come, come, and take a queen / Worth many babes and beggars!" (5.2.45–47). When Proculeius scolds her for intemperance, she replies:

> Sir, I will eat no meat, I'll not drink, sir;
> If idle talk will once be necessary,
> I'll not sleep neither. This mortal house I'll ruin,
> Do Caesar what he can.
>
> (5.2.48–51)

Such is the hyperbole of self-denial: strong, bold, resolute. As she continues, however, her language grows *more* intemperate, as if she is straining to muster the heroic resolve that human frailty would fain deny. She will, she says, refuse to be taken in triumph to Rome: the thought of humiliation must be as painful to her as the prospect of death. But the extremity of her diction reveals how awful the choice would be for her to make:

> Rather a ditch in Egypt
> Be gentle grave unto me! Rather on Nilus' mud
> Lay me stark naked, and let the water-flies
> Blow me into abhorring! Rather make
> My country's high pyramides my gibbet,
> And hang me up in chains!
>
> (5.2.56–61)

Language such as this recalls the plays that helped to shape Shakespeare's tragedy, particularly Daniel's *Cleopatra* which, more than Garnier's or the Countess of Pembroke's versions, emphasized Cleopatra's difficult choice of honor over life—a choice that verifies her previously questionable love for Antony and ennobles her in the process.[17] Shakespeare's heroine is like her Senecan predecessor in fearing most that she may be ridiculed by "the shouting varletry / Of censuring Rome" and, worse, "chastis'd with the sober eye / Of dull Octavia" (ll. 53–56). In the view of J. L. Simmons, these fears help to dramatize "a new Cleopatra rising from Antony's ruin and . . . invest her suicide with high moral significance."[18] If Shakespeare used Daniel's Cleopatra as a model, though, he exaggerated her diction to most histrionic effect. His Cleopatra's ravings about the tortures she is willing to endure are the sort of rant she had used before to defend herself against Antony's charge of treason: "From my cold heart let heaven engender hail, / And poison it in the source"; "Dissolve my life"; "The next Caesarion smite." By pricking our recollection of her earlier rant, Shakespeare implies that she may be using it here to a similar end: to convince her audience—Antony there; Proculeius here—of her credibility, of a heroic absoluteness that she does not feel. The exaggeration of her diction betrays in her a *lack* of the conviction that the heroic idiom customarily signifies. It serves as a defense mechanism to hide the disparity between heroic resolution and those human fears that keep her irresolute. Proculeius seems to recognize some disparity when he observes, "You do extend / These thoughts of horror further than you shall / Find cause in Caesar" (ll. 61–63). He spots her as a wavering mortal far removed from her more absolute Senecan original. In his eyes, as in ours, she is the more sympathetic for that.

Cleopatra's determination to be noble to herself seems assured only when she tests Caesar's good will towards her and finds it wanting. "He words me, girls, he words me," she judges (l. 191); and when Dolabella's intelligence proves her judgment correct—Caesar fully intends to lead her in triumph to Rome—she paints a scene of unendurable humiliation. "The quick comedians," she fears,

> Extemporally will stage us, and present
> Our Alexandrian revels; Antony
> Shall be brought drunken forth, and I shall see
> Some squeaking Cleopatra boy my greatness
> I' th' posture of a whore.
>
> (5.2.216–21)

Cleopatra knows the power of dramatic illusion to mock and degrade what it ought to exalt. Honor, for her as for Antony, entails a preservation of one's image, one's public fame. Knowledge that she will be insulted and defamed, therefore, gives her the courage at last to live up to her idiom and die like a queen. The quick comedians, after all, would be hard pressed to play a noble Roman suicide for laughs. "My resolution's plac'd," she vows, "and I have nothing / Of woman in me. Now from head to foot / I am marble-constant" (ll. 238–40). Her stoic affirmation prepares us to watch her honor the pledge she made to Antony an act earlier.

Even in death, however—a death so magnificently enacted that many claim it fulfills the play's heroic promise—there is some disparity betwen act and intent. Properly speaking, Cleopatra does not make a stoic end. She aspires to a mythic afterlife where, as Antony imagined at his own death, the only shades will be those in the bower where she, a goddess, may ensnare her Mars in venery everlasting. The "high Roman fashion" may be her ideal; but in fact, her death holds too much of promise, too much of worldly pleasure, to make it convincingly Roman. Her last thoughts have nothing to do with the nobleness of life as Romans understood it. Instead, they alternate between erotic reunion with Antony—"If she first meet the curled Antony," she says, seeing Iras fall, "He'll make demand of her, and spend that kiss / Which is my heaven to have" (ll. 301–3)—and political defeat of Caesar—"O, couldst thou speak," she whispers to the asp, "That I might hear thee call great Caesar ass / Unpolicied!" (ll. 306–8). Her concerns are mortal: sex peppered with jealousy, politics seasoned with spite. Neither eroticism nor policy, of course, is consonant with the honor that she claims motivates her act. But her death is the more glorious for that discrepancy, for it affirms most brilliantly what Cleopatra has been in life— a cagey queen and a damned good lover—and apotheosizes her most stunning attribute, her infinite variety. It gives us in full measure what she is best at—theatrical illusion. Her immortal longings are, like those of Ovid's heroic lovers, true to the flesh; and we watch her satisfy them in a spectacle that is indulgently of this world.

The request with which Cleopatra leaves us, then, is the same as the one with which Antony leaves her: Believe in me. They both manipulate the language and the structural forms of heroic tragedy to serve their own ends—to entreat us to believe in their legendary selves. But like their responses to one another, ours to them is equivocal. No matter how much we would like to believe, their heroic claims are too often frustrated to command our full assent. To borrow Cleopatra's phrase, they word us: they would urge upon us an illusion of heroic greatness, and so, on a purely formal level, would the play. But by the time we arrive at this late play we are, like Antony and Cleopatra themselves, not true believers. We do not naively equate conventions with reality as we once did in the early histories; we no longer automatically assume that the heroic idiom defines a true heroism. We weigh the evidence with a trained eye and find too much wanting to sustain our belief in Antony and Cleopatra as conventional heroes or in the play as traditional heroic tragedy.

Undeniably, there is greatness in Cleopatra's end: she does in part become the paragon of heroic love who lives in fame. One of the glories of this play is that it preserves the legendary Antony and Cleopatra even as it challenges us to revise our view of them. When Caesar delivers his conventional eulogy over them—"No grave upon the earth shall clip in it / A pair so famous" (ll. 358–59)—we acknowledge the fitness of it. But recent criticism with its metadramatic bias has tended too much in the direction of belief. In regarding all representations of reality as veiled metaphors *for* the theater, critics have easily assumed that truth and illusion are indistinguishable *in* the theater. This assumption, I suspect, has led them too readily to embrace Cleopatra's fiction as the play's final reality. This embrace needs to be unlocked: critics need to stand at arms' length from Cleopatra, as they have from Antony, to see her not just as she sees herself, but for what her actions make her.

Despite its formal fulfillment of our expectations of heroic tragedy, act 5 continues the methods of detachment that keep our critical faculties alert. Its ironies are of a piece with those that prevented us from being seduced by the heroic fictions of the previous acts and taught us to examine conventions dispassionately. Shakespeare does not ask us suddenly to shift critical gears for Cleopatra's death scene, does not ask us, as Cleopatra asks Dolabella, to forsake all reason. Tragedy is, after all, an art that requires a rational as well as an emotional response. It is not a religious observance. A theater is not a church. The conflict between heroic hyperbole and a diminished human reality in *Antony and Cleopatra* is too fundamental, too pervasive to allow us to make a leap of faith. Even if Cleopatra satisfies her immortal longings by staging an apotheosis unmatched by anyone but Wagner's Tristan and Isolde, she is also a whore, albeit a great one, whose Alexandrian revels have come to a most mortal end. A complete appreciation of Shakespeare's art depends on our awareness of the tension he creates between demands for rational analysis and persuasions to give in to the fiction.

The ending of *Antony and Cleopatra* is analogous to the ending of *King Lear*, where the optimism implicit in Lear's and Cordelia's vow to abjure the world for the paradise of a prison is silenced by Cordelia's death and Lear's return to madness. The force of their *contemptus mundi* lives in our minds even after it has been dramatically discredited. Cleopatra, in her dream of an Emperor Antony, poses the problem more explicitly: Can the force of imagination overwhelm the representation of reality played out on stage? If it can, Shakespeare answers her, it must be the force of her imagination, not ours. His plays do not permit us absolutely to identify with the protagonist's perspective. Just as the Christian affirmation lives, it if lives at all, in the mind of Lear the man rather than in *Lear* the play, so the pagan affirmation lives in Antony and Cleopatra as wishers, not as play.

Those who accept Cleopatra's vision as the play's usually argue that *Antony and Cleopatra* ushers in the period of Shakespearean romance. As Northrop Frye writes, in romance "we surrender ourselves to the story and accept its conventions."[19] To the extent that we surrender our vision to Cleopatra's and are willing to make romance with her, the play is romance. In tragedy, on the other hand, Shakespeare had grown to insist on a psychological complexity alien to the conventional cast of mind. If *Antony and Cleopatra* is considered a profound study of character under stress, we must hold conventions at bay, resist stock responses, never surrender our intellects as we would to romance.

Heroic tragedy, to be sure, is traditionally defined by as many conventions as comedy and romance. For an Elizabethan, heroism was born in myth and nurtured in countless applications of myth to historical figures: thus, in Shakespeare's histories, the heroes of Troy adumbrate the warriors of the roses; the legends of Alexander are indelibly etched in the progress of Henry V. Traditional tragic forms compounded those heroic myths: great men fell from high places, turned with the wheel of fortune, were paid for some great crime or sin or excess by a death that ennobled them even as it damned them. Thus a usurping York could, under the torments of Margaret, metamorphose into an English Hector to make a good end. A Titus Andronicus, awful in his descent to mad revenge, could be praised in death as the Roman Priam. Or a Macbeth, royal butcher that he was, could go greatly to the fire bearing the burdens of a Hercules.

Although, in his early plays, Shakespeare conceived of tragic heroism entirely through the conventions of the received heroic idiom, his greatest achievement was to free tragedy from that servitude and move it towards a dramatization of the hero's inner life, wherein conventions, when they appear, often serve as vehicles against which to measure verisimilitude. Shakespeare echoed traditionally heroic scenes from his earlier plays in his later ones to provide yardsticks for his new "realism"; but even as he exposed the old idiom as artificial, he relied on it, paradoxically, to establish traditional heroic patterns and assumptions without which his more sophisticated *mimesis* could not persuade us to accept his new heroes as rightly great. By the time of *Antony and Cleopatra* he had taught us to regard the idiom as both an essential component of heroic definition yet, in itself, incapable of defining the complex forces at war within the mind of the tragic hero. Antony and Cleopatra may use the idiom to try to mythologize themselves—to ensnare willing believers in their strong toils of grace. But qualified by a context that makes us wary of such an exercise, they fail. From their failure emerges the true tragedy.

Notes

Chapter 1. Heroic Mimesis

1. In his discussion of heroic poetry Sidney closely follows sixteenth-century Italian apologists, especially Minturno. The *Defence,* though probably written in 1580, was not printed until 1595. I quote from Albert Feuillerat's edition of *The Complete Works of Sir Philip Sidney* (Cambridge: At the University Press, 1923), 3:25.

2. Heywood's *Apology,* published in 1612, is quoted from Richard H. Perkinson's facsimile prepared by Scholars' Facsimiles and Reprints (New York, 1941), sigs. B_3–B_4.

3. Samuel Daniel, *The First Fowre Bookes of the Civile Wars Between the Two Houses of Lancaster and Yorke* (London, 1595), 4:42; cited in *Narrative and Dramatic Sources of Shakespeare,* ed. Geoffrey Bullough (New York: Columbia University Press, 1962), 4:421.

4. Coriolanus's speech is open to misinterpretation. The middle three-and-one-half lines constitute a parenthetical attack on what custom wills him to do: to adhere slavishly to "antique time"—that is, to follow conventional patterns of old—will lead only to "mountainous error," not to "the most high and excellent truth" that Sidney insists is the end of heroic emulation. Rather than play the fool by following the pattern himself ("Rather than fool it so"), Coriolanus presumably will seek truth by doing something revolutionary (sweeping the dust), and let the office and honor—terms of ironic disparagement here—go to a conventional hero. The "one that would do thus" is consequently a perpetrator of error: the real irony of the speech resides in the fact that Coriolanus is himself the "one" who is doing "thus". As he finishes the speech, he turns again to beg for more citizens' voices. The ambivalence of the speech results from the conflict between Coriolanus's wry, almost satirical tone and our recognition that the object of his satire is one other than himself. He speaks with a self-directed irony: it is a quality not usually ascribed to Coriolanus.

5. For an analysis of Cominius's speech as a product of epic-narrative tradition, see Reuben Brower, *Hero and Saint: Shakespeare and the Graeco-Roman Heroic Tradition* (New York: Oxford University Press, 1971), 355–61.

6. *Shakespearean Representation: Mimesis and Modernity in Elizabethan Tragedy* (Princeton: Princeton University Press, 1977), 39. Felperin owes something to the studies by Walter Jackson Bate and, more psychoanalytically, Harold Bloom of the writer's struggle to overcome the influence of previous writers' conceptions of "reality;" but Felperin's concern, like mine, is not so much with the psyche of the writer as with the ways in which his art incorporates and reshapes prior art. A. D. Nuttall, too, adopts a conception of "reality" that depends on Shakespeare's simultaneous employment of and deviation from conventions, or formal tropes. His essay "Realistic Convention and Conventional Realism in Shakespeare," *Shakespeare Survey* 34 (1981): 33–37, provides a stimulating rebuttal to Structuralists' belief that all reality may be reduced to a set of codes. And G. R. Hibbard, in *The Making of Shakespeare's Dramatic Poetry* (Toronto: University of Toronto Press, 1981), applies similar ideas with great sensitivity to

Shakespeare's development of a distinctly unconventional language for characterization in the early plays.

7. Of the many books to which I refer in the ensuing chapters, I limit myself here to the most influential: Reuben Brower, *Hero and Saint,* on how the Renaissance formulated its conception of heroic ideals and responded to them, in translations and imitations of the ancients; two books by Eugene M. Waith: *The Herculean Hero in Marlowe, Chapman, Shakespeare and Dryden* (New York: Columbia University Press, 1962), on the transmission of the most significant heroic myth from classical to Renaissance drama, and *Ideas of Greatness: Heroic Drama in England* (London: Routledge and Kegan Paul, 1971), on the formative influence medieval romance had on stage recreations of heroism; Howard Baker, *Induction to Tragedy* (Baton Rouge: Louisiana State University Press, 1939), and Moody E. Prior, *The Language of Tragedy* (New York: Columbia University Press, 1947), on the evolution of a heroic verse in England, from Surrey's *Aeneid* onward; and Fredson Bowers, *Elizabethan Revenge Tragedy, 1587–1642* (Princeton: Princeton University Press, 1940), who, like Baker, tries to wrest studies of Elizabethan heroism from the grip of Seneca; David Riggs, *Shakespeare's Heroical Histories: "Henry VI" and Its Literary Tradition* (Cambridge, Mass.: Harvard University Press, 1971), on the rhetorical origins of heroism in the early tetralogy; and Matthew Proser, *The Heroic Image in Five Shakespearean Tragedies* (Princeton: Princeton University Press, 1965), a New Critical attempt to trace Shakespeare's emergent conception of heroism.

Chapter 2. Emulation Hath a Thousand Sons

1. Though my argument does not hinge absolutely on the relative dating of the plays, I accept the view, now widely shared, that the three parts of *Henry VI* were written by Shakespeare in sequence, beginning in 1590, and furthermore that the Folio texts are more authoritative than the texts of the *First Part of the Contention* and *The True Tragedie of Richard Duke of Yorke,* which apparently are memorial reconstructions. Arguments are summarized and weighed by Andrew S. Cairncross in his New Arden editions of the three plays (London: Methuen, 1962, 1962, 1964).

2. In "The Formation of the Heroic Medium," chap. 2 of his *Induction to Tragedy,* Howard Baker discusses the development of heroic language in the midsixteenth century, from Surrey onward. Wolfgang Clemen devotes the last two chapters of *English Tragedy before Shakespeare: The Development of Dramatic Speech,* trans. T. S. Dorsch (New York: Barnes and Noble, 1961), exclusively to the lament and its forms. Shakespeare, he argues, took time to outgrow the ostentatious eloquence of grief, "the all too rich and ready flow of words" (222) he had inherited from Seneca. In such lament, parallels with mythic and epic figures endow historical characters with grand supernatural associations and lead to a fuller understanding of the speaker's sorrow. This almost religious intensity is also achieved by the speaker's use of the "outbidding topos" (230–31), in which the character is said to have gone the myth one better, just as Henry does Caesar.

3. Edward Hall, *The Union of the Two Noble and Illustre Famelies of Lancastre and Yorke* (1548), lxxxi^v, reprinted in Cairncross's edition of *1 Henry VI,* 134.

4. All references are to *The Complete Plays of Christopher Marlowe,* ed. Irving Ribner (New York: Odyssey Press, 1963). At his own death, Tamburlaine uses imagery that also might have inspired Bedford's line: "Come, let us march against the powers of heaven / And set black streamers in the firmament" (*Part Two:* 5.3.48–49).

5. See Hall, *Union,* Clxiiii^v, cited in Cairncross's edition, 161.

6. Moody Prior accounts for the manner of the conventional Nuntius in *The Language of Tragedy,* 49–50.

7. See Riggs, *Shakespeare's Heroical Histories,* 1–33 and 62–92. Irving Ribner, too, in *The English History Play in the Age of Shakespeare* (Princeton: Princeton University Press, 1957),

suggests the importance of heroic traditions to a proper understanding of the early history plays.

8. Waith, in *The Herculean Hero,* 60–87, assesses the various ways in which Marlowe used the Hercules myth to insulate Tamburlaine from traditional value judgments. Though it may be argued that Tamburlaine is in fact an historical figure, he is nonetheless remote enough to have been regarded as legendary and thus, in a sense, outside the bounds of historical context and social measure. The myth of Alexander, too, permeates the two parts of *Tamburlaine.*

9. Curtis Watson, in *Shakespeare and the Renaissance Concept of Honor* (Princeton: Princeton University Press, 1960), places these divergent concepts of honor—one as fame or reputation; the other, truth to self—in the context of European intellectual development. And in the first two chapters of *Ideas of Greatness,* Waith discusses how the chivalric ideals of medieval romance gradually emerged in Renaissance drama.

10. Arthur B. Ferguson, in *The Indian Summer of English Chivalry* (Durham, N.C.: Duke University Press, 1960), deals at length with the complex fate of chivalric idealism in the context of state: "Always at bottom a personal code, chivalry could not, however, maintain indefinitely its claim to be a code sufficient for the secular life of the governing class as the complexities of Renaissance society called attention with ever growing insistence to the distinction so basic to modern thought between private and public considerations" (128).

11. See Willard Farnham, *The Medieval Heritage of Elizabethan Tragedy* (1937; reprint ed. Oxford: Basil Blackwell, 1956). Lily B. Campbell edited *The Mirror for Magistrates* (1938; reprint ed., New York: Barnes and Noble, 1960); and in *Shakespeare's Tragic Heroes* (1930; reprint ed., New York: Barnes and Noble, 1952) she discusses the intellectual background of the Mirror tradition. Madelaine Doran, in *Endeavors of Art: A Study of Form in Elizabethan Drama* (Madison: University of Wisconsin Press, 1954), 120, traces the *de casibus* form of tragedy back to Senecan origins and to stoicism: Christian moralization is not inherent in the form, therefore. But writers in the Middle Ages soon Christianized it; and as David Bevington demonstrates in *From Mankind to Marlowe* (Cambridge, Mass.: Harvard University Press, 1962), morality-hybrids and chronicle plays readily adapted themselves to the moralized form of *de casibus* tragedy.

12. *The Works of Thomas Nashe,* ed. Ronald B. McKerrow (1910; reprint ed. Oxford: Basil Blackwell, 1958), 1: 212. Emrys Jones, however, in *The Origins of Shakespeare* (Oxford: Clarendon Press, 1977), 155–60, would qualify my assertion. Though the scene of Talbot's death—employing as it does a highly artificial and elevated style—insulates and uplifts him, allows him to die only into fame, Shakespeare nevertheless, according to Jones, fails in its execution. "Whatever Nashe may have thought about their emotional force, these scenes now seem strained and thin, their exaltation something of an effort, their pathos somewhat unmovingly 'official'" (158). And the reason for this failure, Jones suggests, is Shakespeare's lack of enthusiasm for the brand of heroism Talbot practiced: bloody, boastful, vengeful. Shakespeare does not allow us "to accept uncritically the warrior's work of massacre and devastation" (159). If Jones's remarks are anachronistic in their pacifism (though he cites Erasmus for support), and if the evidence he adduces for Talbot's barbarism is spoken largely by Talbot's enemies—the Countess, the Dauphin—he nevertheless forces one to reexamine the Talbot scenes and question why Shakespeare does resort to such stylistic artificiality in them.

13. See "'I am but a shadow of myself': Ceremony and Design in *1 Henry VI*" in *Shakespearean Meanings* (Princeton: Princeton University Press, 1968), 47–77. Burckhardt shows that the hyperbolic language of ceremonial assertion is the idiom common to virtually all the characters in *1 Henry VI:* through it, Shakespeare depicts the War of the Roses as unrealistic and self-defeating in its "relentless reaching for the superlative" (53). Only when Talbot responds to the Countess by stopping short her ceremonial taunt, Burckhardt argues, does Shakespeare allow a voice of tempered realism to put the hyperbole in its place. In this scene only, Talbot functions as a critical commentator on the whole *medium* of the War of the

Roses. Although I do not fully concur with Burckhardt's metadramatic analysis and suspect that Talbot's voice is not quite so realistic as Burckhardt would wish it, my remarks on the scene are nevertheless indebted to his provocative reading.

14. In a stimulating paper called "Self-reflexiveness and Realism in *Henry VI*," presented at the meeting of the Shakespeare Association of American in Minneapolis, April 1982, Peter Berek goes beyond Burckhardt—outdoes him, if you will—by claiming that Talbot is "thoroughly self-conscious" in his response to the Countess: he plays the *role* of bluff soldier and, in his own person, is skeptical of the value of chivalry. Burckhardt had suggested that Talbot deviates from his conventionally heroic character in this scene only to become Shakespeare's spokesman. Berek says he is his *own* spokesman. In this, I part company with him: there is not sufficient evidence to call Talbot a self-dramatizing character or to claim that *1 Henry VI* is a play about play-making.

15. Riggs, *Shakespeare's Heroical Histories*, 104–6.

16. Ibid., 126.

17. Riggs alludes to these passages in a fuller analysis of York's long set-speech in ibid., 122–23.

18. See G. K. Hunter, "Seneca and English Tragedy" in *Seneca*, ed. C. D. N. Costa (London: Routledge and Kegan Paul, 1974), 189. When I speak of Senecan influence on Shakespeare, I focus largely on the rhetorical methods that Shakespeare derived from Seneca through reading the original and through his knowledge of prior dramatists, *not* on any substantive imitation of Senecan drama. In an earlier essay, "Seneca and the Elizabethans: A Case-study in 'Influence'," *Shakespeare Survey* 20 (1967): 17–26, Hunter demonstrates that the nature of such influence in fact amounts to little more than verbal echo: more traditional claims that Seneca pervades Elizabethan tragedy in both substance and ethos, Hunter argues, fail to take into account the eclectic nature of Elizabethan borrowing, especially from native drama and from Ovid. In the first chapters of *English Tragedy before Shakespeare*, Wolfgang Clemen assesses the characteristic rhetoric of Italian and English tragedy in set-speeches of stereotypical emotion—grief, hatred, revenge—that are so glaringly exaggerated that they leave little room for differentiation, both among one another and among the characters who speak them. And Seneca, Clemen asserts, was not so guilty of this as his imitators.

19. See Inga-Stina Ewbank, "The Fiend-like Queen: A Note on 'Macbeth' and Seneca's 'Medea'," *Shakespeare Survey* 19 (1966): 87–88. Ewbank observes that although Ovid's *Tristia*, 3.9, is usually assumed to be the source of Clifford's allusion, Seneca, unlike Ovid, emphasizes the boy's youth ("tender Brother"), and only from Studley would Shakespeare have gotten the word *gobbets*, a word that he uses twice in this play and then never again. Its other appearance is equally lurid. It occurs in the scene where Walter Whitmore slays Suffolk. The lieutenant, declaring his rhetorical aim against Suffolk—"First let my words stab him" (4.1.66)—vents his spleen in terms that would do credit to a Senecan imitator:

> By devilish policy art thou grown great,
> And, like ambitious Sylla, overgorg'd
> With gobbets of thy mother's bleeding heart.

(4.1.83–85)

The quotation of Studley's *Medea* is from *Seneca, His Tenne Tragedies*, ed. Thomas Newton (1581; reprint ed., London: Constable, 1927), 2:61.

20. Inga-Stina Ewbank suggests the connection in "The Fiend-like Queen," 89–90.

21. All references are to *The Works of Thomas Kyd*, ed. Frederick S. Boas (Oxford: Clarendon Press, 1901).

22. Compare Perseda's line, "A kisse I graunt thee, though I hate thee deadlie" (5.4.67) in *Soliman and Perseda*, located in Boas's edition of Kyd. The play is usually ascribed to Kyd, though authorship is uncertain. The echo—one of many from *Soliman and Perseda* heard in *3 Henry VI*—is noted by Cairncross, who also lists verbal echoes of *The Spanish Tragedie* (though not all of them) in Appendix V of his edition.

23. This neglected essay is found in Howarth's *The Tiger's Heart: Eight Essays on Shakespeare* (London: Oxford University Press, 1970), 24–44. It is a remarkably lucid synthesis of perspectives on heroic idealism in works by the major Elizabethan poets and dramatists. Shakespeare's view of history, Howarth tries to demonstrate, is analogous to that of the Old Testament and that of Attic historians. But in calling Shakespeare a realist and an empiricist, he bows too low to the forces of modern skepticism.

24. The object of such images is to fill the hearer with a sense of wonder, to make him ask with cool detachment, "How can such things be?" This object is akin to that of Ovid's *Metamorphoses* and helps to explain the importance of that work as a source for *Titus:* emotional response to violence, such as one is told Senecan drama evokes, is a far different thing. The seminal study of Ovid's influence on *Titus* is Eugene M. Waith's "The Metamorphosis of Violence in 'Titus Andronicus'," *Shakespeare Surey* 10 (1957): 39–49. In *The Making of Shakespeare's Dramatic Poetry,* George Hibbard compares Marcus's speech with Hieronimo's discovery of the dead Horatio, which he thinks Shakespeare was consciously imitating, and concludes, "The attempt to 'overgo' Kyd has ended in a bad 'overdoing' of the effect he aimed at and achieved" (50).

25. In this chapter, I am approximating Robert Y. Turner's argument in *Shakespeare's Apprenticeship* (Chicago: University of Chicago Press, 1974) that rhetoric in the early plays fully determines the limits of character. Rhetoric, by its very nature, assumes a congruity of motive, manifestation, and moral judgment; as such, according to Turner, it stands at odds with mimesis, which is so fraught with irony that it contradicts the force of rhetoric. I disagree with him here, for it seems to me that mimesis can employ rhetoric to serve its own ends even if those ends are ultimately different from those of rhetoric; nor would I agree that Shakespeare conceived his chronicle plays "along the lines of an oration" (34) and thereby intended them to be didactic rather than mimetic (awkward distinction). But the general thrust of his argument anticipates my suggestion that in *Titus,* Shakespeare begins to manipulate rhetoric in such a way as to transcend the limitations of rhetorically defined character and achieve instead an evanescent commodity called life:

> Characters undergo a change comparable to the audience's. In the earlier rhetorical plays they talk like orators, classify other characters by simple categories, and respond to rhetoric much as the playwright expects the audience to be stimulated by his drama. In the later more mimetic plays, characters gain in awareness of themselves and others, are inclined to express their feelings obliquely, as Lucrece does when she responds to the painting of Troy, and exhibit a mixture of bad and good qualities. Their ability to express modulations of feeling requires us to take into account details of story that inhibit ready, categorical judgments. Along with their capacity to express themselves obliquely, usually through descriptive tableaux, many judge themselves. This extra awareness suggests something apart from the composite qualities of character. Different from "characteristics," it creates the impression of a substance underlying and containing the characteristics so that after we have categorized and judged, something is left over. This something, never fully known, helps make plausible the potentiality for change of character. (P. 235)

Chapter 3. Ironic Heroism

1. The sources for *Julius Caesar* are ably discussed by Ernest Schanzer in *The Problem Plays of Shakespeare* (1963; reprint ed. New York: Schocken Books, 1965), 10–70, who attributes the play's ambivalent attitude toward Caesar to Shakespeare's deliberate playing off of the historical (and critical) assessment of him against the popular and laudatory legend. Geoffrey Bullough, in *Narrative and Dramatic Sources of Shakespeare,* vol. 5 : 25–35, pays special attention to Shakespeare's Senecan models, from the pseudo-Senecan Latin *Octavia,* translated by Thomas Nuce in 1561, through Kyd's translation of Garnier's *Cornélie* in 1594, to the academic *Tragedie of Caesar and Pompey, or Caesar's Revenge,* based largely on Appian and probably performed at Trinity College, Oxford, in the 1590s. Schanzer thinks this last play

had direct bearing on Shakespeare: see "A Neglected Source of *Julius Caesar*," *Notes and Queries* 199 (May 1954): 196–97.

2. Shakespeare may have had this scene from *Henry VI* in mind when composing the scene of Caesar's death. In it the crafty Richard suggests that it might be wise to dispose of Queen Margaret along with Edward—"Why should she live, to fill the world with words?" (l. 44)—but is overborne by his brother King Edward, who speaks in conscience, "we have done too much" (l. 43). This opposition of attitudes anticipates that part of the scene in *Caesar* where Cassius, with his accustomed pragmatism, argues for killing Antony but is overborne by the more "prudent" Brutus, only to find that Antony does indeed live to fill the world with words.

3. Bullough provides an extensive synopsis of the play and prints some scenes in their entirety on 196–211. *Caesar's Revenge* was the only play before Shakespeare to dramatize Caesar's murder.

4. Howard Baker cites these instances of the curse in his study of the origins of Elizabethan bombast in *Induction to Tragedy*, 90–91.

5. In *The Problem Plays of Shakespeare*, 52–54, Schanzer argues—rightly, I think—that this and other hunting metaphors in the play were "set off in the poet's mind by Plutarch's description of Caesar as 'hacked and mangled among them, as a wild beast taken of hunters.'" But the germ of a metaphor does not guarantee that the blossom will be predictable: in this case, the style is decidedly Ovidian, not at all Plutarchan.

6. Compare Robert Turner's observation about Shakespeare's growing sophistication as a creator of character in *Shakespeare's Apprenticeship:* "Self-consciousness about language is part and parcel of the characters' encroachment upon the prerogatives of the playwright, who relinquishes many of the decisions he automatically makes when he composes rhetorical drama" (244).

7. Nicholas Brooke objects that the ending of *Julius Caesar,* and particularly Antony's epitaph over Brutus's corpse, tends to push into the realm of conventional heroic tragedy a play that has carefully exposed the speciousness of the values and rhetoric that create an illusion of heroism: thus it gives the play "a fragile tragic value . . . which cannot survive criticism": *Shakespeare's Early Tragedies* (London: Methuen, 1968), 158–62. It is Shakespeare's deliberate irony, I think, to allow Antony to speak over Brutus the praise he would speak over the conventional hero, and to see Brutus as Brutus has tried (unsuccessfully) to see himself throughout—as a man honest, noble of purpose, and motivated only by the general good.

8. A. P. Rossiter makes shrewd observations about the theatrical nature of Richard's role-playing in "Angel with Horns: The Unity of Richard III," in *Angel with Horns,* ed. Graham Storey (New York: Theater Art Books, 1961), 1–22.

9. My discussion of the *eiron* is indebted to J. A. K. Thomson's *Irony: An Historical Introduction* (Cambridge, Mass.: Harvard University Press, 1927), 2–33.

10. See Francis MacDonald Cornford, *The Origins of Attic Comedy* (1914; reprint ed., Garden City, N.Y.: Doubleday, 1961), 182; and for a general account of the *eiron* and *alazon* in their comic interaction, 115ff. Theophrastus defines the two types in his *Characters.* In his *Anatomy of Criticism* (Princeton: Princeton University Press, 1957), Northrop Frye restores the terms to our critical vocabulary and applies them to tragic as well as comic types—the *eiron* as the source of nemesis in tragedy, the *alazon* as an impostor made dizzy by his own hubris; the *eiron* as predestined artist, the *alazon* as predestined victim (40, 216–17). Maynard Mack, too, applies the terms both to comic types and to their tragic counterparts in his "Engagement and Detachment in Shakespeare's Plays," in *Essays on Shakespeare and Elizabethan Drama,* ed. Richard Hosley (Columbia: University of Missouri Press, 1962), 275–96. Mack suggests that in tragedy, an *eiron*'s problem is too much detachment; an *alazon*'s, too much engagement.

11. Thomson, *Irony,* 18.

12. Bernard Spivack's *Shakespeare and the Allegory of Evil* (New York: Columbia University Press, 1958) remains the definitive study of the Vice as a figure who spans the whole of Elizabethan drama, conventional in his manipulation of rhetoric but devoid of any psychologically compelling (or even credible) motive to explain his behavior. Richard's use of heroic

imposture may be partly, not fully, explained by his political egotism; but the delight he takes in villainy is still explicable only in terms of antimimetic traditions. A. R. Braunmuller has recently and succinctly surveyed the hybridization of the Vice with other types—tyrant, Machiavel, revenger, Mankind—in an essay entitled "Early Shakespearian Tragedy and Its Contemporary Context: Cause and Emotion in *Titus Andronicus, Richard III,* and *The Rape of Lucrece,*" in *Shakespearian Tragedy,* ed. Malcolm Bradbury and D. J. Palmer, Stratford-upon-Avon Studies, no. 20 (London: Edward Arnold, 1984), 96–128.

13. Alvin Kernan, for example, discusses Richard as an innocent believer in the golden world in which kingship is guaranteed by divine right and natural hierarchy, and he uses this very quotation to substantiate his point. See "The Henriad: Shakespeare's Major History Plays," *Modern Shakespearean Criticism,* ed. Alvin B. Kernan (New York: Harcourt, Brace, and World, 1970), 247–48. I am otherwise indebted to Kernan's theory that the man of the new order, who replaces a ceremonial with an historical concept of kingship, thinks of himself in terms of role-playing (245–75, passim).

14. This is one of the definitions of irony in Thomson's *Irony,* 166.

15. In *Shakespeare's History Plays* (London: Chatto and Windus, 1944), 278–85, E. M. W. Tillyard interprets Hal's mockery as satire aimed at "the extreme clumsiness" of Hotspur's "would-be nonchalance" in a scene that portrays Hal, by way of ironic contrast, as the perfect courtier—witty, sophisticated, and genuinely nonchalant. Tillyard sees Hal as a traditional Renaissance courtier.

16. In "Rabbits, Ducks, and *Henry V,*" *Shakespeare Quarterly* 28 (1977): 279–96, revised for *Shakespeare and the Problem of Meaning* (Chicago: University of Chicago Press, 1981), Rabkin, surveying much recent criticism, argues that the play's ultimate power lies precisely in "the fact that it points in two opposite directions, virtually daring us to choose one of the two opposed interpretations it requires of us" (279)—as, say, J. H. Walters does in his assertion that Henry is a paragon of chivalry, or antithetically Harold Goddard does in his demonstration that Henry is a model Machiavel. But the play finally demands of us a "complementary" embrace of its alternatives, *not* a synthesis of them: Rabkin here revises his earlier reading of *Henry V* in *Shakespeare and the Common Understanding* (New York: Free Press, 1967), 98–100, in which, paradoxically, he regarded the play as one of the few that was *not* complementary.

17. In "The Figures of Fluellen," an appendix to *New Readings vs. Old Plays: Recent Trends in the Reinterpretation of English Renaissance Drama* (Chicago: University of Chicago Press, 1979), Richard Levin invokes Fluellen's analogy as a paradigm for a masturbatory critical activity he calls Fluellenism: the habit of finding "figures in all things." Levin had previously debunked such fantasies in "On Fluellen Figures, Christ Figures, and James Figures," *PMLA* 89 (1974) and "The 'Fluellenian' Method," *PMLA* 90 (1975).

18. Some of Pistol's allusions are catalogued by A. R. Humphries in his New Arden edition of *2 Henry IV* (London: Methuen, 1966). Eugene M. Waith in *Ideas of Greatness,* 96–97, discusses Pistol's rant as a travesty of the heroic diction Henry will use when he becomes a conqueror-king. Both Harry Levin's suggestion in "Falstaff's Encore," *Shakespeare Quarterly* 32 (1981): 13–14, that Pistol's awareness of old plays is a barometer of Shakespeare's own awareness of the passing of a heroic style, and G. R. Hibbard's argument in *The Making of Shakespeare's Dramatic Poetry,* 1–6, that Pistol's talent for mixing things up depended on Shakespeare's talent for keeping things straight, have been of great use to me. In his book *George Peele* (Boston: G. K. Hall, 1983), A. R. Braunmuller argues similarly that Shakespeare's allusions to Peele and others are his way of declaring independence.

19. Emrys Jones suggests that the Chorus in *Henry V* may provide the best commentary on Talbot's encounter with the Countess. "There is an immense gulf between the scale of the actual historical events and the token representations of them which is all that the conditions of the drama allow," he observes. The Chorus, of course, "is talking overtly about dramatic illusion, while Talbot is entirely concerned with the circumstances of his meeting with the Countess," and yet both insist on the necessity of a "co-operative imagination" to help flesh out and celebrate a legendary military hero. See *The Origins of Shakespeare,* 147–49.

20. Howard Felperin, *Shakespearean Representation,* 47–48, quotes the relevant lines from *The True Tragedy* and suggests that they go a long way toward explaining Hamlet's impatience with early revenge drama.

21. Felperin's interpretation of the closet scene in terms of Morality tradition (49–52), on which I rely here, is extensive and persuasive.

22. There is no play extant that contains the speech. Marlowe's *Dido, Queen of Carthage,* printed in 1594 but written at least three years earlier, contains a Pyrrhus speech, but Shakespeare's is better; and a *Dido and Aeneas,* acted in 1598 by the Admiral's Men, is now lost. Marlowe's play, as Hibbard suggests in *The Making of Shakespeare's Dramatic Poetry,* 16–17, attempts to recreate in dramatic form something of the effect of Virgil's description of the fall of Troy—an admiration that Renaissance poets regarded as the true end of heroic poetry. Hibbard thinks that Shakespeare was striving for a "generalized Marlovian style" not to burlesque heroic diction, but to discover a genuine archaic voice to mediate between himself and Virgil. In any case, the Pyrrhus speech parodies (even if seriously) a comparatively artificial, certainly hyperbolic type of heroic narration; and Shakespeare *may* have been alluding more specifically to a narration in a lost heroic play, "to show that he could better its style and criticise it at the same time," in the words of John Dover Wilson. See his edition of *Hamlet* in the New Cambridge series, 2d ed. (1936; reprint ed. Cambridge: At the University Press, 1971), 183–84n.

23. See "Engagement and Detachment in Shakespeare's Plays," 287.

4. The Matter of Troy

1. Nathaniel E. Griffin, in "Un-Homeric Elements in the Story of Troy," *JEGP* 7 (1907): 32–52, was first to identify Dares and Dictys as the *loci classici* for the medieval denigration of classical heroism. Other useful accounts of Shakespeare's use of sources for this play are Robert K. Presson, *Shakespeare's "Troilus and Cressida" and The Legends of Troy* (Madison: University of Wisconsin Press, 1953); Kenneth Muir, *Shakespeare's Sources,* vol. I (London: Methuen, 1957); Robert Kimbrough, *Shakespeare's "Troilus and Cressida" and Its Setting* (Cambridge, Mass.: Harvard University Press, 1964); and Bullough, *Narrative and Dramatic Sources of Shakespeare,* vol. 6.

2. Lydgate's *Troy Book,* written at the request of Henry V between 1412 and 1420 (and first printed in 1513), followed the Latin history of Guido da Colonna, who in turn relied heavily on the apocrypha of Dictys and Dares. Lydgate's *Fall of Princes,* written between 1430 and 1438 (and printed in 1494) also contained Troy material that Shakespeare is likely to have consulted. Caxton's translation of *The Recuyell of the Historyes of Troye* was completed in 1471. In *Shakespeare's Problem Plays* (Toronto: University of Toronto Press, 1950), 41ff., E. M. W. Tillyard remarks that Shakespeare found the *Troy Book* his most compatible source because it admired the chivalric nature of Homer's heroes but at the same time disparged war as irrational and immoral—an ambivalence that Shakespeare's play in part preserves. Mark Sacharoff, in "The Traditions of the Troy-Story Heroes and the Problem of Satire in 'Troilus and Cressida,'" *Shakespeare Studies* 6 (1970): 125–35, takes an equally complicated stand. Caxton and Lydgate should not be held accountable for Shakespeare's derogation of Homer's heroes, he argues; for though they cast the *Iliad* in chivalric times and thus diminished mythic heroes by confining them to a fixed period, such diminution does not constitute derogation. Indeed, says Sacharoff, Caxton and Lydgate offer ample evidence that they admired Homer's heroes and wished to conceive of them on the grand scale; but grandeur to them meant chivalry. For more factual, if not commonplace, accounts of how Shakespeare may have used Lydgate and Caxton, see Roscoe Addison Small, *The Stage-Quarrel between Ben Jonson and the So-called Poetasters* (Breslau, 1899), 154–67, and Presson, *Shakespeare's "Troilus and Cressida" and The Legends of Troy.*

3. It is unlikely that Shakespeare had read Homer in the original Greek. Presson

overstates his case for Shakespeare's reliance on Chapman, though it is likely that Shakespeare had read the *Seauen Bookes*, which were still quite recent when he came to write his play. In "The Siege of Troy in Elizabethan Literature, Especially in Shakespeare and Heywood," *PMLA* 30 (1915): 673–770, John S. P. Tatlock, though he argues for Shakespeare's debt to medieval redactions of Homer rather than to Chapman, nevertheless provides a useful list of translations of Homer that might have been available to Shakespeare (742).

4. See, for example, G. Wilson Knight, *The Wheel of Fire*, 4th ed. (London: Methuen, 1949); Derek Traversi, *An Approach to Shakespeare*, 3d ed. (Garden City, N.Y.: Anchor Books, 1969); and Brower, *Hero and Saint*.

5. I quote E. C. Pettet, *Shakespeare and the Romance Tradition* (London: Staples Press, 1949), 155. In *Comicall Satyre and Shakespeare's "Troilus and Cressida"* (San Marino, Calif.: Huntington Library Publications, 1938), 195–207, O. J. Campbell argues that Shakespeare aimed in *Troilus* to contribute to the genre popularized by Jonson. Although R. A. Foakes, in *Shakespeare: The Dark Comedies to the Last Plays; From Satire to Celebration* (London: Routledge and Kegan Paul, 1971), 44, essentially agrees with Campbell, he would alter the Jonsonian "humours" parallels Campbell discovers in *Troilus* by ascribing the humours to different characters. This possibility for variance does much to discredit Campbell's theory. More typical of those who regard the play as comic are Frederick S. Boas, who, in *Shakspere and his Predecessors* (1896; reprint ed., London: J. Murray, 1940), calls it "a merciless satire of the high-flown ideal of love, fostered by the medieval cycle of romance" (373), and W. W. Lawrence, who, in *Shakespeare's Problem Comedies* (New York: Macmillan & Co., 1931), 140–42, though he acknowledges that the love plot parodies the excesses of Elizabeth's court, nevertheless rejects Boas's contention that such parody had satirical intent: "Was not Shakespeare rather analyzing life than satirizing chivalry?" (170).

6. T. J. B. Spencer, "'Greeks' and 'Merrygreeks': A Background to 'Timon of Athens' and 'Troilus and Cressida,'" in *Essays on Shakespeare and Elizabethan Drama*, ed. Richard Hosley (Columbia: University of Missouri Press, 1962), 223–33. Furthermore, one should not discount the Elizabethans' identification with Troy in assessing their prejudice against Greeks. Virgil had promulgated the legend that Aeneas was grandsire to Brutus, founder of Britain; and the legend was promoted by chroniclers and poets alike, from Holinshed to Spenser. See T. D. Kendrick, *British Antiquity* (London: Methuen, 1950), 39ff.

7. This is the position of Douglas Cole in "Myth and Anti-Myth: The Case of 'Troilus and Cressida,'" *Shakespeare Quarterly* 31 (1980): 76–84. I take my quotation from p. 78.

8. Benoit de Sainte-Maure's *Roman* was the direct source of Boccaccio's *Il Filostrato*, which in turn became the source for Chaucer's *Troilus and Criseyde*. Hyder E. Rollins's "The Troilus-Cressida Story from Chaucer to Shakespeare," *PMLA* 32 (1917): 383–429, which traces the course of the legend through its various Renaissance manifestations, has been superseded by two recent books, Alice S. Miskimin's *The Renaissance Chaucer* (New Haven: Yale University Press, 1975), which on 189–221 traces the transmission of the legend from Boccaccio onwards, and Ann Thompson's *Shakespeare's Chaucer: A Study in Literary Origins* (New York: Barnes and Noble, 1978). Two other critics address themselves specifically to Shakespeare's response to the legend: Pettet, in *Shakespeare and the Romance Tradition*, 140–56, and M. C. Bradbrook, "What Shakespeare Did to Chaucer's Troilus," *Shakespeare Quarterly* 9 (1958): 311–19.

9. For interpretations of the poem as a *de casibus* tragedy, see D. W. Robertson, "Chaucerian Tragedy," *English Literary History* 19 (1952): 1–37, who interprets it in light of Boethius; and Farnham, *The Medieval Heritage of Elizabethan Tragedy*, 137–60, who interprets it strictly in light of Boccaccio's pattern. It is ironic that Boccaccio wrote *Il Filostrato* not as a tragedy, but as a romance of courtly love.

10. Among those who regard the poem as something more ironic than simply Troilus's tragedy, E. Talbot Donaldson is perhaps the most eloquent spokesman. See "Criseide and Her Narrator" and "The Ending of 'Troilus'" in his *Speaking of Chaucer* (New York: W. W. Norton, 1970).

11. Brower, *Hero and Saint,* 244.

12. The sentence is Pettet's in *Shakespeare and the Romance Tradition,* 146. Willard Farnham, though he would not claim that Troilus is so conscious of the disparity between the real and the ideal as Pettet would, lucidly illustrates how Troilus's idealizing classical images are riddled with a realism that violates them in "Troilus in Shapes of Infinite Desire," *Shakespeare Quarterly* 15 (1964): 257–64.

13. Rossiter, *Angel with Horns,* 135–36.

14. Ornstein, *The Moral Vision of Jacobean Tragedy* (Madison: University of Wisconsin Press, 1960), 249.

15. I apply to him what Alvin Kernan writes about the plot of satire in *The Cankered Muse: Satire of the English Renaissance* (New Haven: Yale University Press, 1959), 31: "Whenever satire does have a plot which eventuates in a change, it is not a true change but simply an intensification of the original condition."

16. Quotation is from *Chaucer's Major Poetry,* ed. Albert C. Baugh (New York: Appleton-Century-Crofts, 1963).

17. John Lydgate, *Fall of Princes,* ed. Henry Bergen (London: Oxford University Press, 1924–27), 1 : 167. See a comparable passage in *Troy Book,* ed. Henry Bergen (London: K. Paul, Trench, Trubner, 1906–35), 1 : 152.

18. Mark Sacharoff's is perhaps the most ingenious way of getting Hector off the hook that critics have yet devised. In "Tragic vs. Satiric: Hector's Conduct in II, ii of Shakespeare's 'Troilus and Cressida,'" *Studies in Philology,* 67 (1970): 517–31, he attempts to clear Hector of the imputation that his having issued a challenge to the Greeks undermines his argument against Troilus. The challenge, he argues, was issued in sport and during a truce; it was not intended, therefore, to result in the decisive encounter that Caxton and Lydgate make of it.

19. Cole, "Myth and Anti-Myth," 81.

20. The quotation is from an untitled paper Dessen submitted to a seminar on Shakespeare's characterization at the meeting of the Shakespeare Association of America in San Francisco in April 1979. "Hector's about-face is crucial for the scene and for the play as the major demonstration of the mentality behind the keeping of Helen and a series of later choices about Cressida, 'fair play,' and 'honor,'" he writes. "Our logic of psychological realism and 'consistency' may be inadequate to deal with a larger theatrical logic based upon surprise and upon an ensemble display of a Trojan mind rather than the mind of a single 'character.'" Dessen develops the idea that Shakespeare in this scene adopts the technique of the "stage psychomachia" in *Elizabethan Drama and the Viewer's Eye* (Chapel Hill: University of North Carolina Press, 1977), 152–54.

21. William Caxton, *The Recuyell of the Historyes of Troye,* ed. H. Oskar Sommer (London: D. Nutt, 1894), 2 : 589–90.

22. The phrase is Nevill Coghill's, in *Shakespeare's Professional Skills* (Cambridge: At the University Press, 1964), 124. Caxton mentions Hector's covetousness with some regularity, with regard to Patroclus's arms (2 : 580), King Menon's arms (2 : 588), and a noble baron's arms (2 : 613, and the likely source for this incident in the play). If Caxton mentions it, Lydgate moralizes upon it (2 : 548–49). After describing in detail Hector's pursuit and slaying of the "Grekysh kyng . . . whiche . . . had ful many riche stoon," Lydgate condemns Hector as unchivalrous in a long apostrophe beginning, "But out! allas! on fals couetyse! / Whos gredy fret,—the whiche is gret pite,— / In hertie may nat lightly staunchid be"; and ending, "For couetyse and knyghthod, as I lere, / In o cheyne may not be knet y-fere."

23. In *Shakespeare and the Popular Dramatic Tradition* (New York: Staples Press, 1944), 103–5, S. L. Bethell suggests that Hector's language extends beyond the significance of the language of covetousness used by Lydgate and makes the incident an allegory similar to the "whited sepulchre" of Holy Scripture, the sumptuous armor standing for outward show that hides inner corruption. But Bethell, like most others, interprets the allegory as a disparaging comment on Hector's "unworthy aims" that "are bound to tarnish the most chivalrous na-

ture"; and thus he really things the incident has the same didactic and morally restrictive aims as Lydgate. In the interpretation, I part company with him.

24. See Brower, *Hero and Saint,* 359–75. Coriolanus's choler and impatience, bloodiness and aloneness, movement from rage to sorrow, and—above all—the yoking of heroic energy to love for his mother, all bring Homer's Achilles to Brower's mind. The analogies are strong, but they remain analogies. Brower provides no substantial evidence that Shakespeare's imagination totally displaced its earlier conception of Achilles for a purer Homeric Achilles. And the fact remains, of course, that Shakespeare refers to Coriolanus as a Hector more than once, never as an Achilles. Brower shifts his ground and admits to seeing a strain of the Homeric Hector in Coriolanus from time to time. In the climactic scene of his capitulation, for example, Coriolanus, "like Hector . . . sees his son as the reincarnation of his own heroism" (368). "In the play, where the bond with the mother is so central to the hero's character, the son is the first to kneel, and in the wholly new passages between Coriolanus and his son, the parallel to Hector suggests that in a domestic and 'natural' moment Coriolanus becomes less Achillean" (379).

25. For Shakespeare's debt to Plutarch, see Bullough, *Narrative and Dramatic Sources of Shakespeare,* vol. 5; Brower, *Hero and Saint,* 205 ff., a good account of how Plutarch modified epic heroism in the context of Roman republicanism; and two more recent studies that deal with Shakespeare's conception of Rome as it was shaped by Plutarch and others: J. L. Simmons, *Shakespeare's Pagan World* (Charlottesville: University Press of Virginia, 1973), and Paul A. Cantor, *Shakespeare's Rome* (Ithaca: Cornell University Press, 1976).

26. Erich Auerbach, *Mimesis: The Representation of Reality in Western Literature,* trans. Willard R. Trask (Princeton: Princeton University Press, 1953), 19,

27. Ann Jennalie Cook, however, has gathered persuasive evidence that the Elizabethan audience was composed of an upper-class intelligentsia, well-read, historically aware, and sensitive to language. Her work follows on that of Alfred Harbage, who posited an audience of several thousand Londoners of a superior sort who patronized the theaters regularly, even daily. Such an audience would have been more likely to appreciate Shakespearean cross-pollination and to interpret each new play in the light of those past; knowing that he *had* such an audience might have encouraged Shakespeare to be more deliberately allusive. See Cook's *The Privileged Playgoers of Shakespeare's London, 1576–1642* (Princeton: Princeton University Press, 1981) and Harbage's *Shakespeare's Audience* (New York: Columbia University Press, 1941).

Chapter 5. The Integrity of the Noble Moor

1. His seminal essay on the language of *Othello* appears in *The Wheel of Fire,* 97–119.

2. Both Reuben Brower, in *Hero and Saint,* 1–28, and Helen Gardner, in *The Noble Moor* (London: Oxford University Press, 1955), have attempted to defend Othello's heroic diction from its critics by invoking the romance tradition.

3. Arthur Sewell, *Character and Society in Shakespeare* (Oxford: Clarendon Press, 1951), 94.

4. It is difficult to separate heroic imagery from Petrarchan conceit in Othello's idealization of Desdemona. Rosalie Colie analyzes the influence of Petrarchanism on the Desdemona-as-warrior imagery in *Shakespeare's Living Art* (Princeton, 1974), 152ff.

5. See, for example, G. R. Elliot, *Flaming Minister* (Durham, N.C.: Duke University Press, 1953), 28–29, and Robert B. Heilman, *Magic in the Web* (Lexington: University Press of Kentucky, 1956), 170–76. Heilman's indispensable reading of the play unfortunately too often denigrates Othello's love as "unredeemed egotism." "Shakespeare succeeds in showing something about the love of the hero for the girl who first caught his eye by adoring his exploits, a love in which an overexplicit temperateness reveals some incompleteness of response and in

which the man of affairs, not quite consciously nourishing a large image of himself that he has seen in the mirror of affairs, has withheld the self from a transforming devotion" (174).

6. G. Wilson Knight pioneered the study of Othello's linguistic transformation in *The Wheel of Fire*, 114–18. He was followed not long after by Wolfgang Clemen in *The Development of Shakespeare's Imagery* (Cambridge, Mass.: Harvard University Press, 1951), 130–32. Other studies include Mikhail M. Morozov, "The Individualization of Shakespeare's Characters through Imagery," *Shakespeare Survey* 2 (1949): 84–87; S. L. Bethell, "Shakespeare's Imagery: The Diabolical Images in 'Othello,'" *Shakespeare Survey* 5 (1952): 62–80; Heilman, *Magic in the Web*, 125ff.; Irving Ribner, *Patterns in Shakespearian Tragedy* (1960; reprint ed., London: Methuen, 1966), 109ff; and Proser, *The Heroic Image in Five Shakespearean Tragedies*, 122ff.

7. Maud Bodkin, *Archetypal Patterns in Poetry*, 2d ed. (London: Oxford University Press, 1963), 223. H. A. Mason, however, in *Shakespeare's Tragedies of Love* (London: Chatto and Windus, 1970), 103–11, traces a possible source for the idea of Othello's predilection for such thoughts back to an essay by G. H. Lewes, "Foreign Actors on Our Stage," which first appeared in *Blackwood's Edinburgh Magazine* 90 (1861).

8. F. R. Leavis, "Diabolical Intellect and the Noble Hero," *Scrutiny* 6 (1937), reprinted in Leavis, *The Common Pursuit* (London: Chatto and Windus, 1952), from which I quote, 140–41. John Holloway, in an appendix to his *The Story of the Night* (1961; reprint ed., Lincoln: University of Nebraska Press, 1966) entitled "Dr. Leavis and 'Diabolical Intellect,'" rejoins that Leavis deliberately distorts the text of the play in order to prove his anti-Bradleyan interpretation of Othello as a man dominated by sensuality and jealousy.

9. Quotations are from the following: Stewart, *Character and Motive in Shakespeare: Some Recent Appraisals Examined* (London: Longmans, Green, 1949), 102–3; Proser, *The Heroic Image in Five Shakespearean Tragedies*, 112; Mason, *Shakespeare's Tragedies of Love*, 107; and Traversi, *An Approach to Shakespeare*, 2:93.

10. *Shakespeare's Mature Tragedies* (Princeton: Princeton University Press, 1973), 115. McElroy's entire assessment of Othello, 89–144, is lucidly and persuasively written. I single it out for my discussion only because it reflects so extremely the dangers of a Bodkinist reading of the play.

11. The phrase is G. R. Elliott's in *Flaming Minister*, 62.

12. Winifred Nowottny's remarks in "Justice and Love in 'Othello,'" *University of Toronto Quarterly* 21 (1952): 330–44, are to the point: "Troilus is aware of the act of choice inherent in ceasing to believe and of the agony that goes with it; Othello, though he understands nothing of this, cannot avoid experiencing it" (336).

13. Heilman, *Magic in the Web*, 176–79, illustrates Iago's technique for setting himself up as Desdemona's rival; my discussion is indebted to him.

14. Norman Rabkin writes eloquently of the "radical simplicity" of Othello's heroic nature in *Shakespeare and the Common Understanding*, 66: "The speed and fullness with which he alters his beliefs to fit his situation once Iago has entered it indicate a character which can exist only in terms of total commitment."

15. See "Justice and Love in 'Othello,'" 332.

16. In *Gli Hecatommithi* (3. 7), the chief source of *Othello*, translated by Geoffrey Bullough in *Narrative and Dramatic Sources of Shakespeare*, 7:243.

17. F. R. Leavis agrees with Eliot that in this speech, "Othello succeeds in turning himself into a pathetic figure, by adopting an *aesthetic* rather than a moral attitude, dramatizing himself against his environment": see Eliot, "Shakespeare and the Stoicism of Seneca" in *Selected Essays*, 2d ed. (New York: Harcourt, Brace, 1950), 111. John Holloway, in *The Story of the Night*, 55–56, defends the convention whereby the hero speaks his own last defense by regarding it as a kind of choric privilege that Shakespeare granted to other of his heroes as well. Walter C. Foreman, Jr., in *The Music of the Close: The Final Scenes of Shakespeare's Tragedies* (Lexington: University Press of Kentucky, 1978), 43–47, more specifically disputes Eliot's claim that Othello is cheering himself up by substituting an aesthetic for a moral attitude.

Aesthetic attitudes do not preclude morality, according to Foreman, and Othello's stance in this speech does, in fact, have the force of moral assertion. I completely concur.

18. See Helen Gardner, *The Business of Criticism* (Oxford: Clarendon Press, 1959), 39. She is also cited by Foreman, *Music of the Close,* 46.

Chapter 6. Timon and the Ethics of Heroism

1. Una Ellis-Fermor, "'Timon of Athens': An Unfinished Play," *Review of English Studies* 18 (1942): 281–82, an essay reprinted in *Shakespeare the Dramatist,* ed. Kenneth Muir (London: Methuen, 1961); and Rabkin, *Shakespeare and the Common Understanding,* 193–94. In the critical introduction to his edition of *Timon* (Harmondsworth: Penguin, 1970), 7–12, George Hibbard lucidly discusses the remoteness and lack of specificity that move *Timon* closer to parable than any other Shakespearean tragedy.

2. Anne Lancashire suggests that the *Everyman* quality of *Timon* makes clear that we are not intended to admire Timon: see "'Timon of Athens': Shakespeare's 'Dr. Faustus,'" *Shakespeare Quarterly* 21 (1970): 42. Other studies of the play as a Morality are David M. Bevington's "'Timon of Athens' and Morality Drama" *College Language Association Journal* 10 (1961): 181–88, and Lewis Walker's "'Timon of Athens' and the Morality Tradition," *Shakespeare Studies* 12 (1979): 159–77. These essays build on earlier analyses of *Timon* as an allegorical satire. G. B. Harrison ascribed the generic label "Reckless Prodigality" to Timon in *Shakespeare's Tragedies* (London: Routledge and Kegan Paul, 1951), 258; and L. C. Knights, in his "Timon of Athens," *The Morality of Art,* ed. D. W. Jefferson (London: Routledge and Kegan Paul, 1969), would agree. A. S. Collins, on the other hand, in "'Timons of Athens': A Reconsideration," *Review of English Studies* 22 (1946): 99, saw Timon as "Ideal Bounty": and Mark Van Doren, as the figure of "Munificence" in *Shakespeare* (New York: H. Holt, 1939), 289. Among those who found specific satirical reference to contemporary situations in *Timon,* most notable were O. J. Campbell, who devoted a chapter in *Shakespeare's Satire* (1943; reprint ed., Hamden: Archon Books, 1963) to demonstrate Timon's culpability, and, antithetically, John W. Draper, "The Theme of 'Timon of Athens,'" *Modern Language Review* 29 (1934): 20–31, whose view of the play as an indictment of contemporary usury I here allude to. Collins, "'Timon of Athens,'" 96, called the play "a satire upon a cold-hearted commercial community fearfully reinforcing its security by a heartless legalism;" and E. C. Pettet, in "'Timon of Athens': The Disruption of Feudal Morality," *Review of English Studies* 23 (1947): 321–36, concluded that the play dramatized how Elizabethan lords, who customarily overspent their estates, were being ruined by the new mercantile society that refused to condone extravagance.

3. Guthrie produced *Timon* for the Old Vic. I quote from his program note, dated May 28, 1952.

4. For brief surveys of Shakespeare's sources, see H. J. Oliver's edition of the play (London: Methuen, 1959), xxxii–xl; J. C. Maxwell's (Cambridge: At the University Press, 1957), xiv–xxii; and Bullough, *Narrative and Dramatic Sources of Shakespeare,* 6:225–50. Robert C. Elliott, in *The Power of Satire: Magic, Ritual, Art* (Princeton: Princeton University Press, 1960), 141–45, traces the roots of the Timon legend to satire; and Willard Farnham, *Shakespeare's Tragic Frontier* (Berkeley and Los Angeles: University of California Press, 1950), 50–67, traces the evolution of the legend through the Renaissance. Particularly important to the Elizabethan conception of Timon was Claude Gruget's *Les Diverses Lecons de Pierre Messie* (1552), which depicted Timon as particularly malicious and bestial in his denial of humanity.

5. I deal at some length with Shakespeare's knowledge of Lucian's *Misanthropos* and account for previous scholarship on the subject in "Shakespeare's Use of the 'Timon' Comedy," *Shakespeare Survey* 29 (1976): 103–16. Rolf Soellner, in attempting to promote two relatively obscure sources as more significant in the shaping of Timon's tragedy than they in fact were (one was Boaistuau's *Theatrum mundi;* the other, Barckley's *A Discourse of the Felicity of*

Man), takes issue with my claims for the comedy, but he (tacitly) agrees with my findings that Shakespeare could have gotten virtually all his Lucian material from the comedy without recourse to the original dialogue. See the appendix, "Date and Sources," to Soellner's *'Timon of Athens': Shakespeare's Pessimistic Tragedy* (Columbus: Ohio State University Press, 1979), 201–18. In an earlier article entitled "The Date and Production of 'Timon' Reconsidered," *Shakespeare Survey* 27 (1974): 111–27, I argued that the comedy, which drew so heavily on Jonson's comical satires, probably followed hard on their heels (since they did not long hold the stage), and was performed at one of the Inns, where Shakespeare may have seen it. If this is so (and how else, other than in manuscript, could Shakespeare have known the comedy?), then it follows that Shakespeare may have conceived of and even begun work on *Timon of Athens* as early as 1602– 3. For that reason, I place my discussion of it between my discussions of *Othello* (c. 1603) and *King Lear* (c. 1605) instead of between *Lear* and *Coriolanus* (c. 1608), where *Timon* is usually placed. The fact that *Timon* appears to be an unfinished work makes the logic of dating even more tentative. In terms of my argument, however, it makes little difference whether one thinks Shakespeare conceived it, started it, or finished it as early as 1603 or as late as 1607.

6. Quotations are from the edition of *Timon* prepared by J. M. Nosworthy and me for The Malone Society Reprints (Oxford: Oxford University Press, 1980). An earlier edition was prepared by Alexander Dyce for The Shakespeare Society (1842); and Bullough prints extracts from the play in *Narrative and Dramatic Sources*, 6:297–339.

7. A. M. Harmon, editor and translator of the Loeb *Lucian* (New York, 1915), 2:325, thinks that Lucian may have followed a Middle Comedy, now lost, by Antiphanes, which may in turn have been influenced by the history of "Master Upright" in the *Plutus* of Aristophanes.

8. References are to *The Works of Lucian of Samosata*, ed. H. W. Fowler and F. G. Fowler (Oxford, 1905), 1:44.

9. I assess Jonson's influence on the comedy in "The Date and Production of 'Timon' Reconsidered," 119–27.

10. J. C. Maxwell makes this point in "Timon of Athens," *Scrutiny* 15 (1948): 197.

11. I quote from the translation by H. Rackham, 2d ed. (Cambridge, Mass.: Harvard University Press, 1934), 8.1.1.

12. See *De Beneficiis*, 1.6.1 in Seneca, *Moral Essays*, trans. John W. Basore (Cambridge, Mass.: Harvard University Press, 1928–35), vol. 3.

13. G. Wilson Knight interprets Timon as such in *The Wheel of Fire*, 235–36. Paul N. Siegel, in *Shakespearean Tragedy and the Elizabethan Compromise* (New York: New York University Press, 1957), 90, suggests that although the analogy is not exact, there are unmistakable allusions early in the play "which invite comparison between Timon's boundless generosity and Christ's overflowing love and between the duplicity of those who feed at Timon's expense and the duplicity of Judas at the Last Supper." Jarold W. Ramsey, in "Timon's Imitation of Christ," *Shakespeare Studies* 2 (1966): 162–73, suggests that because Timon is brought down by his excessive practice of "Christian moral directives," the play challenges the validity of New Testament teaching and condemns Christian idealism as impossible to live by. Roy W. Battenhouse takes issue with Ramsey in *Shakespearean Tragedy: Its Art and Its Christian Premise* (Bloomington: Indiana University Press, 1969), 88–92, by arguing that Timon's ethic is never Christian, but "a man-centered Greekish analogue which unwittingly apes Christian charity." This explanation seems sanest to me. See also Roland Mushat Frye, *Shakespeare and Christian Doctrine* (Princeton: Princeton University Press, 1963), 178–79, 202–4.

14. For an account of Shakespeare's training in moral philosophy that focuses in particular on the importance of Cicero in Elizabethan grammar schools, see T. W. Baldwin, *William Shakspere's small Latine & lesse Greeke* (Urbana: University of Illinois Press, 1944), 2:578–616.

15. Cicero's *De Officiis:* 1.14, translated by Walter Miller (1913; reprint ed., Cambridge, Mass.: Harvard University Press, 1928).

16. Alluding to the interlude called *Liberality and Prodigality* that was revived for Elizabeth in 1602, Muriel Bradbrook, in *Shakespeare the Craftsman* (London: Chatto and Win-

dus, 1969), 146–47, suggests that Timon may have been meant to represent Liberality.

17. I paraphrase the words of John W. Draper, "The Theme of 'Timon of Athens.'" In *An Interpretation of Shakespeare* (Columbia, Mo.: Lucas Brothers, 1948), 247, Hardin Craig concurs with this noble view of Timon in his assertion, "Timon's spending was set down as a mark of his nobility in the ancient world and was so understood in the Renaissance."

18. Campbell, *Shakespeare's Satire*, 186. Clifford Leech, too, in *Shakespeare's Tragedies and Other Studies in Seventeenth-Century Drama* (London: Chatto and Windus, 1950), 116, argues that Timon's "fatal weakness is the desire for munificent splendour."

19. By G. B. Harrison in *Shakespeare's Tragedies*, 258.

20. See Plutarch's essay, "How to Tell a Flatterer from a Friend" in the *Moralia,* trans. Frank Cole Babbitt et al. (New York: G. P. Putnam's Sons, 1927–69), 1:264–395.

21. *The Works of Samuel Johnson, LL.D.,* ed. F. R. Walesby (Oxford: Talboys and Wheeler, 1825), 5:170.

22. In this I disagree with Alice Birney, who, in *Satiric Catharsis in Shakespeare: A Theory of Dramatic Structure* (Berkeley and Los Angeles: University of California Press, 1973), 128, suggests that Apemantus is the "catalytic satirist" for Timon's conversion.

23. Theodore Spencer, *Shakespeare and the Nature of Man,* 2d ed. (New York: Macmillan Co., 1949), 181.

24. Harry Levin, "Shakespeare's Misanthrope," *Shakespeare Survey* 26 (1973): 92–93.

25. William Empson, *The Structure of Complex Words* (New York: New Directions, 1951), 181–82.

26. Elliott, *The Power of Satire,* 166.

27. Birney, *Satiric Catharsis in Shakespeare,* 131.

28. Northrop Frye, *A Natural Perspective: The Development of Shakespearean Comedy and Romance* (New York: Columbia University Press, 1965), 98–100.

29. Farnham, *Shakespeare's Tragic Frontier,* 65–66. Wyndham Lewis, although he is partial to Apemantus and regards Timon, too, as a cynic, nevertheless identifies a radical distinction between Timon's passionate cynicism and Apemantus's philosophical cynicism—one as tragic, the other not. See *The Lion and the Fox* (New York: Harper, 1927), 249–56.

30. Kernan, *The Cankered Muse,* 203. Timon's intensity, writes Kernan, "is no mere rhetorical trick or the inborn envy of a poor creature for his betters, but the expression of agony of a man who fully perceives the 'loss in transformation.'"

31. Elliott, *The Power of Satire,* 165–66.

32. R. P. Draper, "Timon of Athens," *Shakespeare Quarterly* 8 (1957): 198.

33. Discussed by Elliott in *The Power of Satire,* 159.

34. In *The Cankered Muse,* Kernan writes that "the normal 'plot' of satire would then appear to be a stasis in which the two opposing forces, the satirist on the one hand and the fools on the other, are locked in their respective attitudes without any possibility of either dialectical movement of the simple triumph of good over evil" (31).

35. See Knight, *The Wheel of Fire,* 228–31.

36. I quote Harold S. Wilson, *On the Design of Shakespearean Tragedy,* 138. For further discussions of the development in nature imagery as a mode for Timon's purgation, see W. M. T. Nowottny, "Acts IV and V of 'Timon of Athens,'" *Shakespeare Quarterly* 10 (1959): 493–97, and Willard Farnham, *Shakespeare's Tragic Frontier,* 75–76.

37. Bradbrook, *Shakespeare the Craftsman,* 158. Bradbrook attempts to justify her reading historically by speculating that *Timon* was conceived as a "show" for the Blackfriars.

38. Clemen, *The Development of Shakespeare's Imagery,* 176.

Chapter 7. Persistence of the "Old" Lear

1. The most important study of the relationship between *Lear* and native dramatic traditions is Maynard Mack's *"King Lear" in Our Time* (Berkeley and Los Angeles: University of

California Press, 1965). Many studies followed Mack's, using particular analogues to illuminate the meaning of particular scenes or characters, particularly in the Gloucester plot. Notable among them are Alvin Kernan, "Formalism and Realism in Elizabethan Drama: The Miracles in 'King Lear,'" *Renaissance Drama* 9 (1966), and Bridget Gellert Lyons, "The Subplot as Simplification in 'King Lear,'" *Some Facets of "King Lear"*, ed. Rosalie Colie and F. T. Flahiff (Toronto: University of Toronto Press, 1974). Harry Levin anticipated some of their ideas in his early essay on Morality elements in the play, "The Heights and Depths: A Scene from 'King Lear,'" *More Talking of Shakespeare*, ed. John Garrett (London: Longmans, Green, 1959). But Howard Felperin advances on Mack most provocatively and thoroughly in *Shakespearean Representation* by arguing that the main plot of *Lear* involves Morality tradition far more sophisticatedly than the conventional subplot. Up to the point of Lear's reconciliation with Cordelia, Felperin suggests, the play is a "histrionic recreation" of the Morality of kingship that stoops to folly; and despite deviations that make it mimetically more complex, the play, at the moment of Lear's vision of *contemptus mundi*, "has all but reunited with its prototype." But in so far as the ending defies the assurances of morality with a return to madness and absurdity, Shakespeare "redirects our attention to an undetermined reality that exists prior to and remains unavailable to both." The Morality, in other words, provides a traditional model from which the play can deviate in order to establish a reality that may incorporate assumptions from that tradition but not accept those assumptions as adequate in themselves to explain life. See pp. 87–106.

2. I quote Sigurd Burckhardt, who, in *Shakespearean Meanings*, 239–41, argues persuasively that for Lear, words are substantial and creative. Burckhardt suggests that in the first scene, Lear presides over a kind of poetry contest in which his daughters contend for top prize: "he acts on the premise that what they say will be true by virtue of their saying it." This conforms perfectly with the heroic cast of mind.

3. Brower, *Hero and Saint*, 385. The Ovid is from Golding's translation of the *Metamorphoses*, 7.136–37.

4. For this idea I am indebted to Robert Heilman, *This Great Stage: Image and Structure in "King Lear"* (Baton Rouge: Louisiana State University Press, 1948), 168. Yet Ruth Nevo, in *Tragic Form in Shakespeare* (Princeton: Princeton University Press, 1972), 279–82, argues that the difference between Lear and his daughters is more important than the similarity. Lear, however devoted to a measure-for-measure logic, is essentially magnanimous in spirit, she claims; his daughters, essentially selfish. In them, Lear sees an inverted mirror image that provokes him to speculate on man's "true need."

5. See Una Ellis-Fermor, *The Jacobean Drama* (London: Methuen, 1936), 264.

6. In *Shakespeare's Mature Tragedies*, 168ff., Bernard McElroy discusses in much greater detail the course of Lear's wavering and the collapse of his subjective world.

7. Brower, *Hero and Saint*, 395.

8. A. C. Bradley made up a list of parallels between the two plays in *Shakespearean Tragedy*, 2d ed. (1905; reprint ed., London: Macmillan & Co., 1956), Note S, 443–45. Wolfgang Clemen compares their imagery in *The Development of Shakespeare's Imagery*, 171–76. Winifred Nowottny, however, in "Some Aspects of the Style of 'King Lear,'" *Shakespeare Survey* 13 (1960): 49–57, argues that although the two heroes' speeches are alike in subject, Timon's style, "the particularity of detail there, the supple periodicity of syntax sustaining a diction far removed from stereotypes of evaluation," is antithetical to the "free line, the apparent absence of contrivance in the sudden blazes that illuminate the prosy syntax and commonplace vocabulary of Lear's utterances." The transcendence of rhetorical artifice in *Lear*, she argues, suggests that it was written later than *Timon*.

9. D. J.Palmer, in his essay "Elizabethan Tragic Heroes," *Elizabethan Theatre*, Stratford-upon-Avon Studies, no. 9, ed. John Russell Brown and Bernard Harris (New York: St. Martin's Press, 1967), 25, discusses Hieronimo as the prototype for Lear. Not only does Lear raise Hieronimo's question about divine justice with "prodigiously greater intensity," but also "his identification of the world with his torment, his confrontation with Mad Tom . . . his mock trial

of his pelican daughters, his meeting with the blind Gloucester on the way to Dover, and his waking vision of Cordelia as 'a soul in bliss,' are anticipated as devices of characterisation by the transfiguring vision of Hieronimo, who saw in the old man who came to him for justice a projection of his own case." The "pantomime of madness," for Hieronimo as for Lear, "becomes a means of dramatising tragic recognition." Palmer's discussion reinforces my sense that behind Lear there lies a rich and complex network of heroic traditions that must not be overlooked.

10. Peter Alexander, *Shakespeare's Life and Art,* 2d ed. (1939; reprint ed., New York: New York University Press, 1961), 186.

11. Hunter, "The Last Tragic Heroes," *Later Shakespeare,* Stratford-upon-Avon Studies, no. 8, ed. John Russell Brown and Bernard Harris (New York, 1967), 13–14.

12. Many critics would not agree with me. O. J. Campbell, for instance, in *Shakespeare's Satire,* 163–66, calls Lear a vituperative social satirist who, like Timon, liberally uses the verbal stock and the scourge technique of Jacobean satirists. Northrop Frye, in *Fools of Time* (Toronto: University of Toronto Press, 1967), 105ff., claims that Lear, like Timon, utters his curses in a disembodied voice, as though Shakespeare were speaking through him without regard for the dramatic context. Long before, George Orwell, in *Polemic,* 7 (1947): 10, wrote that Lear, in his mad despair, was a mouthpiece for Shakespeare's own disgust at "the rottenness of formal justice and vulgar morality." This idea that Shakespeare expresses extradramatic sentiments through Timon and Lear persists in modern criticism.

13. For similar interpretations of this speech, see Robert Heilman, *This Great Stage,* 122, and D. G. James, *The Dream of Learning: An Essay on the Advancement of Learning, Hamlet, and King Lear* (Oxford: Clarendon Press, 1951), 93–5.

14. In his gloss on the text of his New Arden edition (London: Methuen, 1952), Kenneth Muir cites various uses of the pelican image prior to Shakespeare. In each instance, the parent pelican is described as selflessly sustaining the lives of its young with its blood. Shakespeare makes the metaphor carry a more complex meaning in *Lear.*

15. S. C. Sen Gutpa, in *Aspects of Shakespearean Tragedy* (Calcutta: Oxford University Press, 1972), 140–41, traces the critical misfortunes to which the Fool's prophecy has been subjected. Omitted from the quartos, it has subsequently been rejected by critics as an actor's interpolation—cf. G. Wilson Knight, *The Sovereign Flower* (London: Methuen, 1958), 58—or as a parody of the spurious Chaucerian prophecy printed by Caxton and quoted in Puttenham's *Arte of English Poesie.*

16. Clemen, *The Development of Shakespeare's Imagery,* 143.

17. Enid Welsford, in *The Fool: His Social and Literary History* (1935; reprint ed., Gloucester, Mass.: Peter Smith, 1966), 255–73, explains the Fool's ironic reversals of value according to the traditions of fool literature. Her seminal study has been supplemented by two others: Robert Hilles Goldsmith, *Wise Fools in Shakespeare* (East Lansing: Michigan State University Press, 1955), 60–67, and Marvin Rosenberg, *The Masks of King Lear* (Berkeley and Los Angeles: University of California Press, 1972), 102ff. John Danby's analysis of the Fool's verse style as "handy-dandy" is enlightening. He suggests that such verse reflects the Fool's almost schizophrenic division—his affections lying with Lear, his reason with Goneril and Regan. "The Fool, I think, stands for the unillumined head. . . . He can discern in his cold light the alternatives between which he cannot choose." See *Shakespeare's Doctrine of Nature: A Study of "King Lear"* (London: Faber and Faber, 1949), 102–13.

18. Both William Empson, *The Structure of Complex Words,* 132–33, and William Rosen, *Shakespeare and the Craft of Tragedy* (Cambridge, Mass.: Harvard University Press, 1964), 37–38, question whether the Fool is in fact the high-minded and self-sacrificing character some critics take him to be. The Fool, they argue, may serve as Lear's raisonneur before the storm; but during it, his speeches are reduced to bare necessities, no longer adequate to instruct Lear. Goldsmith, *Wise Fools in Shakespeare,* 65, indulges in the kind of hyperbolic praise of the Fool's heroism against which they argue: "In remaining by Lear, the Fool violates his own sense of

prudence. If this is not devotion, it is the next best thing. Walking clear-eyed into the stormy night and to his probable death on the heath, he comes as close as any fool ever does to the heroic."

19. Robert Hilles Goldsmith assesses the correspondences between Kent and Laches, and other, broader echoes of the comedy in *Lear*, in "Did Shakespeare Use the Old Timon Comedy?", *Shakespeare Quarterly* 9 (1958): 34–37. Goldsmith believes, as I do, that the comedy was written early enough to have been a source for both *Timon* and *Lear*, but he places too much emphasis on tenuous verbal echoes to substantiate his case.

20. Goldberg, *An Essay on "King Lear"* (Cambridge: At the University Press, 1974), 146.

21. The relative merits of a Christian reading of the play have been amply debated by recent critics. Nicholas Brooke, "The Ending of 'King Lear,'" in *Shakespeare 1564–1964*, ed. Edward A. Bloom (Providence: Brown University Press, 1964), 71–87, and William Elton, *"King Lear" and the Gods* (San Marino, Calif.: Huntington Library Publications, 1966), both summarize the opinions of the play's so-called Christianizers in order to provide a context for their own less optimistic readings. Virgil Whitaker, *Mirror up to Nature* (San Marino, Calif.: Huntington Library Publications, 1965), 202–40, and Roy W. Battenhouse, *Shakespearean Tragedy: Its Arts and Its Christian Premises*, 269–302, on the other hand, have reasserted the claim for the play's Christian affirmations.

22. Susan Snyder, *The Comic Matrix of Shakespeare's Tragedies* (Princeton: Princeton University Press, 1979), 179. The quotation does not do justice to Snyder's argument, which poses that in *Lear*, Shakespeare was neither rewriting the *Purgatorio* nor anticipating *Endgame*, but was setting one comic vision against the other and demonstrating that each, in its way, diminishes man. "In their uneasy coexistence," she concludes, "lies the play's peculiar tragic force."

23. Nevo, *Tragic Form in Shakespeare*, 299.

Chapter 8. Bellona's Bridegroom or Dwarfish Thief?

1. I refer the reader to G. K. Hunter's article, "'Macbeth' in the Twentieth Century," in *Shakespeare Survey* 19 (1966): 1–11, which assesses how Macbeth's individuality has been suppressed by studies that emphasize moral generalization and imagery: the play lends itself extremely well to such study. Perhaps the first critic to interpret the play as a Morality was Willard Farnham in *Shakespeare's Tragic Frontier*, 79ff; but his judicious assessment has been taken to extremes by critics such as Edmund Creeth who, in *Mankynde in Shakespeare* (Athens: University of Georgia Press, 1976), 40–72, draws a provocative, if too restrictive, analogy between *Macbeth* and *The Castell of Perseverance*. Howard Felperin, who acknowledges *Macbeth*'s affinities with orthodox Christian tragedy, nevertheless locates another source in medieval mystery cycles, and he holds the "radical equivocation in *Macbeth* in relation to its medieval models" responsible for our "pious mystification or ironic demystification" of the play. See *Shakespearean Representation*, 118–44.

2. Richard Moulton, *Shakespeare as a Dramatic Artist*, 3d ed. (Oxford, 1893), 148.

3. Mary McCarthy is an exception. Her essay "General Macbeth," first printed in *Harper's Magazine* (June 1972) but reprinted and, I venture, widely read in the Signet Classic edition of *Macbeth*, ed. Sylvan Barnet, is worth mentioning only because she, no Shakespeare scholar, distills and exaggerates the opinions of many who are, but does so with unscholarly abandon. To her, "Macbeth's speeches often recall the Player's speech in *Hamlet*. . . He tears a passion to tatters. He has a rather Senecan rhetoric, the fustian of the time." She finds the imagery of his dagger soliloquy "recherché embellishment"; his hyperbole, euphuistic. And the purpose of this "play between poetry and rhetoric, the *conversion* of poetry to rhetoric," she argues, is "treasonous manipulation"—to subvert the traditional order and values implicit in pure poetry. In short, she thinks Macbeth uses heroic verse with an ulterior motive, like

Richard III, to advance his own ends. It is precisely this sort of critical misperception, this distrust of Macbeth's heroic diction, that I hope to correct in the following pages.

4. It is, for example, the one major tragedy that Reuben Brower neglects to discuss in *Hero and Saint,* and Eugene Waith omits it from his study of *The Herculean Hero* and *Ideas of Greatness.* The one source of classical heroism that *has* been acknowledged from time to time is Senecan tragedy, and I shall deal with the Senecanism of *Macbeth* in due course.

5. Paul A. Jorgensen discovers the analogous line from *Hippolytus* in *Our Naked Frailties: Sensational Art and Meaning in "Macbeth"* (Berkeley and Los Angeles: University of California Press, 1971), 72. I quote from Thomas Newton's edition of *Seneca, His Tenne Tragedies* (1581), 1:176. For a fuller discussion of Shakespeare's use of Senecan narration, see J. M. Nosworthy, "The Bleeding Captain Scene in 'Macbeth,'" *Review of English Studies* 22 (1946): 126–30.

6. Eugene M. Waith discusses the paradox that a soldierly virtue representative of spiritual strength may also court brutishness and cruelty in "Manhood and Valor in Two Shakespearean Tragedies," *English Literary History* 17 (1950): 262.

7. Lawrence Danson, in *Tragic Alphabet: Shakespeare's Drama of Language* (New Haven: Yale University Press, 1974), 122–41, is the most recent and subtle analyst of the use of paradox and equivocation in *Macbeth.* Others before him have dealt with the play's antitheses: Kenneth Muir, in the introduction to his New Arden edition (London: Methuen, 1951), xxxi–xxxii, and G. I. Duthie, in "Antithesis in 'Macbeth,'" *Shakespeare Survey* 19 (1966): 25–33.

8. This tension between doubt and resolution in York's soliloquy, of course, anticipates Macbeth's quandary more than his wife's. Lines further on in the soliloquy strengthen my hunch that Shakespeare remembered it when writing *Macbeth.* In them, York gloats over his nobles' error in failing to regard him as a treacherous serpent:

> Well, nobles, well, 'tis politicly done,
> To send me packing with an host of men.
> I fear me you but warm the starved snake,
> Who, cherish'd in your breasts, will sting your hearts.
>
> (3.1.341–44)

Macbeth transforms York's image into a metaphor for a danger he fears—both an outside threat such as Banquo and an inner sense of his own evil:

> We have scorch'd the snake, not kill'd it.
> She'll close and be herself, whilst our poor malice
> Remains in danger of her former tooth.
>
> (3.2.15–17)

Significantly, Macbeth uses the image *after* he has become the "conqueror" his wife has impelled him to become.

9. "The Fiend-Like Queen: A Note on 'Macbeth' and Seneca's 'Medea,'" 82–94. Ewbank elaborates on Shakespeare's apparent reliance on the translation in note 9, p. 93.

10. Quoted in *Seneca, his Tenne Tragedies,* ed. Newton, 2:57. Of the plays I quote, John Studley translated the *Medea* and the *Agamemnon* in 1566 and the *Hippolytus* in 1567; Jasper Heywood, the *Hercules Furens* in 1561. For the sake of uniformity I have chosen not to provide modern translations in my text, although in some instances Shakespeare appears to have adhered more closely to the form and syntax of the Senecan original (an adherence that might be more apparent in a modern translation) than the Tudor imitation. It is quite certain that Shakespeare was familiar with Newton's *Seneca* and almost as certain that he had read Seneca in Latin.

11. The words are Marvin Rosenberg's, from *The Masks of Macbeth* (Berkeley and Los Angeles: University of California Press, 1978), 261. Many of the observations I make about Macbeth's nobility asserting itself even *through* his criminal determination are borne out by Rosenberg's detailed study of the play's past performances.

12. Waith, in "Manhood and Valor," 265–67, assesses at length the differences between Macbeth's and Lady Macbeth's concepts of manhood.

13. I quote Ewbank, "The Fiend-Like Queen," 86. The relevant passage in the *Medea* may be found in Newton's *Seneca*, 2:90.

14. See Hardin Craig, "The Shackling of Accidents: A Study of Elizabethan Tragedy," *Philological Quarterly* 19 (1940): 9–10, and Francis R. Johnson, "Shakespearian Imagery and Senecan Imitation," in *Joseph Quincy Adams Memorial Studies*, ed. James G. McManaway et al. (Washington, D.C.: Folger Shakespeare Library, 1948), 43–46.

15. If, as J. A. K. Thomson suggests in *Shakespeare and the Classics* (London: Allen and Unwin, 1952), 120, Macbeth's apostrophe to sleep in this scene echoes the form and substance of the Chorus's apostrophe in the *Hercules Furens* (and here, Frank Justus Miller's Loeb translation preserves the Senecan syntax better then Heywood's), then there is further evidence that Hercules's horrified apprehension of guilt may have served as a model for Macbeth's:

> And do thou, O sleep, vanquisher of woes, rest of the soul, the better part of human live, thou winged son of thy mother Astraea, sluggish brother of cruel Death. . . . O thou, who art peace after wanderings, haven of life, day's respite and night's comrade . . . let slumber chain his untamed limbs, and leave not his savage breast until his former mind regain its course. (Ll. 1065ff)

But a similar passage appears in Ovid's *Metamorphoses*, 11, 623ff. Thomson concludes that the evidence for a Senecan borrowing is not conclusive; but even if it is not, the fact that Macbeth's apostrophe alludes to *some* heroic source, whether Seneca or Ovid, strengthens my supposition that Shakespeare wishes to use the power of allusion to dramatize moral heroism in Macbeth.

16. Reuben Brower elucidates Seneca's dramatization of the extremes of *virtus* and explains their relationship to Stoic philosophy in *Hero and Saint*, 141–72, and esp. 159ff. Eugene Waith writes more specifically about the Stoic idealization of Hercules, whose "ability to endure [suffering] is the final proof of his heroism," in *The Herculean Hero*, 31–38.

17. Johnson discusses the pervasiveness of this Senecan sentence in *Macbeth* in his essay, "Shakespearian Imagery and Senecan Imitation," 50–52.

18. G. K. Hunter discusses the opposition of religious and theatrical imperatives in Hieronimo in a more general study of how Elizabethan heroes were modeled alternately on the martyr and tyrant of native religious drama in "Tyrant and Martyr: Religious Heroisms in Elizabethan Tragedy," *Poetic Traditions of the English Renaissance*, ed. Maynard Mack and George deForest Lord (New Haven: Yale University Press, 1982); see 93–94.

19. Compare York's attack on Margaret in *3 Henry VI:*

> That face of his the hungry cannibals
> Would not have touch'd, would not have stain'd with blood.
> But you are more inhuman, more inexorable,
> O, ten times more, than tigers of Hyrcania.
>
> (1.4.152–55)

And this from *Hamlet:* "'The rugged Pyrrhus, like th' Hycanian beast'—" (2.2.450). The context here, Aeneas's tale to Dido, reveals how outmoded Shakespeare had come to think such allusions were. Kenneth Muir, in his note to the New Arden edition of *Macbeth*, traces the allusion to Holland's translation of Pliny; but the more obvious source is the *Aeneid*, 4.367: *Hyrcanaeque admorunt ubera tigres.*

20. This possible connection is noted by Jorgensen in *Our Naked Frailties*, 123. "The most obvious source of terror" in Banquo's ghost, he writes, "is in the vivid way he is described physically, surpassing any earlier ghost. Only Seneca could have provided a helpful model. . . ."

21. The first phrase belongs to Maynard Mack, Jr., *Killing the King: Three Studies in Shakespeare's Tragic Structure* (New Haven: Yale University Press, 1973), 168; the second, to

Robert B. Heilman, "The Criminal as Tragic Hero: Dramatic Methods," *Shakespeare Survey* 19 (1966): 15. For a fuller argument that Macbeth shrinks into inhumanity in the last two acts, see Heilman's entire essay, 12–24, and E. A. J. Honigmann, *Shakespeare: Seven Tragedies: The Dramatist's Manipulation of Response* (New York: Barnes and Noble, 1976), 139ff. A notable dissenter from this view is Bernard McElroy, who argues in *Shakespeare's Mature Tragedies*, 233ff, that the tension between Macbeth's ruthless actions and his recognition of their futility lasts out the play. This tension leads him eventually to a spiritual paralysis, according to McElroy.

22. This opinion is defended with admirable clarity by Proser in *The Heroic Image in Five Shakespearean Tragedies*, 84–86. Proser goes so far as to say that Macbeth's reliance on the prophecies is consonant with an "unrelenting belief in himself." Although I disagree with him on this point, I am indebted to him for others.

23. Thomson discovers this connection in *Shakespeare and the Classics*, 123. This is another instance in which Miller's Loeb translation better indicates the similarity between Seneca and Shakespeare:

> Why should I longer stay my soul in the light of day, and linger here, there is no cause; all that was dear to me I've lost: reason, arms, honour, wife, children, strength—and madness too! No power could purge a tainted spirit; by death must sin be healed. (*Hercules Furens*, ll. 1258–62)

Chapter 9. Antony, Cleopatra, and Heroic Retrospection

1. Janet Adelman, *The Common Liar: An Essay on 'Antony and Cleopatra'* (New Haven: Yale University Press, 1973), 160.

2. Reuben Brower notes the Ovidian source for Antony's line in *Hero and Saint*, 124. Elsewhere, Brower suggests that Antony, like Brutus, is motivated more by "the soul's high impulse to regain integrity"—an expression of stoicism that would not offend Christian sensibilities—than by the narrower Roman desire of a soldier to save his honor. See 335ff.

3. For a discussion of the genesis of this phrase and its accrued meanings, see H. T. Price, "Like Himself," *Review of English Studies* 16 (1940): 178–81.

4. G. R. Hibbard, in *The Making of Shakespeare's Dramatic Poetry*, 75–8, discusses the chorus of lamentation in *Romeo and Juliet* as a parody of the lament that Queen Elizabeth, the old Duchess of York, and the children of Clarence make after the deaths of Clarence and Edward IV in *Richard III*, 2.2. In *Antony*, Shakespeare may be continuing his self-parody.

5. Walter C. Foreman, Jr., in *The Music of the Close*, observes the blend of comedy and pathos in Antony's death and suggests how comic conventions enter more pervasively into the structure of Cleopatra's death scene (56–57, 178ff).

6. Brower, in *Hero and Saint*, 350, suggests that Shakespeare, by dropping "an other" from Plutarch's remark that Antony "was overcome, not cowardly, but valiantly, a Romane by an other Romane," shifts the emphasis to a singular and stoic nobility in Antony's death. Antony, in regarding himself as "a Roman by a Roman / Valiantly vanquish'd," means that he has overcome *himself.* Caesar has had nothing to do with it. The other references to stoic self-determination in the scene would support this reading.

7. I concur with Matthew Proser, *The Heroic Image in Five Shakespearean Tragedies*, 214–15, who, recognizing on the one hand the serious nature of such choric commentary, reasons on the other that "the abundance of these remarks in one place may indicate the extent to which *Antony and Cleopatra* is an exploration and gentle mockery of the idea and techniques of tragedy themselves."

8. I borrow the phrase from Paul Cantor, who, reflecting on the parallel scenes, suggests that in both, the tension "between insecurity and the will to lord it over others" results in a tyrannical abuse of power. See *Shakespeare's Rome: Republic and Empire*, 197–98.

9. My suspicion that Shakespeare had Othello's style of heroic anguish in mind when composing Cleopatra's rant is strengthened by a subsequent echo. When the messenger asks,

"Should I lie, madam?", Cleopatra responds, "O, I would thou didst, / So half my Egypt were submerg'd and made / A cistern for scal'd snakes!" (ll. 93–95). Likewise, Othello loathes the thought that he may be keeping his love "as a cistern for foul toads / To knot and gender in" (4.2.61–62). Shakespeare may have associated the two characters in their fear to acknowledge a truth that would strip them of heroic certitude. In both cases, fear leads to a grotesque imagination of torture.

10. For a brilliant discussion of the play's use of the myth, see Adelman, *The Common Liar*, 78–101.

11. Proser, for example, in *The Heroic Image*, 201–2, thinks that "the sense of Antony's old identity makes itself felt here"; Cleopatra "works so beautifully with Antony that the feeling of harmony they create together is inescapable. The sensation that at long last Antony has found his true calling is like that of a dislocated bone settling into place."

12. For a fuller discussion of the relevance of Seneca's Hercules to Antony, see Eugene M. Waith, *The Herculean Hero*, 118–20. Brower mentions the opposition of two conceptions of Hercules in this speech, the mad Hercules of myth and the Stoic hero of self-conquest, in *Hero and Saint*, 333.

13. See 4.3: "'Tis the god Hercules, whom Antony lov'd, / Now leaves him," observes the Second Soldier on hearing unearthly music (ll. 21–22). A recent interpretation of this brief scene by John Coates in "'The Choice of Hercules' in 'Antony and Cleopatra'," *Shakespeare Survey* 31 (1978), argues that Hercules' departure from Antony should be understood as moral allegory, signifying not that Antony has lost his protective spirit, but that he is about to undergo a purgation, a series of trials that ultimately will allow him, like the Hercules of iconographic tradition, to reconcile pleasure with virtue. Hercules may leave Antony to descend to Hades, suggests Coates—a descent that figures Antony's descent into himself, from which he will emerge with a Herculean self-control. See pp. 48–50. This view ignores and implicitly contradicts that of Waith who, in *The Herculean Hero*, 113–21, argues that Antony needs to be seen in a line of Herculean progeny who inspire an admiration that transcends traditional moral bounds and goes hand-in-hand with the play's hyperbole and epic structure. "Sensual indulgence, magnanimity and self-immolation appear to be manifestations of a single bent," writes Waith (116). "So too, through its sheer intensity, does Antony's most Herculean trait, his rage." This understanding of Hercules's function as an analogue of heroic excess for Antony makes more sense to me than discovering in Hercules a moral analogue.

14. Some other critics who share Adelman's belief that Cleopatra's power finally overwhelms our imaginations are Maurice Charney, *Shakespeare's Roman Plays* (Cambridge, Mass.: Harvard University Press, 1961), 20ff.; Phyllis Rackin, "Shakespeare's Boy Cleopatra, the Decorum of Nature, and the Golden World of Poetry," *PMLA* 87 (March 1972): 201–12; and Foreman, *Music of the Close*, 175–201. Foreman would add, "The magic of Cleopatra in the last scene not only asserts the wholeness of her own life but also, like the magic of Isis tending to Osiris, patches up the fragments of Antony's" (56)—a sure indication of how far her mythic powers of persuasion extend.

15. Colie, *Shakespeare's Living Art*, 194. Although Colie's essay focuses specifically on the polarity of Attic and Asiatic styles in representing the worlds of Rome and Egypt, her assumption that the Asiatic style has the power to affirm the play's hyperbolic claims for its heroes resembles that of Adelman and others.

16. See Rackin, "Shakespeare's Boy Cleopatra," 209.

17. For a thorough analysis of the influence that earlier Senecan versions of Cleopatra's tragedy had on Shakespeare, particularly in establishing the moral ambivalence of *Antony and Cleopatra*, see Ernest Schanzer, *The Problem Plays of Shakespeare*, 150–83. For less comprehensive discussions, see J. L. Simmons, *Shakespeare's Pagan World*, 127–33, and Geoffrey Bullough, *Narrative and Dramatic Sources of Shakespeare*, 5 : 231–36. Schanzer's essay includes a substantial discussion of the sources for Antony's tragedy as well.

18. Simmons, *Shakespeare's Pagan World*, 130.

19. Frye, *A Natural Perspective*, 10.

Bibliography

Adelman, Janet. *The Common Liar: An Essay on "Antony and Cleopatra."* New Haven: Yale University Press, 1973.

Alexander, Peter. *Shakespeare's Life and Art.* 1939. Reprint. New York: New York University Press, 1961.

Aristotle. *The Nicomachean Ethics.* 2d ed. Edited and translated by H. Rackham. Cambridge: Harvard University Press, 1934.

Auerbach, Erich. *Mimesis: The Representation of Reality in Western Literature.* Translated by Willard R. Trask. Princeton: Princeton University Press, 1953.

Baker, Howard. *Induction to Tragedy.* Baton Rouge: Louisiana State University Press, 1939.

Baldwin, Thomas Whitfield. *William Shakspere's small Latine & lesse Greeke.* 2 vols. Urbana: University of Illinois Press, 1944.

Battenhouse, Roy W. *Shakespearean Tragedy: Its Art and Its Christian Premises.* Bloomington: Indiana University Press, 1969.

Berek, Peter. "Self-reflexiveness and Realism in 'Henry VI.'" Paper presented at the meeting of The Shakespeare Association of America, Minneapolis. April 1982.

Bethell, S. L. *Shakespeare and the Popular Dramatic Tradition.* New York: Staples Press, 1944.

———. "Shakespeare's Imagery: The Diabolical Images in 'Othello.'" *Shakespeare Quarterly* 5 (1952): 62–80.

Bevington, David M. *From Mankind to Marlowe: Growth of Structure in the Popular Drama of Tudor England.* Cambridge: Harvard University Press, 1962.

———. "'Timon of Athens' and Morality Drama." *College Language Association Journal* 10 (1961): 181–88.

Birney, Alice Lotvin. *Satiric Catharsis in Shakespeare: A Theory of Dramatic Structure.* Berkeley and Los Angeles: University of California Press, 1973.

Boas, Frederick S. *Shakspere and his Predecessors.* 1896. Reprint. London: J. Murray, 1940.

Bodkin, Maud. *Archetypal Patterns in Poetry: Psychological Studies of Imagination.* 2d ed. London: Oxford University Press, 1963.

Bowers, Fredson Thayer. *Elizabethan Revenge Tragedy, 1587–1642.* 1940. Reprint. Gloucester, Mass.: Peter Smith, 1959.

Bradbrook, Muriel C. *Shakespeare the Craftsman.* London: Chatto and Windus, 1969.

———. "What Shakespeare Did to Chaucer's Troilus." *Shakespeare Quarterly* 9 (1958): 311–19.

Bradley, A. C. *Shakespearean Tragedy: Lectures on Hamlet, Othello, King Lear, Macbeth.* 2d ed. 1905. Reprint. London: Macmillan, 1956.

Braunmuller, A. R. "Early Shakespearean Tragedy and Its Contemporary Context: Cause and Emotion in *Titus Andronicus, Richard III,* and *The Rape of Lucrece.*" In *Shakespearean Tragedy.* Edited by Malcolm Bradbury and D. J. Palmer. Stratford-upon-Avon Studies, no. 20. London: Edward Arnold, 1984.

———. *George Peele.* Twayne English Authors Series. Boston: G. K. Hall, 1983.

Brooke, Nicholas. "The Ending of 'King Lear,'" In *Shakespeare 1564–1964.* Edited by Edward A. Bloom. Providence: Brown University Press, 1964.

———. *Shakespeare's Early Tragedies.* London: Methuen, 1968.

Brower, Reuben A. *Hero and Saint: Shakespeare and the Graeco-Roman Heroic Tradition.* New York: Oxford University Press, 1971.

Bullough, Geoffrey. *Narrative and Dramatic Sources of Shakespeare.* 8 vols. New York: Columbia University Press, 1957–75.

Bulman, James C. "The Date and Production of 'Timon' Reconsidered." *Shakespeare Survey* 27 (1974): 111–27.

———. "Shakespeare's Use of the 'Timon' Comedy." *Shakespeare Survey* 29 (1976): 103–16.

———, and J. M. Nosworthy, eds. *Timon.* The Malone Society Reprints. Oxford: Oxford University Press, 1978 (1980).

Burkhardt, Sigurd. *Shakespearean Meanings.* Princeton: Princeton University Press, 1968.

Cairncross, Andrew S., ed. *The First Part of King Henry VI.* The New Arden Shakespeare. London: Methuen, 1962.

———, ed. *The Second Part of King Henry VI.* The New Arden Shakespeare. 1957. Reprint. London: Methuen, 1962.

———, ed. *The Third Part of King Henry VI.* The New Arden Shakespeare. London: Methuen, 1964.

Campbell, Lily Bess, ed. *The Mirror for Magistrates.* 1938. Reprint. New York: Barnes and Noble, 1960.

———. *Shakespeare's Tragic Heroes: Slaves of Passion.* 1930. Reprint. New York: Barnes and Noble, 1952.

Campbell, Oscar James. *Comicall Satyre and Shakespeare's "Troilus and Cressida."* San Marino, Calif.: Huntington Library Publications, 1938.

———. *Shakespeare's Satire.* 1943. Reprint. Hamden: Archon Books, 1963.

Cantor, Paul. *Shakespeare's Rome: Republic and Empire.* Ithaca: Cornell University Press, 1976.

Caxton, William. *The Recuyell of the Historyes of Troye.* Edited by H. Oskar Sommer. 2 vols. London: D. Nutt, 1894.

Charney, Maurice. *Shakespeare's Roman Plays.* Cambridge, Mass.: Harvard University Press, 1961.

Chaucer, Geoffrey. *Chaucer's Major Poetry.* Edited by Albert C. Baugh. New York: Appleton-Century-Crofts, 1963.

Cicero, *De Officiis.* Edited and translated by Walter Miller. 1913. Reprint. Cambridge, Mass.: Harvard University Press, 1928.

Clemen, Wolfgang. *The Development of Shakespeare's Imagery.* Cambridge, Mass.: Harvard University Press, 1951.

————. *English Tragedy before Shakespeare: The Development of Dramatic Speech.* Translated by T. S. Dorsch. New York: Barnes and Noble, 1961.

Coates, John. "'The Choice of Hercules' in 'Antony and Cleopatra.'" *Shakespeare Survey* 31 (1978): 45–52.

Coghill, Nevill. *Shakespeare's Professional Skills.* Cambridge: At the University Press, 1964.

Cole, Douglas. "Myth and Anti-Myth: The Case of 'Troilus and Cressida.'" *Shakespeare Quarterly* 31 (1980): 76–84.

Colie, Rosalie. *Shakespeare's Living Art.* Princeton: Princeton University Press, 1974.

Collins, A. S. "'Timon of Athens': A Reconsideration." *Review of English Studies* 22 (1946): 96–108.

Cook, Ann Jennalie. *The Privileged Playgoers of Shakespeare's London, 1576–1642.* Princeton: Princeton University Press, 1981.

Cornford, Francis MacDonald. *The Origins of Attic Comedy.* 1914. Reprint. Garden City, N.Y.: Anchor Books, 1961.

Craig, Hardin. *An Interpretation of Shakespeare.* Columbia, Mo.: Lucas Brothers, 1948.

————. "The Shackling of Accidents: A Study of Elizabethan Tragedy." *Philological Quarterly* 19 (1940): 1–19.

Creeth, Edmund. *Mankynde in Shakespeare.* Athens: University of Georgia Press, 1976.

Danby, John. *Shakespeare's Doctrine of Nature: A Study of "King Lear."* London: Faber and Faber, 1949.

Danson, Lawrence. *Tragic Alphabet: Shakespeare's Drama of Language.* New Haven: Yale University Press, 1974.

Dessen, Alan. *Elizabethan Drama and the Viewer's Eye.* Chapel Hill: University of North Carolina Press, 1977.

————. Untitled paper presented at the meeting of The Shakespeare Association of America, San Francisco. April 1979.

Donaldson, E. Talbot. *Speaking of Chaucer.* New York: W. W. Norton, 1970.

Doran, Madeleine. *Endeavors of Art: A Study of Form in Elizabethan Drama.* Madison: University of Wisconsin Press, 1954.

Draper, John W. "The Theme of 'Timon of Athens.'" *Modern Language Review* 29 (1934): 20–31.

Draper, R. P. "Timon of Athens." *Shakespeare Quarterly* 8 (1957): 195–200.

Duthie, George Ian. "Antithesis in 'Macbeth.'" *Shakespeare Survey* 19 (1966): 25–33.

Dyce, Alexander, ed. *Timon.* London: The Shakespeare Society, 1842.

Eliot, T. S. "Shakespeare and the Stoicism of Seneca." Introductory essay to *Seneca, His Tenne Tragedies,* edited by Thomas Newton. London, 1927. Reprinted in *Selected Essays, 1917–1932.* New York: Harcourt, Brace, 1932.

Elliott, G. R. *Flaming Minister: A Study of "Othello."* Durham, N.C.: Duke University Press, 1953.

Elliott, Robert C. *The Power of Satire: Magic, Ritual, Art.* Princeton: Princeton University Press, 1960.

Ellis-Fermor, Una. *The Jacobean Drama: An Interpretation.* London: Methuen, 1936.

———. " 'Timon of Athens': An Unfinished Play." *Review of English Studies* 18 (1942): 270–83. Reprinted in Una Ellis-Fermor, *Shakespeare the Dramatist.* Edited by Kenneth Muir. London: Methuen, 1961.

Elton, William R. *"King Lear" and the Gods.* San Marino, Calif.: Huntington Library Publications, 1966.

Empson, William. *The Structure of Complex Words.* New York: New Directions, 1951.

Ewbank, Inga-Stina. "The Fiend-like Queen: A Note on 'Macbeth' and Seneca's 'Medea.' " *Shakespeare Survey* 19 (1966): 82–94.

Farnham, Willard. *The Medieval Heritage of Elizabethan Tragedy.* 1936. Reprint. Oxford: Basil Blackwell, 1956.

———. *Shakespeare's Tragic Frontier: The World of his Final Tragedies.* Berkeley and Los Angeles: University of California Press, 1950.

———. "Troilus in Shapes of Infinite Desire." *Shakespeare Quarterly* 15 (1964): 257–64.

Felperin, Howard. *Shakespearean Representation: Mimesis and Modernity in Elizabethan Tragedy.* Princeton: Princeton University Press, 1977.

Ferguson, Arthur B. *The Indian Summer of English Chivalry: Studies in the Decline and Transformation of Chivalric Idealism.* Durham, N.C.: Duke University Press, 1960.

Foakes, Reginald A. *Shakespeare: The Dark Comedies to the Last Plays; From Satire to Celebration.* London: Routledge and Kegan Paul, 1971.

Foreman, Walter C., Jr. *The Music of the Close: The Final Scenes of Shakespeare's Tragedies.* Lexington: University Press of Kentucky, 1978.

Frye, Northrop. *Anatomy of Criticism: Four Essays.* Princeton: Princeton University Press, 1957.

———. *Fools of Time: Studies in Shakespearean Tragedy.* Toronto: University of Toronto Press, 1967.

———. *A Natural Perspective: The Development of Shakespearean Comedy and Romance.* New York: Columbia University Press, 1965.

Frye, Roland Mushat. *Shakespeare and Christian Doctrine.* Princeton: Princeton University Press, 1963.

Gardner, Helen. *The Business of Criticism.* Oxford: Clarendon Press, 1959.

———. *The Noble Moor.* London: Oxford University Press, 1956.

Goddard, Harold C. *The Meaning of Shakespeare.* Chicago: University of Chicago Press, 1951.

Goldberg, S. L. *An Essay on "King Lear."* Cambridge: At the University Press, 1974.

Goldsmith, Robert Hilles. "Did Shakespeare Use the Old Timon Comedy?" *Shakespeare Quarterly* 9 (1958): 31–38.

———. *Wise Fools in Shakespeare.* East Lansing: Michigan State University Press, 1955.

Griffin, Nathaniel E. "Un-Homeric Elements in the Story of Troy." *Journal of English and Germanic Philology* 7 (1907): 32–52.

Guthrie, Tyrone. Program Notes for the Old Vic production of *Timon of Athens*. 28 May 1952.

Harbage, Alfred. *Shakespeare's Audience*. New York: Columbia University Press, 1941.

Harrison, George B. *Shakespeare's Tragedies*. London: Routledge and Kegan Paul, 1951.

Heilman, Robert B. "The Criminal as Tragic Hero: Dramatic Methods." *Shakespeare Survey* 19 (1966): 12–24.

———. *Magic in the Web: Action and Language in "Othello."* Lexington: University Press of Kentucky, 1956.

———. *This Great Stage: Image and Structure in "King Lear."* Baton Rouge: Louisiana State University Press, 1948.

Heywood, Thomas. *An Apology for Actors*. Edited by Richard H. Perkinson. New York: Scholars' Facsimiles and Reprints, 1941.

Hibbard, George R. *The Making of Shakespeare's Dramatic Poetry*. Toronto: University of Toronto Press, 1981.

———, ed. *Timon of Athens*. The New Penguin Shakespeare. Harmondsworth: Penguin Books, 1970.

Holloway, John. *The Story of the Night: Studies in Shakespeare's Major Tragedies*. 1961. Reprint. Lincoln: University of Nebraska Press, 1966.

Honigmann, E. A. J. *Shakespeare: Seven Tragedies: The Dramatist's Manipulation of Response*. New York: Barnes and Noble, 1976.

Howarth, Herbert. *The Tiger's Heart: Eight Essays on Shakespeare*. London: Oxford University Press, 1970.

Humphries, A. R., ed. *The Second Part of King Henry IV*. The New Arden Shakespeare. London: Methuen, 1966.

Hunter, George K. "The Last Tragic Heroes." In *Later Shakespeare*. Edited by John Russell Brown and Bernard Harris. Stratford-upon-Avon Studies, no. 8. New York: St. Martin's Press, 1967.

———. "'Macbeth' in the Twentieth Century." *Shakespeare Survey* 19 (1966): 1–11.

———. "Seneca and the Elizabethans: A Case-Study in 'Influence.'" *Shakespeare Survey* 20 (1967): 17–26.

———. "Seneca and English Tragedy." In *Seneca*. Edited by C. D. N. Costa. London: Routledge and Kegan Paul, 1974.

———. "Tyrant and Martyr: Religious Heroisms in Elizabethan Tragedy." In *Poetic Traditions of the English Renaissance*. Edited by Maynard Mack and George deForest Lord. New Haven: Yale University Press, 1982.

James, D. G. *The Dream of Learning: An Essay on the Advancement of Learning, Hamlet, and King Lear*. Oxford: Clarendon Press, 1951.

Johnson, Francis R. "Shakespearean Imagery and Senecan Imagination." In *Joseph Quincy Adams Memorial Studies*. Edited by James G. McManaway, Giles E. Dawson, and Edwin E. Willoughby. Washington, D.C.: Folger Shakespeare Library, 1948.

Johnson, Samuel. *The Works of Samuel Johnson, LL.D.* Edited by F. R. Walesby. 11 vols. Oxford: Talboys and Wheeler, 1825.

Jones, Emrys. *The Origins of Shakespeare.* Oxford: Clarendon Press, 1977.

Jorgensen, Paul A. *Our Naked Frailties: Sensational Art and Meaning in "Macbeth."* Berkeley and Los Angeles: University of California Press, 1971.

Kendrick, Thomas Downing. *British Antiquity.* London: Methuen, 1950.

Kernan, Alvin. *The Cankered Muse: Satire of the English Renaissance.* New Haven: Yale University Press, 1959.

———. "Formalism and Realism in Elizabethan Drama: The Miracles in 'King Lear.'" *Renaissance Drama* 9 (1966): 59–66.

———. "The Henriad: Shakespeare's Major History Plays." In *Modern Shakespearean Criticism: Essays on Style, Dramaturgy, and the Major Plays.* Edited by Alvin B. Kernan. New York: Harcourt, Brace, and World, 1970.

Kimbrough, Robert. *Shakespeare's "Troilus and Cressida" and Its Setting.* Cambridge, Mass.: Harvard University Press, 1964.

Knight, G. Wilson. *The Sovereign Flower.* London: Methuen, 1958.

———. *The Wheel of Fire.* 4th ed. London: Methuen, 1949.

Knights, L. C. "Timon of Athens." In *The Morality of Art.* Edited by D. W. Jefferson. London: Routledge and Kegan Paul, 1969.

Kyd, Thomas. *The Works of Thomas Kyd.* Edited by Frederick S. Boas. Oxford: Clarendon Press, 1901.

Lancashire, Anne. "'Timon of Athens': Shakespeare's 'Dr. Faustus.'" *Shakespeare Quarterly* 21 (1970): 35–44.

Lawrence, W. W. *Shakespeare's Problem Comedies.* New York: Macmillan, 1931.

Leavis, F. R. "Diabolical Intellect and the Noble Hero." *Scrutiny* 6 (1937): 259–83. Reprinted in F. R. Leavis. *The Comon Pursuit.* London: Chatto and Windus, 1952.

Leech, Clifford. *Shakespeare's Tragedies and Other Studies in Seventeenth Century Drama.* London: Chatto and Windus, 1950.

Levin, Harry. "Falstaff's Encore." *Shakespeare Quarterly* 32 (1981): 5–17.

———. "The Heights and Depths: A Scene from 'King Lear.'" In *More Talking of Shakespeare.* Edited by John Garrett. London: Longmans, Green, 1959.

———. "Shakespeare's Misanthrope." *Shakespeare Survey* 26 (1973): 89–94.

Levin, Richard. "On Fluellen Figures, Christ Figures, and James Figures." *PMLA* 89 (1974): 302–11.

———. "The 'Fluellenian' Method." *PMLA* 90 (1975): 292–93.

———. *New Readings vs. Old Plays: Recent Trends in the Reinterpretation of English Renaissance Drama.* Chicago: University of Chicago Press, 1979.

Lewes, G. H. "Foreign Actors on Our Stage." *Blackwood's Edinburgh Magazine* 90 (1861).

Lewis, Wyndham. *The Lion and the Fox: The Role of the Hero in the Plays of Shakespeare.* New York, Harper, 1927.

Lucian. *The Works of Lucian of Samosata.* Edited and translated by H. W. Fowler and F. G. Fowler. 4 vols. Oxford: Clarendon Press, 1905.

———. *Lucian.* Edited and translated by A. M. Harmon. Vol. 2. New York: Macmillan, 1915.

Lydgate, John. *Fall of Princes.* Edited by Henry Bergen. 4 vols. London: Oxford University Press, 1924–27.

————. *Troy Book.* Edited by Henry Bergen. 4 vols. London: K. Paul, Trench, Trubner, 1906–35.

Lyons, Bridget Gellert. "The Subplot as Simplification in 'King Lear.'" In *Some Facets of "King Lear": Essays in Prismatic Criticism.* Edited by Rosalie L. Colie and F. T. Flahiff. Toronto: University of Toronto Press, 1974.

McCarthy, Mary. "General Macbeth." *Harper's Magazine* (June 1972). Reprinted in the Signet Classic *Macbeth,* edited by Sylvan Barnet, 229–40. New York: New American Library, 1963.

McElroy, Bernard. *Shakespeare's Mature Tragedies.* Princeton: Princeton University Press, 1973.

Mack, Maynard. "Engagement and Detachment in Shakespeare's Plays." In *Essays on Shakespeare and Elizabethan Drama in Honor of Hardin Craig.* Edited by Richard Hosley. Columbia: University of Missouri Press, 1962.

————. *"King Lear" in Our Time.* Berkeley and Los Angeles: University of California Press, 1965.

Mack, Maynard, Jr. *Killing the King: Three Studies in Shakespeare's Tragic Structure.* New Haven: Yale University Press, 1973.

Marlowe, Christopher. *The Complete Plays of Christopher Marlowe.* Edited by Irving Ribner. New York: Odyssey Press, 1963.

Mason, H. A. *Shakespeare's Tragedies of Love.* London: Chatto and Windus, 1970.

Maxwell, J. C. "Timon of Athens." *Scrutiny* 15 (1948): 195–208.

————, ed. *Timon of Athens.* The New Cambridge Shakespeare. Cambridge: At the University Press, 1957.

Miskimin, Alice S. *The Renaissance Chaucer.* New Haven: Yale University Press, 1975.

Morozov, Mikhail M. "The Individualization of Shakespeare's Characters through Imagery." *Shakespeare Survey* 2 (1949): 83–106.

Moulton, Richard. *Shakespeare as a Dramatic Artist: A Popular Illustration of the Principles of Scientific Criticism.* 3d ed. Oxford: Clarendon Press, 1893.

Muir, Kenneth, ed. *King Lear.* The New Arden Shakespeare. London: Methuen, 1952.

————, ed. *Macbeth.* The New Arden Shakespeare. London: Methuen, 1951.

————. *Shakespeare's Sources.* London: Methuen, 1957.

Nashe, Thomas. *The Works of Thomas Nashe.* Edited by Ronald B. McKerrow. 5 vols. 1910. Reprint. Oxford: Basil Blackwell, 1958.

Nevo, Ruth. *Tragic Form in Shakespeare.* Princeton: Princeton University Press, 1972.

Nosworthy, J. M. "The Bleeding Captain Scene in 'Macbeth.'" *Review of English Studies* 22 (1946): 126–30.

Nowottny, Winifred M. T. "Acts IV and V of 'Timon of Athens.'" *Shakespeare Quarterly* 10 (1959): 493–97.

————. "Justice and Love in 'Othello.'" *University of Toronto Quarterly* 21 (1952): 330–44.

————. "Some Aspects of the Style of 'King Lear.'" *Shakespeare Survey* 13 (1960): 49–57.

Nuttall, Anthony D. "Realistic Convention and Conventional Realism in Shakespeare." *Shakespeare Survey* 34 (1981): 33–37.

Oliver, H. J., ed. *Timon of Athens.* The New Arden Shakespeare. London: Methuen, 1959.

Ornstein, Robert. *The Moral Vision of Jacobean Tragedy.* Madison: University of Wisconsin Press, 1960.

Orwell, George. "Lear, Tolstoy and the Fool." *Polemic* 7 (1947): 2–17.

Palmer, D. J. "Elizabethan Tragic Heroes." In *Elizabethan Theater.* Edited by John Russell Brown and Bernard Harris. Stratford-upon-Avon Studies, no. 9. New York: St. Martin's Press, 1967.

Pettet, Ernest Charles. *Shakespeare and the Romance Tradition.* London: Staples Press, 1949.

————. "Timon of Athens: The Disruption of Feudal Morality." *Review of English Studies* 23 (1947): 321–36.

Plutarch. *Moralia.* Edited and translated by Frank Cole Babbitt et al. 15 vols. New York: G. P. Putnam's Sons, 1927–69.

Presson, Robert K. *Shakespeare's "Troilus and Cressida" and the Legends of Troy.* Madison: University of Wisconsin Press, 1953.

Price, H. T. "Like Himself." *Review of English Studies* 16 (1940): 178–81.

Prior, Moody E. *The Language of Tragedy.* New York: Columbia University Press, 1947.

Proser, Matthew N. *The Heroic Image in Five Shakespearean Tragedies.* Princeton: Princeton University Press, 1965.

Rabkin, Norman. "Rabbits, Ducks, and 'Henry V.'" *Shakespeare Quarterly* 28 (1977): 279–96. Reprinted in Norman Rabkin, *Shakespeare and the Problem of Meaning.* Chicago: University of Chicago Press, 1981.

————. *Shakespeare and the Common Understanding.* New York: Free Press, 1967.

Rackin, Phyllis. "Shakespeare's Boy Cleopatra, the Decorum of Nature, and the Golden World of Poetry." *PMLA* 87 (1972): 201–12.

Ramsey, Jarold W. "Timon's Imitation of Christ." *Shakespeare Studies* 2 (1966): 162–73.

Ribner, Irving. *The English History Play in the Age of Shakespeare.* Princeton: Princeton University Press, 1957.

————. *Patterns in Shakespearean Tragedy.* 1960. Reprint. London: Methuen, 1966.

Riggs, David. *Shakespeare's Heroical Histories: "Henry VI" and Its Literary Tradition.* Cambridge, Mass.: Harvard University Press, 1971.

Robertson, D. W. "Chaucerian Tragedy." *English Literary History* 19 (1952): 1–37.

Rollins, Hyder E. "The Troilus-Cressida Story from Chaucer to Shakespeare." *PMLA* 32 (1917): 383–429.

Rosen, William. *Shakespeare and the Craft of Tragedy.* Cambridge, Mass.: Harvard University Press, 1964.

Rosenberg, Marvin. *The Masks of King Lear.* Bekeley and Los Angeles: University of California Press, 1972.

————. *The Masks of Macbeth.* Berkeley and Los Angeles: University of California Press, 1978.

Rossiter, A. P. *Angel with Horns and Other Shakespeare Lectures.* Edited by Graham Storey. New York: Theater Arts Books, 1961.

Sacharoff, Mark. "The Traditions of the Troy-Story Heroes and the Problem of Satire in 'Troilus and Cressida.'" *Shakespeare Studies* 6 (1970): 125–35.

———. "Tragic vs. Satiric: Hector's Conduct in II,ii of Shakespeare's 'Troilus and Cressida.'" *Studies in Philology* 67 (1970): 517–31.

Schanzer, Ernest. "A Neglected Source of 'Julius Caesar.'" *Notes and Queries* 199 (1954): 196–97.

———. *The Problem Plays of Shakespeare.* 1963. Reprint. New York: Schocken Books, 1965.

Seneca. *Moral Essays.* Edited and translated by John W. Basore. 3 vols. Cambridge, Mass.: Harvard University Press, 1928–35.

———. *Seneca, His Tenne Tragedies.* Edited by Thomas Newton. 1581. Reprinted, with an introduction by T. S. Eliot. 2 vols. London: Constable, 1927.

———. *Seneca's Tragedies.* Translated by Frank Justus Miller. 2 vols. New York: G. P. Putnam's Sons, 1917–29.

Sen Gutpa, S. C. *Aspects of Shakespearian Tragedy.* Calcutta: Oxford University Press, 1972.

Sewell, Arthur. *Character and Society in Shakespeare.* Oxford: Clarendon Press, 1951.

Sidney, Philip. *The Complete Works of Sir Philip Sidney.* Edited by Albert Feuillerat. 4 vols. Cambridge: At the University Press, 1922–26.

Siegel, Paul N. *Shakespearean Tragedy and the Elizabethan Compromise.* New York: New York University Press, 1957.

Simmons, J. L. *Shakespeare's Pagan World: The Roman Tragedies.* Charlottesville: University Press of Virginia, 1973.

Small, Roscoe Addison. *The Stage-Quarrel between Ben Johnson and the So-Called Poetasters.* Breslau: M. and H. Marcus, 1899.

Snyder, Susan. *The Comic Matrix of Shakespeare's Tragedies.* Princeton: Princeton University Press, 1979.

Soellner, Rolf. *"Timon of Athens": Shakespeare's Pessimistic Tragedy.* Columbus: Ohio State University Press, 1979.

Spencer, T. J. B. "'Greeks' and 'Merrygreeks': A Background to 'Timon of Athens' and 'Troilus and Cressida.'" In *Essays on Shakespeare and Elizabethan Drama in Honor of Hardin Craig.* Edited by Richard Hosley. Columbia: University of Missouri Press, 1962.

Spencer, Theodore. *Shakespeare and the Nature of Man.* 2d ed. New York: Macmillan, 1949.

Spivack, Bernard. *Shakespeare and the Allegory of Evil: The History of a Metaphor in Relation to his Major Villains.* New York: Columbia University Press, 1958.

Stewart, J. I. M. *Character and Motive in Shakespeare.* London: Longmans, Green, 1949.

Tatlock, John S. P. "The Siege of Troy in Elizabethan Literature, Especially in Shakespeare and Heywood." *PMLA* 30 (1915): 673–770.

Thompson, Ann. *Shakespeare's Chaucer: A Study in Literary Origins.* New York: Barnes and Noble, 1978.

Thomson, J. A. K. *Irony: An Historical Introduction.* Cambridge, Mass.: Harvard University Press, 1927.

———. *Shakespeare and the Classics.* London: Allen and Unwin, 1952.

Tillyard, E. M. W. *Shakespeare's History Plays.* London: Chatto and Windus, 1944.

———. *Shakespeare's Problem Plays.* Toronto: University of Toronto Press, 1950.

Traversi, Derek. *An Approach to Shakespeare.* 3d ed. 2 vols. Garden City, N.Y.: Anchor Books, 1969.

Turner, Robert Y. *Shakespeare's Apprenticeship.* Chicago: University of Chicago Press, 1974.

Van Doren, Mark. *Shakespeare.* New York: H. Holt, 1939.

Waith, Eugene M. *The Herculean Hero in Marlowe, Chapman, Shakespeare, and Dryden.* New York: Columbia University Press, 1962.

———. *Ideas of Greatness: Heroic Drama in England.* London: Routledge and Kegan Paul, 1971.

———. "Manhood and Valor in Two Shakespearean Tragedies." *English Literary History* 17 (1950): 262–73.

———. "The Metamorphosis of Violence in 'Titus Andronicus.'" *Shakespeare Survey* 10 (1957): 39–49.

Walker, Lewis. "'Timon of Athens' and the Morality Tradition." *Shakespeare Studies* 12 (1979): 159–77.

Walter, John H., ed. *King Henry V.* The New Arden Shakespeare. London: Methuen, 1959.

Watson, Curtis Brown. *Shakespeare and the Renaissance Concept of Honor.* Princeton: Princeton University Press, 1960.

Welsford, Enid. *The Fool: His Social and Literary History.* 1935. Reprint. Gloucester, Mass.: Peter Smith, 1966.

Whitaker, Virgil K. *The Mirror up to Nature: The Technique of Shakespeare's Tragedies.* San Marino, Calif.: Huntington Library Publications, 1965.

Wilson, Harold S. *On the Design of Shakespearian Tragedy.* Toronto: University of Toronto Press, 1957.

Wilson, John Dover, ed. *Hamlet.* The New Cambridge Shakespeare. 2d ed. 1936. Reprint. Cambridge: At the University Press, 1971.

Index

+23 19/05